TECHNOCRIMES

by

AUGUST BEQUAI

Lexington Books

D.C. Heath and Company • Lexington, Massachusetts • Toronto

Library of Congress Cataloging-in-Publication Data

Bequai, August.
Technocrimes.

Bibliography: p.
Includes index.
1. Computer crimes. 2. Computer crimes—United States. I. Title.
HV6773.B48   1987   364.1'68   85-45801
ISBN 0-669-12342-0 (alk. paper)
ISBN 0-669-13842-8 (pbk. : alk. paper)

Published simultaneously in Canada
Printed in the United States of America
Casebound International Standard Book Number: 0-669-12342-0
Paperbound International Standard Book Number: 0-669-13842-8
Library of Congress Catalog Card Number: 85-45801

The paper used in this publication meets
the minimum requirements of American National Standard
for Information Sciences—Permanence of Paper
for Printed Library Materials, ANSI Z39.48-1984.

86 87 88 89 90 8 7 6 5 4 3 2 1

TECHNOCRIMES

For
HAXHI BEQUAI,
*who believed in ethics
and social justice.*

Contents

Preface IX

1. Unleashing the Electronic Genie I

    *The Computer Comes of Age • Then Came the
    Chip • The Basics of Computer Technology • Going
    Cashless and Paperless • A Growing Dependency*

2. High-Tech America Revisited 15

    *The Pitfalls of Dependency • High Tech Gone
    Amiss • Opening Pandora's Box*

3. The Electronic Delinquents 29

    *What's Hacking All About? • Who's to Blame?
    • The Hackers' Netherland • Of Pirates and
    Electronic Bulletin Boards • The Need for Innovative
    Solutions*

4. Democratizing Crime: The Myth of the
    Supercriminal 45

    *The Universe of Computer Crime • Anyone Can Do
    It • Enter the Twilight Zone • A Short History of
    Computer Crime • Enter the Keyboard Bandit • Computer
    Diddling*

5. Organized Crime Goes Electronic 61

    *The Electronic Mafiosi • Preying on Business
    and Government—High-Tech Style • High-Tech Recruits*

6. From Russia with Love 77

    *Of Spies and Chips • The Pipeline to Moscow • Lenin's
    Heirs • The VPK's Shopping List • In the Service of the*

*KGB and the GRU • Industrial Espionage—Russian
Style • A Tunnel without End • A Balancing Act*

7.   Ripping Off James Bond Is Easy   97

*Snafus—Washington Style • Ripping Off the Feds • Scope
and Modus Operandi • Blame It on High Tech*

8.   Why the Cops Can't Cope   109

*On Deaf Ears • Silence Is the Rule • High-Tech Theft
Pays • The Need for New Laws • Training Is
Needed • An International Problem*

9.   High-Tech Terrorism   129

*League of Terror • Anatomy of Terror • High-Tech
Targets Abound • Dante's Inferno Revisited*

10. Tapping King Solomon's Mines   143

*What Are EFT Systems? • Jesse James Goes
Electronic • Making EFT Systems Secure*

11. The Orwellian Specter   165

*Police Automation Is Threatening • Additional
Concerns • The Need for Legal Safeguards • The
Potential for Corporate Abuse*

Conclusion   177

Bibliography   181

Index   183

About the Author   193

Preface

I N November 1979, 127 tourists boarded an Air New Zealand DC-10 destined for Antarctica. All seemed well. As they approached Antarctica, the American research base at McMurdo gave the plane clearance to descend below the clouds so that its passengers could get a better view. But several minutes later, the ill-fated DC-10 crashed into an active volcano. What went wrong? Early reports blamed the pilot. But an intensive government investigation found otherwise. Apparently, the DC-10's flight computer had been erroneously programmed to fly directly into the 12,200-foot volcano.

Most of us are aware of the explosive growth of computer technology. But few of us grasp the depth and breadth of the high-tech revolution, which some say may be even more important and far-reaching than the Industrial Revolution. Although the Industrial Revolution was limited by its main resource, steam power, which fueled its furnaces and engines, the high-tech revolution is fueled by human intellect, an inexhaustible resource. We live in the dawn of the computer age—on the threshold of a second renaissance.

The high-tech revolution is no simple matter to grasp, for it is both complex and in a state of rapid flux. It is also emotionally laden: hailed by some as the technological savior of our ailing industrial base, it is vilified by others as a renegade force, threatening our privacy and political freedoms.

While acknowledging that no modern society could stay intact for long without the tools of the high-tech revolution, this book identifies the potential for abuse of computer technology. This is a technology that can be easily corrupted by unethical people—criminals, political malcontents, and others who may use it to rob and manipulate society with impunity. In a sense, this book is a travelogue into our high-tech future, where all-too-realistic phantoms may haunt us. Contemplate a world in which new and more frightening methods of crime and mass destruction emerge. Ponder a cashless and paperless society, where the police track down the politically "undesirable" in a matter of microseconds, where terrorists and criminals murder by computer, and where industrial spies and saboteurs armed with portable computers threaten the West's entire financial foundation. *Technocrimes* journeys to the dark side of the high-tech revolution.

The unprecedented and accelerated changes brought about by the high-tech revolution constitute an awesome challenge to our political, social, and economic institutions. This book depicts what awaits us if we fail to understand and address the challenges of the postindustrial society.

Starkly reminding us that even great civilizations can fall victim to their creations, *Technocrimes* raises the specter of a highly evolved society: a brave new world lacking in ethics, where humanity finds itself at the mercy of machines.

It must be remembered that there is nothing more difficult to plan, more doubtful of success, nor more dangerous to manage than the creation of a new system.

— Machiavelli, *The Prince* (1513)

1

Unleashing the Electronic Genie

The most idealistic nations invent machines.
— D.H. Lawrence

THE global electronic pathways grow daily. Computer networks now link U.S. businesses with their counterparts in Europe, Africa, Asia, and Latin America. Compared by Austrian Chancellor Bruno Kreisky to the "networks of railroads, highways, and canals . . . [of] another age," they exemplify a new epoch in human evolution, one that we have yet to fully comprehend. One can aptly call these pathways a source of new life.

Computers do just about everything today: navigate ships and airplanes, run hospital life-support systems, process billions of dollars daily, and even guide the weapons of Armageddon. Plans are even afoot to develop a new generation of supercomputers, machines that will replicate our thoughts and emotions. The electronic genie is out of the bottle.

The computer industry is one of the fastest-growing sectors of the U.S. economy. In 1962, total revenues for the computer industry were estimated to be $1 billion; by 1984, they exceeded $50 billion, and experts forecast in excess of $500 billion by the end of the century. The combined annual sales of software, telecommunications, and automated business systems now exceed $250 billion.

The high-tech revolution is moving fast all over the world. In Western Europe, for example, the business and professional sectors purchased 392,000 PCs (personal computers) in 1982; by 1984, PC sales were put at 950,000, with forecasts that they would exceed 5 million by 1990. According to International Data Corporation (IDC), the West German microcomputer market is growing at 30 percent annually. The United Kingdom is one of the world's largest and most developed markets for technological products; its data processing expenditures are forecasted to exceed $28 billion by 1989.

The computer markets of Asia and Latin America are also growing swiftly. The Asian market is increasing at an annual rate of 40 percent; Japan is now the world's second-largest computer market, having spent over $22 billion to date on computers. In Latin America, Brazil's microcomputer market is increasing at approximately 50 percent annually. Mexico has over 21,000 computer sites and the demand is skyrocketing.

Well into the 1960s the computer revolution was largely the province of North America and Western Europe, and it was restricted mainly to academia, government, and large businesses. Everything changed with the introduction of the personal computer in 1974. The revolution made its way not only into the homes of America, but also into the towns and villages of Afro-Asia. The personal computer has democratized the high-tech revolution.

The Computer Comes of Age

Modern technology is given credit for the computer. But historians will tell you otherwise; they trace its roots back to ancient history, when Boston's famed high-tech highway—Route 128—was a thick forest.

Credit for inventing the ancient ancestor of the modern computer, the abacus, must go to the Chinese. More than 4,000 years ago they discovered that by sliding beads on a string, they could perform complex calculations. The Japanese, even then quick to spot a good idea, modified the abacus to meet their own needs, and called it *soroban*. The abacus is still in use today—and it operates without electricity.

No individual or nation can lay claim to the development of the computer. People have been toying with calculators of some sort since the dawn of civilization. Like a staircase, each development brought us closer to where we are today. Consider the following:

> More than 3,000 years ago the British erected Stonehenge, a monument of massive stones arranged in concentric circles. A puzzle to archeologists for a long time, they now speculate that it was a giant astronomical calculator.

> In 1967 scholars discovered two of Leonardo da Vinci's books in Madrid's National Library. The fifteenth-century genius had sketched plans for a sophisticated calculator.

Still a teenager in 1642, the French mathematician Blaise Pascal constructed a mechanical device that could add and subtract. It never caught on because the bureaucrats of Europe feared that it would take their jobs away.

In 1692, the German mathematician Gottfried Wilhelm Leibniz wrote that "it is unworthy of excellent men to lose hours like slaves in the labor of calculations." In order to help them, he devised a machine that could multiply and divide.

The nineteenth-century English mathematician Charles Babbage developed plans for a giant mechanical calculator: the analytical engine. Had the analytical engine been constructed, it would have occupied an area the size of a football field and it would have required several steam engines for power. It resembled the modern computer: it had a memory device called the "store," a control unit, and an output device. But it needed a system to direct its operations. Lady Lovelace, long a confidante of Babbage and the erratic daughter of Lord Byron, came to the rescue. She devised a program to operate the machine. Although Babbage never built his analytical engine, Lovelace's program gained her a place in the annals of computer technology.

In 1887 the U.S. Census Bureau needed a machine to help tabulate the upcoming census. In response, Herman Hollerith invented a punch card that could store information about an individual's race, sex, age, and marital status. Hollerith's punch card soon became the favorite input device for many of the mechanical calculators and early computers of the 20th century. Hollerith also established a company to market his invention; it was the forerunner of the International Business Machines Corporation —IBM.

During World War II the German engineer Konrad Zuse built a computer that was used to construct rockets. At the same time, the English engineer Alan Turing designed a computer that was instrumental in cracking Germany's military codes.

By the late 1930s mechanical calculators gave way to electronic ones. The first of these was IBM's Mark I. Constructed at Harvard University during World War II, the Mark I could multiply two 23-digit numbers in five seconds. Then, in 1953, the Burroughs Corporation manufactured the UDEC, which weighed several tons and housed more than 10,000 vacuum tubes. But the first commercial computer, UNIVAC I, did not arrive until 1956, when the Sperry Corporation constructed it for the U.S. Census Bureau.

More milestones followed. A new generation of computers made its debut. In 1961, the Control Data Corporation built the CDC-1604, the first of the supercomputers; it was fully transistorized. Then, in 1975, Seymour Cray introduced the Cray-1, which was soon followed by the Cray-2, the fastest computer of its time. By 1984, the United States and Japan were neck-and-neck in a race to develop supercomputers with 100,000 times the computing power of any computer yet devised. The computer industry was now big business.

The dream of the computer industry is to have a computer in every home by the year 2000. If sales are any indicator, that goal may nearly become a reality. In 1980, 724,000 Americans purchased personal computers (PCs). By 1983, sales exceeded 5 million. Forecasters predict that by 1988 computer sales will pass the 16 million mark. Overall software sales for all types of computers are now growing 20 to 30 percent annually; businesses of all sizes now use microcomputers to perform a variety of functions.

More than 40,000 Americans now "telecommute"—work from the comfort of their homes via their computers. Some experts predict that by the year 2000, over 20 percent of our population may telecommute. And in the continuous push to upgrade computers, Japan's Toshiba Corporation has constructed a super-microcomputer, the TOSBAC G8050, that can carry out 18 million instructions. The G8050 also has a memory almost equal to that of a large (mainframe) computer.

What is behind such phenomenal growth? It's simple: government and technology. In 1984 the federal government spent more than $44 billion on research and development, much of it in the high-tech sector. The government loves computers because they play an important role in making sure that we pay our taxes, serve in the military when called upon, and comply with all the other rules and regulations of the bureaucracy. Computers were initially designed with government in mind.

Technological breakthroughs must also be credited for this phenomenal growth. One of the more important of these came in 1959, when Texas Instruments and Fairchild Semiconductor simultaneously announced that they had produced integrated circuits. This meant that manufacturers could now pack more computing power into less space. The introduction of microprocessors in 1971 by Intel Corporation marked another important breakthrough that spawned the personal computer revolution now in full swing.

Then Came the Chip

Personal computers have inundated both our homes and offices. By simply plugging your personal computer into one of the more than 2,000 data bases in the United States, you can check the price of stocks, obtain airline schedules, read movie reviews, and even determine the generic names of your prescription drugs.

The growth of personal computers has been phenomenal. Annual sales now exceed the $15 billion mark; software sales for personal computers are expected to reach $16 billion by 1990. Books on personal computers have increased along with computer sales. Between 1980 and 1984 the number of books grew eight-fold, reaching 4,000 in a mere four years. This number does not include the more than 300 magazines devoted to the topic. Mainframe computers have steadily lost their share in the face of the onslaught of personal computing. Mini- and microcomputers comprise over 60 percent of the market today. For as little as $100, a personal computer can be hooked up to one of the many readily available data banks, thus giving it the ability to do many of the same jobs as mainframe computers.

The success of personal computers is due to the microchip; the microchip is to the computer what gasoline is to the automobile. One-fourth the size of a fingernail, and etched with circuits powerful enough to assemble autos and guide missiles, the microchip has made it possible to reduce dramatically both the size and price of computers.

The microchip has played an important role in spawning the information age. Its history began in 1947, when scientists at Bell Telephone Laboratories developed the transistor to replace the bulky and expensive vacuum tubes that operated the giant computers of that day. Unlike vacuum tubes, transistors were small, used very little energy, gave off little heat, and didn't burn out. They were welded to a circuit board and took up little space. But the transistor had problems: for one thing, it easily broke off the circuit board.

The scientists went back to their drawing boards, and in 1959 they came up with the integrated circuit, or silicon chip. Each chip contained several electronic circuits. By the early 1970s, scientists were able to place several thousand integrated circuits on one quarter-inch silicon chip.

Far more powerful than the old Mark I, a single chip today houses more than 100,000 transistors, thus allowing greater computing power in much less space. For example, the IBM 360 model—popular in the 1960s—was five feet high and six feet wide, cost $300,000 and could perform 33,000 calculations per second. By contrast, a desktop computer costs less than $3,000 and can perform more than 700,000 calculations per second.

The chip consists of thousands of electronic circuits crammed onto a silver-grey fleck of silicon. It is made out of the world's second most abundant element: silicon, found in rocks and sand. On this silicon base scientists pattern minuscule switches; these are then joined together by microscopic wires etched from thin films of metal. If you were to place a chip under a microscope, its intricate terrain would resemble the bridges, streets, and buildings of a giant metropolis being viewed from a satellite far out in space.

But chips perform a variety of tasks. Some have memories that can store large volumes of data; others serve as amplifiers and transmit that data. Still others act as microprocessors that combine a variety of computing functions; the microprocessor is merely a computer engraved on a chip, and contains both logic and memory. Its applications are numerous: it can set a thermostat, control a car's engine, or guide a robot. One day, it is thought, engineers will be able to cram more than one billion electronic switches onto a single chip: 1,000 times the number of transistors in many of the chips in use today.

The Basics of Computer Technology

Although computers differ in speed and the manner in which they operate, there are nevertheless several components common to all of them.

Hardware. This term refers to the equipment and devices that go into the construction of a computer. Hardware includes the equipment used to take in the information (input); process it (central processing unit); store it (media storage); transmit it (data communication); and translate it into a language or format (output) that a user will understand.

Software. Computers operate only in response to written instructions (programs). Programs contain step-by-step instructions that control the manner in which the hardware operates. Programs fall into two categories. One consists of instructions to solve a specific problem—such as handling the payroll, billing, or inventory control of a company. The other category is system software, which guides many of the internal operations of the computer—for example, translating programs into a language the computer understands, scheduling the jobs the computer should perform, and even monitoring the computer's activities.

Data base. This term refers to the information stored in the computer. Collections of logically related records in the data base are called files. For example, a personnel file would include such things as an individual's name, address, social security number, and rate of pay. Files are stored on disks or diskettes and are used as needed.

Data processing. The systematic method by which a computer handles data and produces the desired results. Computers can process, store, cross-reference, and retrieve large amounts of data.

Central processing unit (CPU). The CPU is the computer's brain, which varies in size. In a personal computer, it can be as small as a single chip (microprocessor). Like the human brain, the CPU controls the flow of information, interprets the instructions received from the program, and issues commands to the other components of the computer. It can also store data and instructions for future use.

Communications. A large mainframe computer can be connected to more than 100 terminals at the same time. By using a terminal, a user can gain entry to the mainframe's data base from a great distance. When a user strikes the keyboard, a modem (modulator/demodulator) connected to the terminal converts the information to electrical pulses that are sent by telephone lines or microwaves to the mainframe computer, many miles away. Time-sharing systems (systems accessed by many users who have rental time on them) and data bases operate largely in this manner.

People. The computer merely follows directions. It depends on human intervention for its daily operations. Some of the more important functions in computer systems are carried out by:

Data entry operators, who convert information into a language that the computer understands. Their responsibility is to verify the information and catch errors.

Computer operators, who control and monitor the daily operations of the computer system. They are also responsible for handling many of the problems that require human intervention.

Programmers, who test, implement, and maintain the programs. They are also responsible for modifying the programs to meet the changing needs of the system.

Systems analysts, who are responsible for designing and implementing the system according to the user's needs.

Data base administrators, who design and control the system's data base and provide guidelines for the use, control, and security of its files.

Controls. Computers perform only as well as the people who operate them; their effectiveness is equally hampered by both intentional and unintentional acts. These can take the following form:

Errors resulting from omissions, neglect, or the incompetence of the system's staff.

Frauds involving the unlawful use of the system. Frauds are often committed by individuals in positions of trust or by those who have a working knowledge of the system.

Power outages, which are intentional or unintentional disruptions of power to the system. Outages can often damage sensitive hardware and disrupt communications within the system.

Fire, which, according to some experts, is the worst single disaster affecting computer-based systems.

Water from a malfunctioning sprinkler system or leaking pipe, which can cause serious damage to the system.

Natural calamities such as earthquakes, tornadoes, lightning, and floods, which can easily disrupt a system's operations and make it inoperable.

Experts agree that security is an important element in the overall operation of a computer system. Although total computer security is not possible, efforts must be made to maximize the safety of the system. Few modern organizations can long survive if their systems become inoperable.

Among the recommended computer safeguards are:

Access controls. Posting personnel at the entrance of the computer facility can make it difficult for saboteurs and criminals to gain entry and cause damage or loss.

Protected location. By locating the computer system in an area away from potential sources of hazard, one can enhance the system's effectiveness and safeguard its operations.

Back-up power supplies. Computers need an uninterrupted supply of electricity. Back-up sources should be available in the event of power fluctuations or blackouts.

Personnel screening. Computer crimes and abuses are a people problem. They often occur when too many people have access to the system, know its passwords, or are familiar with its overall operations. Experts advise that only those persons with a legitimate need should have access to the system. Duties should be separated, and passwords should be changed frequently.

Cryptography. Encrypting data can play an important role in safeguarding computer communications. A thief would find it difficult to decipher encrypted data.

Computers not only come in all sizes and shapes, but they also serve different functions.

Mainframes. These large computers come in various sizes and prices. Buyers are often the military, government, large corporations, and universities. A large mainframe can carry a price tag of more than $1 million, and will often require a skilled staff to maintain it. Mainframes can perform a variety of tasks, have great computing power, store large amounts of data, and accommodate a large number of input/output devices. A small mainframe can cost anywhere from $100,000 to $1 million, has less storage capacity than a large mainframe, accommodates fewer input and output devices, and has less computational power. Small mainframes are often used by large organizations that want to lessen the workload of their large mainframes.

Supercomputers. These large computers are customized to meet the needs of the client. Several hundred of these specialized giants are currently in use; most of them have been purchased by government laboratories. While a top-of-the-line mainframe often costs about $3 million and many personal computers are sold for less than $1,000, the price tag on a supercomputer can range from $5 million to $15 million. The first supercomputer, the ILLIAC IV, was designed at the University of Illinois in the late 1960s and manufactured by the Burroughs Corporation. Its price tag: $30 million.

Supercomputers are designed for one purpose: to process a large amount of information very rapidly. Unlike the general-purpose mainframe, which can handle a wide variety of jobs, supercomputers are ideally suited for routine and repetitive tasks, such as weather forecasting, cracking military codes, designing airplanes, predicting nuclear weapons explosions, and a multitude of complex military-related problems. For example, the largest user of supercomputers in the world is the Los Alamos Nuclear Weapons Laboratory in New Mexico.

The present market for supercomputers is small. Many are constructed by hand; only sixty or so are sold each year. Even so, this represents a $300 million annual market. In the 1970s the supercomputer market was dominated by Control Data Corporation (CDC). Seymour Cray left CDC to start his own firm and soon became CDC's competitor. The Cray Research Corporation now sells about 40 percent of the world's supercomputers.

Several other companies have arrived in the market since then; among them are Denelcor, ETA Systems, Hitachi, and Fujitsu. The U.S. Commerce Department estimates that the annual demand for supercomputers could exceed 1,000 by 1990; this translates into a $2 billion annual market. For the present, at least, the supercomputer market will continue to remain small because of the high price tag.

Minicomputers. Although small in size, the "minis" have the same computing power as the older mainframes. One can purchase a mini for as little as $2,000. The price tag will largely depend on the minicomputer's capacity and peripheral equipment; but, in general, prices are coming down. As organizations continue to decentralize their computing operations, minis are gaining increasing popularity. Minis can be used either on a stand-alone basis, or they can be connected to a large mainframe to form a network. Minis have revolutionized the business environment.

Microcomputers. First sold as toys, microcomputers—or personal computers—are profoundly shaping the way in which we do business and carry out our daily financial transactions in America. Guided by an electronic brain that consists of a small chip, the "micro" has greater computational power than the large mainframes of the late 1950s.

Superprograms. Mad computers with human-like characteristics are the stuff that sells science fiction films. The most famous example of this is the deranged computer in *2001: A Space Odyssey,* which killed the astronauts in the film so that it could control the spaceship. Soon, however, intelligent computers may not be fiction. Programs make computers run, and artificial intelligence (AI) programs are the wave of the future. Experts predict that the coming fifth-generation computers will be run by superprograms that give computers intelligence. However, there is concern that AI could give rise to serious abuses—many of which we have yet to grasp.

Going Cashless and Paperless

According to Future Computing, by the year 1989, there may be more than 50 million personal computers in use in the United States. PCs, even given the periodic sales slumps, are fast proliferating in our homes and workplaces. In large part, their phenomenal success must be attributed to the variety of tasks that they can perform.

The PC revolution is the main reason that America is now going cashless and paperless. If you have any doubts, merely look around at some of the ways computers have already transformed everyday life.

Data banks. Personal computers can now be hooked up, via telephone lines, to one of the many data banks around the country that store large amounts of information on a variety of subjects.

Networking. By hooking up to a data bank, a subscriber can use his or her PC to exchange electronic mail.

Education. Chalk and blackboards are now being replaced by computers in our schools. Special software that allows students to communicate with their school's computer is now available. Some schools are even wiring thousands of PCs into a giant network so that students can communicate both with each other and with the school's system.

Medicine. Doctors are increasingly turning to micros to assist in the diagnosis of disease. For example, some hospitals are using micros to help their physicians identify rare infectious diseases. Even patients are turning to computers for medical consultation. A survey at one hospital found that patients thought their computer was friendlier than their doctor.

Electronic newspapers. Newsprint is quickly giving way to electronic blips. Readers can now get their news by simply tapping into a data bank.

Home banking. In many parts of the United States, consumers can now bank and shop from the convenience of their homes—largely as a result of the micro revolution. For example, a consumer can transfer funds, pay utility bills, and check account balances through a home computer. The automated payment systems—often referred to in the trade jargon as electronic funds transfer systems (EFTS)—appear to be an inevitable part of the computer society.

Electronic lawyers. Future barristers may never again have to set foot inside a law library. They will be able to carry out their legal research by simply tapping their computers into one of the many growing legal data banks. By providing the computer with a secret code, the barrister will have much of the legal literature at his or her fingertips.

Telecommuting. Work-at-home schemes have been with us for hundreds of years, and many such cottage industries have fallen by the wayside. But not telecommuting. Working at home by computer is rapidly gaining popularity in America—especially with the physically handicapped. We may yet see the advent of the much-heralded electronic cottage industries.

Bulletin boards. There are currently more than 3,000 electronic bulletin boards throughout the United States; their numbers grow daily. Many are maintained by computer-user clubs, and are free of charge to the user. As with old-style bulletin boards, users can tack messages on them for others to read. In this case, however, the messages are tacked on electronically by computer. To read the messages, a user merely needs a modem (modulator/demodulator), a telephone, and a PC. The modem enables the user to communicate with a bulletin board via the telephone lines. Information on such bulletin boards is readily available from any local computer store.

A Growing Dependency

The global community is rapidly becoming dependent on computer technology. The United States ranks at the top of this roster; we have become a nation of high-tech junkies. Our computer dependence grows daily, and some experts fear that this trend will be to our long-term detriment. If you have any doubt about this dependence, then consider the following:

Banks, credit unions, savings and loans, and credit card companies are quickly adopting automated payment systems. The workhorse of this cashless society is the computer. Millions of computers and terminals will be needed to operate these automated payments systems.

The auto industry is fast shifting to robotics. By the year 1990, it may employ more than 20,000 robot workers. These robots are controlled and guided by computers. Plans are even afoot to construct robots that can see, touch, and speak.

The present airline reservation system is so dependent on computers that it could not long operate without them. In the event of a computer shut-down, our transportation system could come to a halt.

If the telephone companies did not use computers, it would take the entire population of the United States to operate the current system.

Federal, state, and local government could not provide many of the present services if their computers were taken away. For example, the Social Security Administration (SSA) would fall on its face if its computers were made inoperable. As a result of computer malfunctions the SSA cannot account for several billion dollars.

Our hospitals are so dependent on computers for monitoring drug usage, scheduling patient visits, running life-support systems, and maintaining vital medical records, that they would find it impossible to function at their present efficiency level if their computers were taken away.

Computer technology is very tempting. The computer industry knows this and plays on our weakness for gadgetry with slick brochures and advertisements. The high-tech bait can prove to be alluring. For example:

A computer the size of a wristwatch, which will soon be marketed, will allow us to communicate with our banks, offices, and homes from thousands of miles away.

Some computers now allow users to view several files simultaneously on a single screen.

One company has come out with a touch-sensitive display screen that enables a user to control the computer by simply touching the screen.

Lightweight portable computers with compact display screens are rapidly invading the market.

A superchip is now available with over 200,000 transistors housed on one three-eighths-inch-square slice of silicon.

On balance, computer technology has been of immense benefit. It has enriched our lives. But we are also paying a price for this enrichment:

Computers have replaced people and caused job losses in many industries.

A catastrophic computer failure could easily cripple a large corporation or government agency. For example, over 90 percent of all Fortune 500 Corporations would not be able to operate if their computers became inoperable.

It is alleged that terrorists used a microprocessor to detonate the powerful bomb in Brighton, England, that almost killed Prime Minister Margaret Thatcher. Four others lost their lives and more than thirty people were wounded. Technological terrorism is a growing problem.

Government and business maintain increasing numbers of computer files on individuals; as a result the potential for abuses of privacy is both real and growing.

A programming error that went undetected for over six years cost the Australian government dearly: between $150 million and $235 million disappeared in overpayments to pharmacists who dispensed National Health prescriptions. Since there was no evidence of fraud on the part of the pharmacists, the government stands little chance of recouping its losses.

Robot workers can be hazardous to human workers in industry. One employee of the Ford Motor Corporation plant in Flat Rock, Michigan, was killed when a giant robot crushed his head.

Large-scale computer systems continue to grow; both business and government have come to view them as essential to their operations. Microcomputers and telecommunications are on the verge of merging; electronic message systems are here to stay. Computer technology is now irrevocably implanted in our social fiber.

But where do we go from here? Both business and government—within and outside the United States—will tell you that we need larger and more efficient computers. Yet for the humanist, the computer revolution seems to be pointless. In part, the humanists are correct. On the surface, at least, the computer revolution is devoid of any real purpose—except to sell more computers and increase the profits of the industry. If it is conducted outside of an ethical framework, the computer revolution could lead to serious abuses; there is every indication that the abuses have already begun.

2

High-Tech America Revisited

We must go on, conquest beyond conquest . . . all the universe
or nothingness.

— H.G. Wells

F UELED by human intellect and manned by an army of technicians, engineers, and scientists, the computer revolution has given rise to the informational man. Like a chameleon, the computer assumes many roles: filing cabinet, bank, watchman, robot, communications network, missile guidance
system, and researcher, to cite just a few of its uses.

Few people would dispute that the computer revolution has become the
dominant driving force in the postindustrial society. But computer technology
has also made postindustrial society more susceptible to the darkest fears of
Aldous Huxley's *Brave New World*: electronic eavesdropping, new types of
crime, computer warfare and terrorism, and other dangers. We would do well
to revisit our brave new world in the context of the computer revolution.

The Pitfalls of Dependency

In Washington, D.C., more than 4,000 welfare recipients were terminated
from the city's welfare rolls when its computers broke down. Many went
hungry or flocked to the churches for assistance. In Indianapolis, the police
arrested Dennis L. Bunch when the Municipal Court's computers erroneously
listed him as having missed a court appearance. Mr. Bunch spent eight days
in jail before the computer error was finally rectified.

But high-tech errors also have a lighter side. When Sherlene Bloomquist
wrote to Sears Roebuck and Company complaining about a 29 cent error in

her account, the company's computers complied. In fact, they proved to be overgenerous—they credited her account for $161 billion.

The number of hardware- and software-related snafus grows daily. Some experts fear that in our rush to embrace the computer revolution, we may have neglected safety considerations. Computer errors, malfunctions, and equipment breakdowns pose a serious long-term problem, one that we have not adequately addressed.

The University of Minnesota Graduate School of Business Administration conducted a study of corporations in the area. The study found that a majority of the businesses would be forced to shut down most—if not all—of their operations in the event of a serious computer shutdown resulting from malfunctions in the hardware or software.

In the case of a company with annual sales of over $200 million, the study found that if data processing capabilities broke down, projected losses for the first week, would exceed $90,000. By the second week, losses would exceed $800,000, and would be more than $2 million by the third week. The researchers also discovered that human error, and not natural causes, accounted for over 80 percent of system malfunctions and failures. Humanity's overdependence on technology carries with it a heavy price tag. If H.G. Wells were alive today, he would surely warn us of the dangers of computer dependency.

Regardless of whether by error or design, technology that runs amiss can threaten the fragile fiber of our postindustrial society. We would do well to remember that the historian Arnold Toynbee has amply documented the rise and fall of twenty-one major civilizations since the advent of human settlements. The computer society could easily join the junk yard of history. As Toynbee has observed, civilizations are frail social, political, and economic edifices, lacking in permanence.

High Tech Gone Amiss

Computer breakdowns and malfunctions have now become daily occurrences in business and government. Corporate officials complain that computer errors are costing them millions of dollars in losses; one bank executive confided that such an error may have cost his bank $12 million. The U.S. Government Accounting Office (GAO) warns that computer breakdowns could result in social havoc and serious loss of life.

One such scenario almost came to life when a faulty air traffic control computer caused a fully loaded passenger jet to fly for six miles at the wrong altitude in New York's crowded and dangerous skies. A federal official later remarked, "We were dangerously lucky." A South Korean 747 jetliner that accidentally strayed over Soviet territory as a result of a computer malfunction was not so lucky; Soviet jets intercepted it and shot it down.

The U.S. Senate Committee on Government Operations first blew the whistle on the pitfalls of computer technology in 1976. It reported that "computers make decisions that can cause incorrect actions for an extended period of time," and called on the federal government to secure its computer systems. The committee also documented numerous cases in which computers, made inoperable by sabotage or human error, had caused both financial losses and human suffering. For example, it noted that power fluctuations at one federal computer center had caused over fifteen computer system failures, with losses exceeding $500,000. And how a computer error caused New York City welfare recipients incalculable suffering.

In 1977, the Swedish Ministry of Defense, known for its calm and collected manner, added its voice to the chorus. One of its committees reported that the level of computer vulnerability in the West was unacceptably high, and warned that the West's growing dependency on computers increased the threat of both internal and external attack. Four years later the Swedish government was even more specific: computer dependence, it said, has made the West extremely vulnerable to financial fraud, sabotage, and terrorist attacks.

Likewise, the National Security Agency (NSA), in a communiqué issued in August 1984 to more than 2,000 corporations, warned that computer systems were vulnerable to attack and sabotage by political malcontents and criminals. The Australian and Norwegian governments, as well as England's Scotland Yard, the FBI, and the Paris-based Organisation for Economic Cooperation and Development, have raised similar concerns. As if to prove them correct, terrorists have started to attack computer centers, and use microcomputers to detonate powerful explosive devices.

But computer errors or malfunctions can exact heavy costs by themselves, without the intervention of criminal attack or sabotage. For example, in November 1979 and June 1980, the Pentagon's computers rang a false alarm: "America is under Soviet missile attack." Luckily, the error was discovered before the United States launched missiles in retaliation. In 1980, bank regulators in Massachusetts nearly closed 100 banks when the computers of a company that processed the data for the banks malfunctioned. A state official later remarked, "We were lucky to catch it on time." And a fire at the Military Personnel Records Center in St. Louis, Missouri, destroyed much of the computer center, along with 15 million records.

Experts note that our dependence on computers is an outgrowth of two technological developments: dramatic improvements in computers, and the proliferation of computer networks. In addition, the rapid speed of newer computers and their overwhelming storage capacity make the timely detection and correction of errors and malfunctions difficult, time-consuming, and costly. Once erroneous data enters a giant network, locating it can prove as difficult as finding a pin in a haystack.

To date, we have been lucky. No major computer-related catastrophe has befallen our society. But some would atribute this more to chance than to vision. Even the American Federation of Information Processing Societies, known for its conservatism, has called for a serious study of the risks posed by our computer dependency. We would be ill-advised to dismiss the potential for informational catastrophes.

Opening Pandora's Box

The Spanish Conquistadores had little trouble conquering the New World. They did it easily, by simply using the network of good roads that their Indian adversaries had constructed. Likewise, the electronic pathways of computer networks make our society vulnerable both internally and externally. It would serve us well to weigh the glitter of high technology against its less-desirable trappings.

Civil Liberties

Groups opposed to technology date back to the early days of the Industrial Revolution. Small but vocal groups opposed to our high-tech revolution have likewise made themselves visible. One of the first of these was the International Society for the Abolition of Data Processing. Similar groups have sprung up in Western Europe and the United Kingdom. Some members of the high-tech community cavalierly dismiss these groups as being afraid of change, composed of timid souls who fear the new and unknown.

But a sizeable number of the the apprehensive voices belong to members of the high-tech community. They fear that we may well have gazed into the secrets of Pandora's box without fully understanding the ramifications. Some are most concerned about loss of privacy. The late U.S. Senator Frank Church expressed his alarm when he observed that there would be no place to hide in the computer society. Computer snooping can also lend itself to serious political manipulation.

There is justifiable basis for concern, especially as computers increasingly govern our daily lives. Computers perform over 100,000 calculations each second for every man, woman, and child in America. Our names pop up in some computer at least forty times a day. Moreover, federal, state, and local government agencies keep more than thirty-five files on each one of us, while the Census Bureau collects over 5 billion facts about American citizens.

Privacy and civil liberties cannot survive long without each other. But privacy is fast becoming a thing of the past in our computer society:

> The National Security Agency's (NSA) computers eavesdrop twenty-four hours a day, seven days a week, on all overseas communications. NSA also occasionally monitors communications within the United States.

> Much of the confidential data stored in the computer systems of financial institutions, retailers, and manufacturers is susceptible to unauthorized tapping.

> The computerization of our telephone system has made it very vulnerable to electronic snooping.

> As computer systems are linked to national and international networks, it will become even easier to track a person's movements.

> By using a device called an addressable converter, cable companies can now keep track of what programs a customer watches.

Congressman Robert W. Kastenmeier observed that "the essence of personal privacy protection is the assurance that private communications are protected." Sadly, this is not the case today. Our massive data banks and instant retrieval systems, make George Orwell's telescreens seem outmoded by comparison. The only thing missing now is a giant network that would link together all private and government computer systems—and that, too, may be in the offing. William B. Finneran, a member of the New York State Commission on Cable Television, has said that "the technical capability for collecting large amounts of personal information is already [here]." And computer pioneer Joseph Weizenbaum warns that we may be rapidly becoming a nation of sheep. Events may soon prove both of them correct.

Disasters

In 1844, the first words that Samuel Morse tapped on his telegraph were "What hath God wrought!" If Morse were alive today, he might add: "He hath wrought the high-tech revolution." For today's limits are imposed not by our technology, but rather by our imaginations. For example, plans are afoot to construct a computer that talks and responds in many languages and is tuned to a person's brain waves. This miraculous device would be based on a microchip that can hold 2 billion bits of information. The computer would be small enough to be worn as a wrist watch, but sufficiently powerful to communicate with other computers around the world.

While the computer age has produced marvels, it has also produced disasters, or so-called informational catastrophes. The consequences for our society could prove serious. Already we have faced the tragic and costly results of computer malfunctions:

> Because of a faulty computer, the Boston Water and Sewer Commission was forced to delay its billing by several weeks, at a cost of millions of dollars.

> A fire at the First Data Corporation computer facility in Massachusetts caused over $3 million in damages. More than 500 of its time-sharing customers went without service for over a week.

> In South Carolina, the state government's faulty computer was responsible for $55 million in unaccountable annual expenditures.

> The 1978 Santa Barbara earthquake made twelve key computer systems inoperable—some for up to fifty-eight hours.

> A government study concluded that an inoperable hospital computer may have been responsible for the death of at least one patient.

> A survey by IBM of 352 major computer breakdowns found that fire and flooding accounted for over 60 percent of the incidents; human error and bombings accounted for the others.

Computers malfunction. The causes can range from negligence on the part of human operators to natural phenomena. Some experts even believe that electromagnetic changes in the human body can affect the workings of computers. A survey of 500 Canadian users found that over 40 percent had experienced some computer-related problem in the preceding year. The unreliability of hardware and software is well documented. Yet both the U.S. and Soviet military are toying with the idea of a missile warning system, in which computers would be programmed to launch a nuclear attack, on their own, if their sensors detected approaching missiles. The threat of Armageddon is palpable today.

Civil Strife

Automation is fast displacing jobs in the automotive and textile industries. By the year 2000 manufacturing jobs will account for only 11 percent of the labor force, down from nearly 24 percent in 1980. Agricultural jobs are also on the decline, from four to three percent, because of automation. By 1993, up to 1.3 million workers may lose their jobs as 260,000 robots enter the workforce. A new elite is on the ascent; a new power structure centered around informational wealth is springing up. The social dimension that will confront us in the coming years will be between the "knows" and "know-nots."

The smokestack industries are not alone; computerization is also quickly displacing many white-collar workers. The news for such employees is not good. Court stenographers in many states are now being replaced by computerized tape-recording systems that keep track of proceedings in several courtrooms at once. A strike in 1983 by 675,000 American Telephone and Telegraph Company employees proved ineffective, largely because several thousand supervisory personnel were able to operate the telephone system with the aid of computers. And striking Consolidated Edison workers in New York were not able to shut off service to the company's 3.5 million customers largely because a small cadre of supervisors kept the system going with the assistance of the company's computers.

The Industrial Revolution wrought profound social upheaval and widespread civil strife in Europe. The streets of Paris, Rome, and Vienna became battlegrounds. Acts of sabotage by employees became common; some employees even joined the ranks of the revolutionaries.

Likewise, to a lesser extent, the computer revolution has witnessed its share of employee sabotage and civil strife. For example:

Angry employees in Great Britain have periodically threatened to destroy their employers' computers unless given pay raises.

In Harrison, New York, a group calling itself the United Freedom Federation successfully bombed the offices of one of the large local employers.

Angry public assistance recipients in Massachusetts have threatened to destroy the welfare department's computers.

Disgruntled workers sabotaged the weather service computers operated by the Metropolitan Life Insurance Company.

Striking New York University employees threatened to destroy the school's $3.5 million computer center.

Because many high-tech companies are small—the majority employ fewer than 200 people—our high-tech prophets are often asked, "Where will the millions of displaced workers find new jobs?" Since the manpower needs of the high-tech sector are limited, training people for jobs in this industry will prove of limited value. As early as 1970, British Prime Minister Edward Heath warned that the long-term threat to the West came not from nuclear war, but rather from civil strife.

Corporate Secrets

Corporate snooping is not a new phenomenon. Companies have always wanted to know the business plans and strategies of their competitors. Corporate intelligence-gathering, although unethical, is often legal as long as the snooper doesn't resort to outright stealing. Big companies that have been known to systematically collect information on competitors include Westinghouse, Emerson Electric, Digital Equipment Corporation, General Electric, and Wang Laboratories.

But many corporations continue to do it the old-fashioned way. Their techniques often differ little from those employed by businesses in the nineteenth century. Industrial spying can take several forms, including hiring a competitor's employees with promises of more pay, or picking the brains of a competitor's customers, suppliers, and former employees. Companies may also infiltrate a competitor's business operations with spies, or take a competitor's products apart to analyze their components (known as "reverse engineering"). But these outdated techniques can prove costly and time consuming. High-tech snooping is easy and inexpensive. The computer revolution has given rise to vast electronic data bases that store information on every company in America, even multinationals; their data is easy to retrieve.

The illegal way of retrieving data, which some companies choose anyway, is to hire an industrial spy who gains unauthorized access to the data base and copies it. This involves the risk—admittedly minuscule—of criminal and civil prosecution, as well as adverse publicity. The legal, and increasingly the preferred way, is to buy information from one of the more than 2,000 data retrieval services in the United States. A data base service called Investext, published by Business Research Corporation, will provide a subscriber with the full text of a research report prepared by a security analyst on a competitor. Selective Dissemination of Information, provided by Dialog Information Services, can give a subscriber an update on a competitor's data base. Or, Economic Information Systems, published by Control Data Corporation, can provide a subscriber with the locations of a competitor's plants, the number of people it employs, the estimated dollar volume output, and the market share its production represents.

High-Tech Terror

In France, terrorists used Soviet-made RPG7 antitank rockets to blow up a nuclear power plant. Luckily, the rockets only damaged the plant's concrete outer shell. The Pacifist and Ecologist Committee claimed responsibility. In the United States, a Puerto Rican terrorist group (FALN) is said to have been behind more than 120 bombings; its targets included the New York and American Stock Exchanges.

Terrorism, both within and outside the United States, is growing. Much of it is directed against U.S. corporations. The *National Law Journal* has described terrorism as being well organized, "since many terrorist groups have access to millions of dollars and the use of sophisticated training facilities of other governments." And computers are fast replacing business executives and diplomats as the targets of terrorism.

Technoterrorism can be both easy and devastating; to an organization, the loss of its computers can prove critical. For example, the bombing of the Pentagon's computers brought some of its operations to a standstill for up to twenty hours. By destroying a university computer, saboteurs destroyed critical research data, the loss of which cost clients millions of dollars.

In a realistic exercise, seven military counterterrorist experts with false credentials easily infiltrated a closely guarded nuclear power plant. Once inside, they had little difficulty in seizing hostages and gaining control of the plant's computer center. Experts agree that well-organized and trained groups bent on violence could easily take control of key computer facilities in the United States, since few of them are secure. Once inside the facility, the terrorists could hold it hostage in return for money or some other demand.

Lack of Technoethics

An insurance company employee was caught using his employer's computer to run a mail-order business on the side; a private investigator paid an employee of the California Department of Human Resources to run a computer check on several individuals. And a disgruntled employee who was dismissed from his job erased the computer files of his fellow employees; a bank manager who was angry with a female employee for rejecting his amorous advances altered her computerized personnel record.

As these cases amply illustrate, technoethics in the private and public sectors leave much to be desired. Unfortunately, many private and public sector employees feel that there is nothing wrong with peeping at a fellow employee's files, altering or deleting data, copying software, leaking confidential data, and even using their employer's computer for personal business. Lamenting the need for ethics in the computer age, the Data Processing Management Association has called for a "commitment to ethical behavior."

But what constitutes proper computer ethics remains ambiguous. A survey of 100 corporations by the National Association of Accountants found that only fifty-two percent of those responding said that their companies had any guidelines dealing with the use of computers; only 22 percent provided their employees with any written guidelines. And the Educational Fund for Individual Rights reports that over 90 percent of the companies it studied have no guidelines on what constitutes the proper use of computers by their employees.

Slowly, both business and government are coming to realize that technoethics are needed for their workforces. It is dawning on management that an employee merely needs the correct password to access its most valuable trade secrets and marketing plans. Corporate America has an additional inducement: the courts and legislatures are threatening to pass computer security laws, unless businesses adopt voluntary guidelines. In addition, software manufacturers are planning to take legal action against employers who permit the copying of their software, some consumer activists are calling for federal legislation on computer ethics, and private individuals are bringing a plethora of lawsuits against businesses that have failed to safeguard their computers.

Few dispute that ethical considerations should govern the transfer of information between computers, their use, and access to the data they store. Most companies have done little, if anything, to address the ethics problem; when they have done so, their guidelines are often cosmetic and ambiguous. For example:

Company A's guidelines specify that computers should not be used for private purposes; they fail to specify what constitutes a private purpose.

Company B prohibits its employees from misappropriating computer time, but it fails to define misappropriation. Nor are the rules applied equitably.

Company C allows its employees to take their computers home, provided that they use them only for company business; it fails to specify what constitutes authorized company business.

Desktop computers now give employees access to large volumes of information on a multitude of individuals both inside and outside the organization. Ensuring that an employee does not abuse this power can often prove difficult; it could even constitute an invasion of privacy if, for example, the surveillance involved the electronic monitoring of computer use. Although union officials look askance at electronic monitoring by companies, somehow the widespread perception that it's okay to snoop into computer files and electronic mail needs to be changed.

Technostress

The proponents of automation, through advertisements and public relations efforts, remind us daily that computerization will: make us happier, rejuvenate our ailing industries, eradicate racial and class differences, give rise to a generation of superchildren, and allow us to work in the comfort of our homes. Like all myths, the high-tech myth has its vision of a better society. Some critics charge that computerization has merely introduced a new form of tension into our lives—"technostress."

Technostress is a buzzword that merits watching. It refers to many of the health-related drawbacks of working with computers; its existence has been confirmed by research. For example, the National Institute for Occupational Safety and Health reported that some of today's most stressful jobs involve computers. A survey by the National Association of Working Women found that female VDT (visual display terminal) operators suffer a disproportionate number of miscarriages, deaths of newborn infants, children born with defects, and premature deliveries. A study of twenty-six computer centers in the United States and Canada by the Data Entry Management Association also pointed to the reality of technostress. It found that computer operators and clerical employees at the centers complained of back pain, nervousness, fatigue, neck and shoulder pain, burning eyes, stomach pains, skin rashes, swollen muscles and joints, and eyestrain.

There is evidence that some VDTs may be emitting harmful levels of radiation. But computer industry sources deny these claims; they dismiss the evidence as doubtful. "Computer technology," they note "is safe and clean." They charge that these studies were conducted by persons and groups unfavorably disposed toward the computer industry.

Among the other ills identified with computerization are the sense of isolation and the sense of loss of control that it produces in some workers. Using computers to keep track of worker productivity—how many breaks they take, the number of phone calls they make, and how fast they type—merely aggravates such feelings. Even some industry sources privately acknowledge that technostress is a problem. Denying its existence will not make it go away; at least in part, it is an outgrowth of our computer age.

Robotics

In 1982, IBM entered the nascent robot market with a one-armed programmable robot system that could be connected to a personal computer. The Japanese have unveiled a robot that can read books to the blind, and General Dynamics Corporation is constructing robots that can be programmed to train marine mammals.

The robots have arrived. Guided by artificial intelligence, they will soon run factories, administrate hospitals, mine the deep seas, explore space, perform rescue missions, attend to agriculture, teach in our schools, and even tend our cows. Robotics, however, is still in its infancy.

Up to now Japan has been the leader in this field, followed closely by the United States, West Germany, and Sweden. But the United States is catching up fast. Our robot population is expected to reach 72,000 by 1988; experts forecast that it will exceed 260,000 by 1993. But robotics carries a price for humans: before the end of this century, one third of America's workforce may find itself replaced by robots.

Robots are the shock troops of the computer age. Plans are on the drawing boards to develop an entire generation of sophisticated home robots, which could become household fixtures by the end of this century. However, robots are more than merely mechanical servants; they are the link between the computer and the world at large. They are guided by a microcomputer that can be programmed to direct them to perform specific tasks; once programmed, they often need little human intervention.

But robotics also has its dark side. When robots malfunction, disaster can ensue. A malfunctioning computer at the University of Florida's Center for Intellectual Machines and Robots caused a robot to go berserk and destroy valuable property. In Japan, a malfunctioning robot killed one of the mechanics sent to fix it.

Experts predict that by the end of this century, robots will possess many human attributes. They will be able to distinguish human voices, smell smoke, taste food, and—armed with artificial intelligence—even duplicate our innermost feelings. There is even talk in some legal circles of enacting a bill of rights for robots. The robots are fast taking over.

Test-Tube Computers

The daily newspapers are replete with news about test-tube babies, but scientists are looking even further down the pike: a generation of test-tube computers. The idea is to use genetics to turn molecules and bacteria grown in a laboratory into powerful computer circuits. In other words, to replace the billions of molecules that now make up a silicon chip with a single laboratory-grown molecule that can be used to construct super sophisticated computers. The Japanese, quick to see a valuable commercial opportunity, are quickly moving into this area.

Plans are also on the drawing board in the United States to devise living computer chips. Researchers at the National Institutes of Health have already isolated amino acids (the building blocks of life) that can be used to construct powerful computer chips. EMV Associates, a high-tech research firm based in Rockville, Maryland, plans to have a prototype of the amino acid computer chip within the next five years.

These living chips would be more than one billion times as powerful as their silicon counterparts. Visionaries also dream of implanting living chips between neurons in the brain, giving humans the ability to communicate more directly with computers. At a whim, the brain would be able to communicate with computers many miles away. There are even plans to turn brain cells into tiny computers by linking them to giant communication networks; this would also enable the brain to communicate with computers located many thousands of miles away. The computer revolution knows no bounds.

Science fiction writers have pictured a future with colonies in space, floating cities in our oceans, superhuman robots, and genetic engineering. All this is in the offing. It will be made reality by the computer revolution—by ultrafast computers that think and communicate not only with other computers but also with humans. But the computer age also raises disturbing legal, moral, and political questions.

3

The Electronic Delinquents

Put another password in,
Bomb it out, then try again.
Try to get past logging in,
We're hacking, hacking, hacking.

— Cheshire Catalyst

AMERICA'S schools are off and running in the high-tech race. From 1983 to 1984, the number of schools with computers almost doubled; it doubled again in 1985. More than two out of three public schools now own computers—at least one computer for every fifty students. And the Medard H. Nelson Elementary School in New Orleans now offers computer courses not only for its students, but also for their parents. Many of the 1,100 students (grades 7 to 11) at the Gompers Secondary School in East San Diego spend up to twenty hours a week "working out" on the school's computer terminals.

The 1980s have witnessed a dramatic growth in the number of young men and women who have turned to computers for both schoolwork and fun. The purchase of computer equipment for and by young people in the last several years has increased so rapidly that a report by the consulting firm of Market Data Retrieval characterized it as "explosive, astonishing, and phenomenal."

Yet this growth has also given rise to a phenomenon the *New York Times* has labeled "electronic vandalism." Hacking, as it is commonly called, has become part of our daily vocabulary. The Phantom, Roscoe, and Cable Pair are names that have become part of the hackers' folklore. Electronic bulletin boards are now found in every city in America. They are quickly replacing the street corner as the place to meet and socialize with one's peers—all for the price of a home computer and modem.

The antics of young hackers have aroused great concern. While some young people still scale fences and play ball, the modern hacker roams at will through the mazes of the electronic underworld, tapping into some of the nation's most sophisticated computer networks. The hackers' escapades have not only proven costly, they also threaten the privacy of millions of Americans. Today's hacker is the stepchild of the computer age.

What's Hacking All About?

Hacking encompasses a wide range of computer-assisted activities—some legal, others criminal, and many unethical. It is an emotionally laden topic. To the business and law enforcement communities, the hacker is a trespasser and thief. To the news media and avid computer fans, the hacker is a modern-day joy rider, roaming the electronic highways.

There is no agreement on exactly what constitutes hacking. It is all a matter of who you talk to, as the following comments make clear:

NEWS REPORTER: An adolescent phenomenon, a rite of passage in the computer age.

INVENTOR: I hope my kid grows up to be like them.

CONSULTANT: A hacker is someone who programs computers for the sheer fun of it. [Hacking is] a meritocracy based on ability.

SCHOOL ADVISER: Youngsters with a penchant for breaking the security of computer systems.

PROSECUTOR: An electronic game of Peeping Tom.

POLITICIAN: We can't write off those incidents as harmless teenage pranks.

EXECUTIVE: Mischievous kids who want to have fun.

SECURITY OFFICER: Yahoos who electronically invade other people's computers, usually for the challenge.

PROFESSOR: The closest analogy is joy riding.

HACKER: The "fifth generation" people. The generation that will build America's artificial intelligence computers.

The hacker phenomenon cuts across the broad spectrum of our society. Hackers range in age from ten to sixty, and in computer literacy from novice to computer scientist. While some observers view the hackers' antics as simply pranks, others view them as unethical and sometimes dangerous. Consider these incidents:

A college student used his school's computer to set up a blind date— only to regret it.

The hacker-revolutionary, "Milo Phonebill" (a pseudonym), posted the following message on an electronic bulletin board: "The 'ESTABLISH-MENT' seems to be in an uproar about the. . . . assaults on their high-tech toys."

A ninth-grader, armed with a $250 home computer, tapped into the Pentagon's computer system and deleted valuable data. At the time of his arrest, the police found that he had more than thirty pages of Pentagon computer listings and passwords.

A thirteen-year-old gained access to a dozen New York City computers that are tied to a nationwide network.

Three men who caused $250,000 worth of damage to a San Francisco company's system were also able to gain access to "The Ark"—Digital Equipment Corporation's internal software development system in Maynard, Massachusetts.

A group of men and women, ranging in age from fourteen to twenty-two, set up a computer club to arrange sexual encounters and exchange information on computer sabotage.

Nobody knows how hacking got started. How did joy riding get started? Suffice it to say that the first computer antics date back to the mid-1960s and they often involved college students, who called themselves hackers. Proud of their computer pranks, many of them were computer jokesters—a tradition still in full force.

But hacking really became visible in the early 1980s, as a result of two major developments: the proliferation of inexpensive personal computers, and the dramatic growth in computer literacy, especially among the younger generation. According to Infocorp., a San Jose market research organization, there were over 900,000 computers in use in American homes by 1983. More than 200,000 of these were equipped with modems (inexpensive devices that make it possible for home computers to communicate with computer systems long distances away, via the telephone lines).

In addition, many present-day computer enthusiasts grew up during the social turmoil of the early 1970s. They were influenced by the escapades of the yippie-inspired "phone freaks" and raised under the tutelage of the "me generation." For example, one of the early nominees to the Hacker's Hall of Fame was John Draper (aka Cap'n Crunch), a pioneering phone freak who constructed one of the first "blue boxes," devices used to break into long-distance telephone lines. Arrested for his telephone antics in 1976, he was sent to Northampton State Prison in Pennsylvania. In an interview in the June 1984 issue of *Info World,* Draper defined hacking as "taking things apart, figuring out how they work; whether it's the telephone system, the Telenet system, or copyrighted programs, it doesn't matter."

But why hack? There are a variety of answers. Like the hackers of the early 1970s, many of today's hackers do it for the fun and challenge; they can aptly be called electronic joy riders. The case of the MIT Cookie Monster illustrates this best. A prankster had programmed the MIT computer to flash the word "cookie" across the screens of unsuspecting users. If the user did not "feed" the monster by typing in the word "cookie," the Cookie Monster would obliterate whatever was on the screen.

There is also a positive, serious side to hacking. Not all hackers are pranksters. For example, Explorer Post 692 in Virginia is not a traditional scout troop. Every Tuesday evening about twenty of its members, mostly high school students, employ their hacking skills to test the security systems of local business computers. Similarly, students at Western Washington University are encouraged to periodically test the safeguards of the school's computer system. And members of the Hacker's Club at Columbia University develop computer programs for public use. For many, hacking is a serious endeavor. Unlike the thrill-seeker, the serious hacker wants his or her efforts to serve the betterment of society and to advance the more positive aspects of computer technology.

But the dark side to hacking surfaces periodically. For example, industrial spies and thieves have been known to disguise their activities as the work of hackers. It is a simple matter for an industrial spy who has discovered a system's entry code to cover his tracks by posting the code on one of the many electronic bulletin boards, foiling even the best of security measures. To date, the FBI has identified more than 200 such spies and thieves in California alone. They range in age from eighteen to twenty-nine, and have little in common with the youngster who hacks for fun. Law enforcement agencies have also discovered computer clubs, where the latest computer access techniques are exchanged and plans for computer heists are discussed. One such group was identified in 1981; it already had twice sabotaged the computers of the telephone directory assistance facility in Pasadena, California.

The darker side of hacking has also spawned underground newsletters, which provide their readers with tips on how to break into business and government computers. In one of its issues, one such New York City newsletter, *TAP*, gave detailed instructions for accessing the Princeton University computer system. Pirate bulletin boards also abound. Many of them even provide step-by-step instructions on how to plant a spy program in a computer system. The spy program tricks an authorized user into revealing the secret password.

Who's to Blame?

Despite the many abuses, it would be unfair and inaccurate to portray the majority of hackers as criminals who surreptitiously enter systems to steal, copy, or alter valuable data. Admittedly, a small number have done this, but most hackers—even some who have had brushes with the law—are not aware that their acts may be illegal. Given the current state of computer law, even judges and lawyers have difficulty discerning lawful from unlawful hacking. In fact, much of the present hacking activity, although unethical, may not necessarily be unlawful.

Schools must also share some of the blame for the irresponsible conduct of many young hackers. In their pursuit to train students in computer technology, schools have neglected to sensitize them to the need for computer ethics. Nor have teachers set an example. An official of the Minnesota Educational Consortium put it this way, "Computer piracy is rampant, and teachers are among the worst offenders. The kids not only copy, they see their teachers copying." Technoethics appears to have fallen by the wayside in many of our schools.

It is inaccurate to portray hackers as whiz kids who sit for hours in front of their screens in a dark room and match wits with corporate and government computers. It is equally inaccurate to characterize hackers as political rebels, fighting against the evils of bureaucratic America. The hackers' call to the "electronic barricades" may make for interesting press, but has little resemblance to the real world. Most hackers have a greater interest in Calvin Klein than Karl Marx; they are not modern-day Jacobins. Hacking should be seen for what it is: the sometimes misdirected and sometimes malicious activities of mostly young individuals.

The Hackers' Netherland

James L. Hallers II was described by Texas A&M University officials as a straight-A student. Thanks to Hallers, his friends were also straight-A students. In pursuit of academic excellence, Hallers used his home computer to tap into the university's mainframe and change the grades. He was later discovered, prosecuted, and jailed for one night.

Han Shan S. Scott Anderson was a good student at San Jose State University. His friends and family were shocked when he was arrested and charged by the police with tapping into several California computer systems. Anderson was alleged to have also used the university's computer to play "Star Trek" and other games with students as far away as Sweden and Taiwan. The police suspected that he may have erased programs belonging to other students, as well as those of a nationwide group of college hackers.

Bloodstock Research Information Services, based in Lexington, Kentucky, keeps computerized records on the breeding and racing history of every thoroughbred in the United States. Customers are given a secret account number, which allows them to access Bloodstock's data banks. When company officials suspected that someone had broken into their system, they notified the FBI. Eventually the calls were traced to a group of twenty hackers in California. The FBI surmised that the son of one of Bloodstock's customers, a doctor who dealt in thoroughbreds, had passed his father's secret account number to his friends. The FBI also suspected that this same group of hackers had broken into other computers in the United States and other countries.

Cases like these can make it tempting to view hackers as spoiled, middle-class brats who are contemptuous of the privacy of others because neither their families nor their schools have taught them otherwise. They have rightly been called the stepchildren of our high-tech society—offspring devoid of ethics. However, hacking is a more complex phenomenon; it cannot be attributed solely to a lack of social values. Rather, it is the outgrowth of several social and technological forces, the more prominent of which are discussed in following sections.

Personal Computers

For Susan Headley (a k a Susan Thunder), for example, hacking started in her teens, when she joined a group of California computer enthusiasts. For more than four years, she and her fellow hackers spent many hours each day accessing government and business computers. On October 25, 1983, she detailed for a U.S. Senate Subcommittee how she and her friends had used their personal computers to alter credit ratings, insert obscenities, and even to attempt to shut down the entire California telephone system.

A California high school student who had taken a computer course at a local college was quick to put his new-found skills to use. Armed only with a personal computer, he accessed the main computing system of the University of California. Arrested and convicted of malicious mischief, he was placed on probation. But a year later he was arrested again and charged with stealing more than $50,000 worth of computer equipment from the university's Engineering Department. The overzealous hacker had intended to use his booty to access local business computers.

Over fifteen percent of the total population now use a personal computer either at home or at work. Many experts attribute the phenomenal growth of hacking, at least in part, to the proliferation of low-cost computers both domestically and overseas. Armed with one, a ten-year-old child can tap into any one of many databases.

High-Tech Literacy

During a two-week period, the telephone lines at the Dalton School, an expensive private school in Manhattan's fashionable Upper East Side, were used to make over forty calls to the Telenet System. The intruders had also penetrated the computer systems of more than twenty Canadian companies and universities; in one instance, they erased one fifth of the data in a Canada Cemente La Forge Computer.

When the FBI was called in on the case, agents went to the school armed with a search warrant. Upon their arrival, the principal acompanied them to the computer room on the fifth floor, where they seized several bags containing computer printouts and a terminal log sheet. With the assistance of computer experts, the agents finally cracked the case—to find that the intruders were several eighth-grade students.

In the spring of 1984, the Howard County, Maryland, police department received an anonymous tip: A young hacker had been using information supplied by other computer pirates to place free long-distance telephone calls and to copy bootlegged computer programs. Armed with a search warrant, the police descended on the hacker's home and seized the evidence. They were baffled. "How does a young kid in the suburbs of Maryland tap into computers clear across the country?," one of them asked. Further, "Who was the 'Kernel,' 'Bandit,' and 'Space Invader'?" Frustrated, the police called on computer experts for a crash course in programming.

Dealing with street delinquents is one thing, but high-tech delinquents—as the police are finding out—is an entirely new ball game. But in this case, the police were lucky: the young hacker agreed to help. He showed them how he communicated with other hackers around the country, he gave them a lesson on tacking up information on electronic bulletin boards, and he told them how to place free telephone calls to Paris and London. He also gave them a real gem—an exclusive demonstration of his "dirty dialing" program, in which the computer automatically dialed every number in a given exchange until it connected with another computer. A police official later remarked that it was a good thing he was on their side.

When the first computer course opened in 1977, only eighty-four students enrolled. Now hundreds of thousands of youngsters attend computer camps every year, and almost every school in the United States offers some sort of course on computers. A college professor has even taught his three-year-old daughter how to operate his home computer.

Young Americans are the most computer literate segment of our population. But with technoliteracy has also come the temptation to hack. A young hacker summarized it best: "It gives us a sense of pride to show we can crack the system's security. It's also fun."

Intercomputer Networks

Several years ago, FBI agents carried out well-coordinated raids against hackers in several large cities; among them were Buffalo, New York, San Diego, Detroit, Los Angeles, Phoenix, and Oklahoma City. An FBI spokesman was quoted as saying, "We're giving it high priority." Among those snared was the Wizard of Arpanet; he watched tearfully as the FBI seized his computer. The agents also closed in on the infamous Cracker, the mysterious San Diego hacker who is said to have helped engineer break-ins into several telecommunications systems around the country.

Youth gangs are part of the American scene; names like the Shadows, Dragons, and White Knights are synonymous with street gangs. But the Phalsers were not a typical youth gang. Its members did not hang out on street corners; instead, they frequented America's electronic bulletin boards. Armed solely with their home computers, members of this computer gang are said to have tapped into the GTE electronic mail network. Other computer gangs are known to have raided the networks of financial institutions, credit bureaus, and even the Department of Defense.

Intercomputer networks are the electronic highways that bring hackers from all over the world together. In large part, the rise of these networks was made possible by the microcomputer and telecommunications revolutions. Some of the better-known of these networks are GTE Telecommunications, Cyclix Communication, and Compuserve.

Intercomputer networks consist of one or more computer systems linked together by communication lines. These networks can be easily accessed by anyone who has a personal computer linked to a modem and who has the correct password. The modem enables the hacker to connect his computer, via the telephone, to other computers in the network; the password is the key to the network's electronic pathways.

Lack of Visibility

While Wisconsin law enforcement officials looked on, two reporters for the *Wisconsin State Journal* used a home computer to access the state's computer system. The demonstration put to rest any doubts that state tax records, food stamp authorizations, welfare payments, and other confidential data were vulnerable to hacking. The reporters had received the passwords and routines needed to access the system from an undisclosed source. It was later discovered that the access code had also been displayed on an electronic bulletin board, where many could have seen it and made it public.

The reporters had little experience with computers. To tap the system, they used a friend's Apple II home computer, which had been equipped with a telephone communication link for the purpose of the demonstration. Although previous audits of the Wisconsin computer system had found it to be vulnerable to penetration, state officials had done nothing to remedy the situation.

In a separate case, students at the University of California were able to crack the school's UNIX operating system and leave messages in the university's electronic mail system. They later gave school officials a demonstration of how simple it had been to conceal the intrusion.

Armed with access codes, hackers can penetrate virtually any computer system inside or outside the United States—even those in the faraway cities of Asia. Without much difficulty, they can alter, modify, or destroy data; they can also erase the evidence of their intrusions. Hacking, like most other computer-connected abuses, is often invisible—difficult to detect and guard against. Even secure systems are not always safe from an intelligent and determined hacker.

Challenge

A fifteen-year-old Arkansas high school student used his Victor Technologies VIC 20 home computer to break into the school district's Honeywell DPS8/44 mainframe. When asked why he did it, he replied: "To show it could be done." When police in Ann Arbor, Michigan, arrested an electronic peeping Tom, who had tapped into a university computer system, and inquired about his motives, he responded, "for the challenge."

Computers and thrills are one and the same in the minds of many youths. Thrills are probably what a seventeen-year-old Chicago high school student had in mind when he used his home computer to tap into the De Paul University system. His prank cost the university over $20,000 in damages. When arrested, he protested: "But all I did was beat the system!"

The fun and thrill of beating the system is as American as Mom and apple pie. For the hacker, accessing computer systems has become a rite of passage. Our society stresses competition; winning is often an end in itself. Overcoming obstacles, regardless of the price or means employed, brings with it both recognition and rewards. Today's hacker, no less than his elders, is often motivated by the challenge of beating the system. Electronic machismo has fast become an integral part of our computer society.

Fun and Frolic

The FBI had been on the lookout for a group of hackers in Irvine, California, who had tapped into the electronic mail system of GTE Telenet, which serves more than 200,000 terminal users and 1,200 computer systems worldwide. The suspects had "never been in trouble before." When arrested and asked why they did it, one of them replied, "for fun and games."

In Massachusetts, officials at the MIT Laboratory for Computer Science confirmed rumors that the FBI had been investigating intrusions into its computers. It was alleged that several of the laboratory's computer files had been erased and a complete system had been made inoperable ("crashed"). When questioned by the FBI, a fourteen-year-old suspect confessed that he did it "for the fun of gettin' in."

But regardless of whether one considers hacking a rite of passage, fun and frolic, or a pastime, few will deny that it can often prove disruptive to the rights of others. Occasionally, it results in malicious destruction and outright thievery. Thus, it is imperative that we learn to channel the hacker's enthusiasm and energy into more constructive avenues that will advance our technological revolution and benefit society.

The Need for Technoethics

A student in Marlborough, Massachusetts, is said to have tapped the local high school computer to "peep" at his classmates' grades. A newsletter in Tacoma, Washington, keeps readers up to date on the latest devices that companies are using to secure their computer systems. But perhaps the best illustration of lack of computer ethics in our society is the young hacker who broke into the computer system of a New York hospital. When asked why he did it, he replied, "There was nothing wrong with it."

The lack of ethics in the computer rooms of business and government in America may be linked to the amorality of our society. Disgruntled employees often justify their computer antics by pointing to the ethics or lack thereof of their superiors. Young hackers are no different; they merely mimic the behavior of their elders. Although schools are entering the computer era at a frantic pace, few of them offer any courses in computer ethics. Apparently, many even tolerate the hacker's pranks.

Courses in computer ethics are needed so that young computer enthusiasts can learn to respect the rights and privacy of others. Some efforts are currently underway in this area. Drexel University and several other universities and colleges are looking at basic courses in computer ethics; and some public schools, like those in Red Bank, New Jersey, now offer such courses. Even first-graders are required to take them.

By themselves, the best laws and police training will not deter computer misuse. Deterrence must, as a first step, start in our classrooms, where the young must be taught respect for the rights of others. Corporate America must also display leadership in this area. Take, for example, the case of "System Cruncher" and "Vladimer," two gang hackers who were charged with breaking into the computer systems of several universities. Hollywood offered them movie contracts—hardly a good example.

Of Pirates and Electronic Bulletin Boards

In the summer of 1983, a leading news story awoke the nation to the dangers of hacking. It started the morning of June 3, when Chen Chui, a systems manager at New York's Memorial Sloan-Kettering Cancer Center, reported to work at the hospital's computer center. He noticed that something was wrong with the computer. The VAX 11/780 held the records of more than 6,000 patients. It also monitored the hospital's radiation treatment machines, and some seventy hospitals around the country used it to calculate the radiation dosages for their patients. After an examination, Chui concluded that someone had tampered with a section of the computer's memory; the files had been altered to authorize access to new accounts. Since Chui did not recognize these accounts, he became suspicious.

Certain that someone had penetrated their computer system, hospital officials rang the alarm. The New York City police and the FBI were called in, and a trace was put on the system. The game of cat and mouse went on for almost two months. During this period, the intruder made more than fifty attempts to enter the system. In mid-August the pieces of the puzzle finally came together, and the police identified the intruder. They were stunned, as was the entire nation, to find that the elusive criminal was part of a gang of Milwaukee-based hackers who called themselves the 414s.

As the investigation proceeded, it became apparent that the 414s had probably been involved in at least sixty other computer break-ins involving corporate and government computers both in the United States and Canada. Among the computers violated were those of the Security Pacific National Bank in Los Angeles and the Los Alamos National Laboratory. One of the 414s, seventeen-year-old Neal Patrick, was asked to testify before a congressional subcommittee. To a packed audience, with television cameras glaring, he remarked, "We were just playing a game." Another member of the group later told the press that the break-ins "were really easy to pull off."

Although the escapades of these inexperienced teenagers seemed impossible in the face of sophisticated corporate and government security, under closer scrutiny it became obvious that the break-ins of the 414s were not dazzling technological feats. The group had simply stumbled onto a treasure trove of secret access codes and instructions for gaining entry into major computer systems across the country—codes openly posted on electronic bulletin boards. Much of the information had been posted by other hackers at the OSUNY (Ohio Scientific Users of New York) electronic bulletin board in New York. Armed with the necessary passwords, all that the young hackers needed was a home computer (Patrick had used his father's TRS-80 Model II), a modem, and some understanding of how computers worked. The rest is history.

Tom Tcimpidis could tell you all about electronic bulletin boards. He used to operate one, until the Los Angeles police and security officials for the Pacific Telephone Company arrived at his home and confiscated the equipment for his bulletin board system: a Heathkit terminal, about 150 floppy disks, his disk drive, and a monitor. They alleged that his bulletin board had been used by more than 5,000 people to post credit card numbers and access codes.

There are currently over 3,000 electronic bulletin board systems (commonly referred to as BBSs) in the United States. More than 100 of these are located in the New York City area alone. They go by such names as Pirate Cove, Paladin's Palace, Staten Island Smart Terminal (SISTER), Secret Service, Earth News Central, and Atari Inn. Their users have flamboyant monikers, such as Flying Corsair, Stainless Steel Rat, Dark Lord, and Mr. Xerox. A BBS is run by a "syop," or system operator, who has equipped his personal computer with special BBS software, a modem, and telephone lines. Many syops are teenagers. For example, Demon BBS (based in New York) was run by a seventeen-year-old hacker. And some BBSs, such as Timecor in Boston, charge a fee; others, like New York's Arthur Tree, are open by invitation only.

Most BBSs are open twenty-four hours a day, seven days a week. They have become the high-tech version of the old town square. Users drop in to exchange messages and ideas, and to joke, philosophize, flirt, and even arrange dates. Many BBSs perform valuable services; their syops often erase offensive language, passwords, and other hints on accessing computer systems. Many of the boards also carry disclaimers that flash on the user's screen. For example: "This operator shall not be liable to any person for any loss or damage caused by this board or its use." However, whether these disclaimers offer the syops any legal safeguards remains to be seen; the courts have not yet addressed this thorny legal issue.

Police officials estimate that there are more than 400 pirate bulletin boards in the United States. These services are used by hackers to post such valuables as passwords, telephone access codes (for such services as Telenet, MCI, and Sprint), ways to break into computer systems, and ways to evade police taps. Pirate BBSs are where the Milwaukee 414s found the passwords to the Los Alamos and Sloan-Kettering computers, where Computer Yabler found the password to the Dow Jones computers, where Cracko offered to exchange the access code to the Brookhaven National Laboratory computer, and where Cracker made public the GTE Telenet access code. The BBS is where the action is in the hackers' world. Hacking would prove difficult without this new electronic institution. But, to date, neither the legislatures (the U.S. Congress included) nor the courts have defined the legal status of BBSs.

The BBS has also become a favorite vehicle for software pirates, hackers who break into commercial computer programs for the purpose of copying them. Access codes and detailed instructions for copying such programs are often exchanged on BBSs. Pirates frequently use long-distance telephone lines to transmit the copied software, billing the call to a legitimate customer's account.

Some law enforcement sources estimate that the majority of the BBSs in the New York area are misued by software pirates.

The Need for Innovative Solutions

The government is worried. The U.S. Office of Management and Budget (OMB) warns that the activities of hackers could "undermine the confidence of the public in our ability to protect the data that is essential to the operation of agency [government] programs." Meanwhile, in the private sector, hackers and phone freaks are costing telephone companies more than $100 million in annual losses. In response to the hackers' threat, the U.S. Department of Defense has doubled its computer security staff; the National Communications Security Committee—which includes high-ranking officials from the CIA, Pentagon, Federal Emergency Management Agency, and other federal agencies—has recommended additional safeguards for governmental computers.

In general, the response to hacking has been twofold: A call for tighter security and new laws to combat hackers. Several corporations have taken active steps to safeguard their computer systems. For example, the Grumman Aerospace Company has already spent more than $1 million on coding devices to secure its systems from unauthorized intrusions; GTE Telenet Communications Corporation now offers users of its Telemail electronic mail service special data-scrambling software, which is designed to prevent unauthorized access. In many states and in the U.S. Congress, efforts are underway to amend existing criminal laws to make hacking a criminal offense; some states have already done so.

Yet even the most stringent security measures are not foolproof. For example, a fifteen-year-old hacker was able to obtain the passwords to 8,000 data banks from one of the more "secure" systems; a disgruntled employee had provided him with the system's access code. Security, moreover, is expensive. The business community currently spends more than $50 million annually on cryptographic equipment alone. In addition, security measures can limit legitimate users' access to a system; many users find this confining. Commenting on computer security, one user observed, "We're in the business of making money and not playing cops and robbers. Security is a drain."

As for the enactment of criminal legislation directed at hackers, U.S. Senator Charles Mathias, Jr., summarized the dilemma: "Threatening inquisitive 15-year-olds with criminal prosecution isn't a very appetizing prospect, or a likely one." Both federal and local prosecutors are currently inundated with computer abuses involving adults, so the prospect of prosecuting juveniles is both unappealing and unrealistic, especially since most of the hackers come from middle-class families.

Hacking must be seen in the proper perspective. Most of the criminal abuses are committed by a very small percentage of the hacker population. For many young computer enthusiasts, hacking simply provides an outlet for their energies; left to their own devices, even well-intentioned hackers can abuse the rights and privacy of their fellow citizens. As matters stand now, even a well-meaning hacker could accidentally cause an informational catastrophe, a high-tech Three Mile Island. It is only a matter of time.

Perhaps we should create an electronic Peace Corps to harness the energies of hackers in the service of the lesser-developed nations and peoples of the world. Global computer networks, linked together by inexpensive satellite communications (it will soon cost less than a dollar to send a 1,000-word message anywhere in the world), could enable American students and young professionals to communicate with and assist persons in the Third World. Global networks already exist in embryonic form, as exemplified by the present Corinet computer network that ties the United States with the Caribbean, Africa, and Southeast Asia. Employing the marvels of high technology, electronic Peace Corps volunteers could transmit the best that America has to offer to those in need.

Likewise, the talents and energies of young hackers could be used to assist the less-fortunate in our own society. Electronic bulletin boards could easily be converted into electronic classrooms to help the disadvantaged, disabled, and elderly. A domestic electronic Peace Corps would also help channel the enormous enthusiasm of young and idealistic hackers.

Yet there is no quick fix for the high-tech malady of hacking. Faced with the problem of constructively directing youths toward responsible and judicious use of advanced technology, we must match the imaginations of these hackers to create both private and public programs which would deter hacker-related abuses and promote the positive contributions that hackers could provide. The computer industry could easily lead the way.

4

Democratizing Crime:
The Myth of the Supercriminal

I can resist everything but temptation.
— Oscar Wilde

W HILE leaving his New York City apartment, Stephen Jones, twenty-two, was arrested by two police detectives and charged with burglary. Witnesses later identified him at his trial as the thief who had broken into a neighborhood grocery store. His total take: less than $200 worth of groceries. Facing a ten-year prison term, the defendant told his lawyer, "I never seem to win." Jones entered prison and the system consigned him to oblivion.

At the same time, Jerry Neal Schneider, twenty-one, was arrested in Los Angeles and charged with stealing more than $1 million worth of equipment from the Pacific Telephone and Telegraph Company. Computer security expert Gerald McKnight called it "one of the most amazing robberies in the history of crime." Schneider had used the victim's computer to funnel valuable equipment to a company that he controlled; at the time of his arrest, Schneider's company employed ten persons, who helped him gather and sell the loot. After spending forty days in jail, Schneider commenced a $500-a-day consulting career and became a superstar in the annals of high-tech criminology.

Crime, not the economy, is paramount in the public's mind. The skeptic should take a look at the U.S.A. Crime Clock: a serious crime is committed every three seconds, a theft every four seconds, a burglary every ten seconds, a robbery every sixty-three seconds, and with every passing day, an average of two banks are robbed in New York, Los Angeles, and San Francisco. Ten cities will see their banks robbed every other day. Americans are obsessed with crime. The private sector alone currently spends more than $20 billion annually on an array of security services and devices; expenditures may exceed $100 billion by 1995.

Yet crime in America is taking a turn. While serious street crimes have been declining in the last several years, high-tech crimes have been on the increase. The largest heist in American history, more than $2 billion, was carried out with the assistance of a computer, not a gun.

According to the FBI, the average take in a bank robbery is $4,000; the average computer heist exceeds $400,000. The American Society for Industrial Security calls computer-connected crimes a "multi-billion dollar annual business." The Business School of City University, London, found that existing audit techniques are inadequate for detecting computer-connected thefts and abuses; most computer heists go undetected for an average of three years. And *Fortune* magazine warns that the "risks of computer crime are very high." If Bonnie and Clyde were alive today, they would go electronic.

The Universe of Computer Crime

Critics have long charged that New York City's food stamp program is a "black hole" of waste and fraud: almost $60 million worth. A federal task force proved them right. But according to task force sources, the food stamp recipients were not the real villains—they accounted for less than two percent of the losses. Most of the losses were connected to check-cashing companies, wholesale grocers, and criminals. These operators were assisted by dishonest insiders, who had programmed the city's computers to issue phony food stamp authorization forms.

Perhaps to show that the Soviets can do it as well, three women employees of a state-owned factory in Vilnius, Lithuania, took their employer for more than 78,584 rubles ($120,000 in U.S. currency, equivalent to more than twenty-five years of the average Soviet worker's salary) in a phantom employee scheme. They altered the factory's computerized payroll and created a phantom workforce. Twice each month the happy proletarians banked the wages of the ghost employees. It took the Soviet authorities more than four years to detect the fraud. When it finally surfaced, the local newspaper, *Soviet Lithuania*, called it a "capitalist act."

Crimes by computer are a growth industry; no industry, sector of the economy, or country is immune. Not even the world's dictatorships. A MIS Training Institute survey of 600 attendees at the 5th Annual Conference on Control, Audit and Security of IBM Systems, confirmed this. It found that:

59 percent of the respondents said that their organizations had experienced losses to computer crime in the last two years.

63 percent of those crimes were committed by insiders: programmers, operators, and supervisory and nonsupervisory personnel.

40 percent of the people apprehended did it for personal gain, 26 percent for the challenge, 8 percent as competition, and the remainder for publicity or as a result of peer pressure.

Although experts agree that technocrimes are increasing, there is no consensus on exactly what constitutes these offenses. In part, this uncertainty arises because both the technology and the techniques used by criminals rapidly change. Thus, the definitions are many. Take your choice:

Using a computer as the instrument of a business crime.

Fraud, embezzlement, blackmail, and other crimes committed by the manipulation or misuse of computers.

Any intentional act, or series of acts, designed to deceive or mislead others that has an impact or a potential impact on an organization's financial statements. Electronic data processing must be involved in the perpetration or cover-up of the act or series of acts.

Direct involvement of computers in committing a crime.

Any illegal act where a special knowledge of computer technology is essential for its perpetration.

A form of white-collar crime committed by computer.

Confused? Well, don't be. Simply put, these crimes should be thought of as illegal acts in which the computer is either the vehicle used to commit the act—as in an embezzlement—or the target of the act—as in sabotage. The objective of the criminal is often to gain an economic advantage; computers have been widely used since the early 1960s to steal money, property, services, and valuable information. Occasionally—as in the case of a disgruntled employee or political malcontent—the objective may be to simply damage or bring the system to a halt, causing its owner serious economic losses.

If you are still confused, don't worry. Even the experts are not sure. But this has not stopped the thieves; in fact, they are busier than ever:

Employees of a furniture company took more than $180,000 in merchandise by simply manipulating its computerized inventory data.

Monolithic Memories of Sunnyvale, California, charged two of its employees with the theft of more than $3 million in computer chips.

A San Jose, California, computer manufacturer charged that several of its former employees had sold trade secrets valued at $15 million to a competitor.

Two insiders at the Slavenburg Bank in Rotterdam, The Netherlands, used their employer's computer to embezzle more than $60 million.

Two Certified Food programmers are said to have used the company's computer to run their own business.

A programmer for the National Bonded Company in Louisiana used his company's minicomputer system to steal more than $100,000.

Two disgruntled Los Angeles programmers sabotaged their company's computer, causing more than $200,000 in losses.

A former employee of Optimum Services is said to have tapped its computers to copy a valuable program.

A Westinghouse employee is said to have embezzled more than $1 million by programming the company's computer to make payments to bogus companies.

You may wonder who are the targets of computer crime. Traditionally, they have been corporations and government agencies. Ripping-off "Fortune 500s" became almost a sport in the pre-1980 period. But change is in the air. Hospitals, law firms, nonprofit organizations, time-sharing networks, and anyone else who uses or owns a computer is fair game for the post-1980 computer criminal. Everyone and everything is now a target. There are no safe havens.

In the 1960s and 1970s computer heists were often the closely guarded monopoly of computer operators, programmers, magnetic tape librarians, electronic engineers, and other "techno types." This is no longer true. Now any person armed with a little bit of knowledge and access to a keyboard can become a computer criminal in three easy steps: (1) buy an inexpensive personal computer ($500 is often more than adequate); (2) read the instructions that come with the computer; and (3) master the keyboard.

Three factors account for the spread of computer crime, factors not too dissimilar from those connected with the hacking phenomenon. First of all, the explosive growth of computer crime is directly connected to the widespread use of simple and easy-to-operate computers in every area of our lives. The other two developments that have contributed to the dramatic rise of computer crime are the proliferation of computers that can be easily accessed through telephone lines, and the soaring number of individuals who now have access to their employers' computers.

By simply equipping a computer with a modem, even the proverbial little guy can talk to other computers thousands of miles away over the telephone lines, and can hook up to numerous data bases that provide the latest business news developments twenty-four hours a day. Presently, more than 30 million Americans have that capability. Mao Tse Tung spoke of the individual's supremacy over technology. It can aptly be said that the computer has amplified that supremacy. The superstar in the pantheon of high-tech crime is the computer.

Anyone Can Do It

The advances in computer technology in the last several years have been so great, and security has trailed so far behind, that it is now almost child's play to steal electronically. Even an amateur with access to a keyboard can do it. If you don't believe it, then take a look at this list of "hardened criminals":

Michele Cubbage, twenty-seven, was a housewife in Oxon Hill, Maryland. There was nothing unusual about her; she had no computer training. She learned from watching the television program *60 Minutes* how easy it was to steal by computer. And she did, taking People's Security Bank for more than $36,000.

Until May 1983, Stanley Slyngstad worked for the Washington State Division of Vocational Rehabilitation. An unemployed friend of his needed money to buy a truck, and Stanley decided to help. He took more than $17,000 from his employer by programming the department's computer to issue twenty-five bogus checks to "people who were down on their luck." Stanley had never stolen a nickel before this; neither did he know what "computer crime was all about."

Eryie Ann Edgerly, thirty-seven, and Jennie L. Barger, thirty-eight, were two inconspicuous Maryland housewives. Their neighbors were startled to learn that the two had been implicated in a $500,000 fraud involving a

Washington, D.C., pension fund. They did it by filling out phony computer sheets, which listed Eryie as a beneficiary; the computer issued a total of 608 checks to her.

In England a salesman for a chemical company defrauded his employer out of more than $100,000 by programming the computer to double his sales commissions. This was his first brush with the law.

Criminals are trading in their guns for computers, since the chances of being caught are minuscule. The FBI will tell you that they are "less than one in 20,000." The take is often big. According to Tom Whiteside of *The New Yorker* magazine, "a million dollars from a computer crime is considered respectable but not an extra-ordinary score." Often nobody gets hurt—physically, that is.

However, many of these offenses would not be possible without the direct or indirect involvement of dishonest insiders. According to the U.S. Department of Commerce, "thefts committed by employees are behind at least 60 percent of crime-related losses." Banking and the service industries are especially vulnerable. A 1984 congressional study found that about two thirds of all bank failures in the United States between 1980 and mid-1983, were connected to misconduct by insiders. Increasingly, these dishonest insiders are using computers.

Enter the Twilight Zone

When it comes to traditional crime, we know that nearly 24 million of the nation's 86 million households will experience at least one crime, and over 70 million Americans live in households that will be touched by crime. In the realm of business crime, we know that stealing high-tech trade secrets is big business in America. But no one really knew how big until November 1983, when IBM filed a lawsuit against National Semiconductor Corporation and Japan Hitachi, charging that the defendants had been stealing its trade secrets for over three years. Acording to IBM, the stolen information was worth somewhere between $750 million and $2.5 billion.

Statistics abound for traditional crime, but no one knows the annual losses caused by computer crime. Nor does anyone know the cost of investigating and prosecuting these cases. Unfortunately, for too long we have put the study of computer crime on the back burner. This is not to say that there is no study of computer crime, but rather that it is in its infancy. And the estimates available are disturbing. More than 90 percent of all computer criminals evade prosecution; and one out of every ten men and women working with computers will attempt to steal at least once in his or her lifetime. Out of 283 organizations surveyed by the American Bar Association, 72 reported annual losses to computer crime of between $2 and $10 million. And according to a study by the National Center for Computer Crime Data in Los Angeles, a survey of 130 prosecutor's offices in thirty-eight states was able to uncover only seventy-five computer crime cases. One case involved a prosecutor in Colorado who asked a motor vehicle employee to delete a pair of speeding tickets from the defendant's computer system.

Although annual losses associated with computer crime can only be estimated, most experts agree that these losses fall somewhere between $100 million and $5 billion. Figures vary, for example:

U.S. Chamber of Commerce: more than $100 million. "These [annual] estimates do not include the cost involved in combating [computer crimes]."

American Bar Association: between $145 million and $730 million. "The annual losses incurred as a result of computer crime appear, by any measure, to be enormous." And, "if the annual losses attributable to computer crime sustained by the relatively small survey group are conservatively estimated, in the range of half a billion dollars, then it takes little imagination to realize the magnitude of the annual losses sustained on a nationwide basis."

American Society for Industrial Security: as high as $3 billion. "The problem of computer crime will continue to grow with the influx of more computers into the marketplace."

Business Week: up to $3 billion. "While the amount of computer fraud is often overstated, . . . losses in the 100 or so cases of computer fraud reported annually run in the $100 million range."

U.S. Department of Justice: more than $100 million. "Computers have been involved in most types of crime, including fraud, theft, larceny, embezzlement, bribery, burglary, sabotage, espionage, extortion, and kidnapping."

U.S. Congress: perhaps as high as $1 billion. "Although estimates of the current costs of computer crime run into the billions, the true magnitude of the computer security problem is not known."

While both officials and official sources paint a depressing picture of the rampant growth of computer crime, computer manufacturers and their representatives tell a different story. They say that the annual losses attributed to computer crime have been vastly exaggerated. They blame the press and security consultants for the overstatement and accuse them of trying to increase circulation and fan business. But if you ask the press and consultants, they will tell you that the computer industry is trying to keep the lid on the problem because it fears adverse publicity.

However, regardless of what the exact figures are, there is no escaping the conclusion that, as computers continue to proliferate, computer criminals have a bright future.

A Short History of Computer Crime

Computer crime is not solely a phenomenon of the 1980s. Computers were used in an assortment of abuses as early as the 1950s. Although we don't know the extent of such abuses, we do know that the first recorded computer crime case surfaced in 1958 and that the first federal prosecution occurred in 1966. Computer criminals have been active for more than twenty years on both sides of the Atlantic—especially since the mid-1960s. For example, some better known cases were:

1964. Robert F. Hancock attempted to sell $5 million worth of ill-gotten software to the Texaco Company.

1967. The computers of the Strategic Air Command Headquarters in Omaha were tapped. The intruder gained access to confidential military data.

1969. The Canadian International Development Agency discovered that one of its computer tapes had been shipped to a nonexistent company. Computers at Boston University were sabotaged with acid.

1970. The Fresno State College computers were bombed, with damages exceeding $400,000. Also, two employees of a Swedish company sold copies of their firm's computer tapes to competitors.

1971. An English salary clerk used his company's computer to embezzle a mere $720. In the United States, disgruntled employees of the Honeywell Corporation sabotaged the Metropolitan Life computer network and made it inoperable for more than a month.

1973. A teller at New York's Dime Savings Bank used its computer to embezzle more than $1 million. Top management at Equity Funding, a Los Angeles-based insurance conglomerate, used computers to create more than $2 billion in bogus insurance policies and assets.

1983. Two former officials at Southern Illinois University pleaded guilty to a $1.3 million purchasing and leasing scam.

1984. A U.S. Customs Service clerk was arrested and charged with accessing a government computer and modifying data without proper authorization. And two members of Wisconsin's widely heralded 414 computer group pleaded guilty to two counts each of making harassing telephone calls with their modem-equipped computers.

1985. Officials at the University of Southern California investigated allegations that counterfeit degrees, supported by transcripts that were illegally placed in the university's computer system, were sold for as much as $25,000 each. A brokerage firm margin clerk altered computer records to turn 1,700 shares of Loren Industries stock worth less than two dollars each into a number of Long Island Lighting shares selling for more than ten times that price.

1986. The American Medical Association filed a lawsuit charging the GTE Telenet Communications Corporation with sabotaging its on-line medical information service. A financial analyst changed the District of Columbia treasurer's secret computer code to deny his superiors access to financial codes.

The computer antics go on. But few people—both in the private and public sectors—paid any attention until hacking made national headlines. Many businesses, fearing adverse publicity, were reluctant to report these offenses. Concerned with sales, the high-tech industry likewise down-played the problem.

And a major factor hindering efforts to study computer offenses is the speed with which they can be committed. Unlike a burglary, which can take hours to commit, a computer heist can be pulled in less than five milliseconds. The thief can easily erase all records of the intrusion, making it difficult to study the offense. But the study of computer crime, long the province of a handful of mavericks, is beginning to come into its own.

Enter the Keyboard Bandit

According to the *Kiplinger Washington Letter*, the "possibilities [for computer crime] are almost unlimited. And virtually every business today is a potential victim." A survey of 319 organizations published in *Computerworld* in February confirmed this: it disclosed that 65 percent of the respondents had been the victims of some type of computer manipulation, while 70 percent said that they had suffered some form of misuse of their computers. A survey by the Data Processing Management Association (DPMA) of 200 of its members found that 70 percent were concerned that their computers were not sufficiently secure. Many also said that their companies stood to lose over $140,000 a day in the event of a computer break-in or some other type of security breach. And a survey of 100 companies by Price Waterhouse and Company found that only 19 percent of the companies had taken any steps to secure their data. According to one expert, "Computer security in most companies enjoys a lower priority than their leaky roofs."

One reason for this low priority is that security is expensive. Few companies are willing to pay for the needed resources. It will take at least half-a-dozen years for computer security to catch up with the computer thief. The best security will no more succeed in making a system foolproof than modern technology has succeeded in making safes and vaults inpenetrable. It's simply a question of the thief's sophistication and the resources.

Computer manufacturers design computers so that they can be easily used by anybody—even a thief. Consequently, computers are vulnerable to fraud and abuse. The following five characteristics of the computer also help keyboard bandits.

Computers Are Functional

In Alexandria, Virginia, four persons were charged with unlawfully accessing the computers of major corporations and federal agencies. Among the companies involved were Coca Cola, Raytheon Corporation, 3M, and American Hospital Supply Corporation; the accused were also said to have broken into the computers of the U.S. Department of Agriculture and the National Aeronautics and Space Administration. And in Los Angeles, a federal grand jury indicted six persons for manipulating one of the nation's largest credit data banks; its computers are said to store information on more than 50 million Americans. It is alleged that, for fees ranging up to $1,500, the ring would doctor a person's credit rating. More than 100 persons are said to have paid to have their bad credit ratings erased.

Computers perform many functions: they record, process, store, and transmit large amounts of data. They are designed to serve as giant electronic filing cabinets, easily accessible to users from faraway locations. Therein lies their weakness: computers are excellent performers, whether for good or for ill.

Computers Are Superfast

A former employee and a legal secretary of the Dade County, Florida, State Attorney's Office are said to have been paid $2,500 for promising to erase a criminal record from the county's Criminal Justice Information System. Since any one of 250 terminals has access to the system, it would have been a simple matter, taking only seconds, to erase the record.

In Los Angeles, two persons were charged with conspiring to steal over $9 million from the city's Treasurer's Office. The duo managed to siphon off $810,000 before being discovered. The transfer of funds took only seconds to complete. Since computers operate in milliseconds, many computer heists go undetected.

Computers Are Simple

The simplicity of computer systems makes them vulnerable, especially where dishonest employees are involved. Most computer functions are open to abuse, for example:

Input: A dishonest operator can easily introduce false data into the system, or modify or alter existing records.

Programming: A thief can insert instructions into a program that direct the computer to divert money or property to a source not originally intended.

Output: Valuable marketing plans, mailing lists, or trade secrets can be copied and sold to a competitor.

Communication: Through public or private telephone circuits, data can be transmitted between computers, or between computers and remote terminals. The communication function is especially vulnerable to electronic penetration; for example, a thief armed with the proper access code and a terminal can easily gain access to the system and copy the data or software stored in it.

Computers Make Mistakes

A Los Angeles accountant was charged with stealing nearly $1 million from the United California Bank. His defense: a computer mistake. His attorney argued that a keyboarding error had accidentally credited his client's account with $927,288. A superior court jury agreed and found him not guilty.

According to the *Wall Street Journal*, as much as 85 percent of the "destruction of valuable computer data" involves inadvertent acts. People that operate computers make mistakes; few juries will convict a defendant who can convince them that it was the outcome of a simple mistake.

Computer Fraud Is Difficult to Detect

According to the American Institute of Certified Public Accountants (AICPA), computer frauds can "continue for long periods of time—some for years—before they are detected." Many surface accidentally. A computer programmer proved the AICPA correct. With the aid of his employer's computer, he stole more than $10,000; the fraud continued undetected for six years. In another case, a computer operator robbed his employer of more than $50,000; it took the victim four years to discover the heist.

From the AICPA we also learn that the majority of computer frauds are detected only accidentally—for example, as a result of a routine audit, while auditors are checking unusual activity, as a result of an anonymous tip, or because of numerous customer complaints. But even when the fraud is uncovered, according to the AICPA, "there is also a general reluctance of many companies to disclose information about fraud." For example, when a Fortune 500 corporation discovered that one of its executives had been involved in a large computer fraud, rather than prosecute, it transferred him to one of its subsidiaries.

Computer Diddling

Computer thieves have employed an array of techniques to defraud their victims. Many of these criminal acts have involved one or more of the following: the system's equipment and its supporting facilities (hardware), programs and operating systems (software), information handled by the system (data), and services provided by the system (resources). And most computer crimes fall under one or more of the following areas: destructive acts, data abuses, theft and counterfeiting of hardware, pirating of software, financial thefts, and unauthorized use of services. And the computer crimes discovered so far are merely the tip of the iceberg. The future bodes an increase in all areas of computer crime.

Destructive Acts

A computer operator for a trucking company in New York City, angry because his employer worked him too hard, destroyed more than $2 million in billing information that he was supposed to have entered into the company's computer. An electrical instrument manufacturer in Pennsylvania charged a disgruntled employee with destroying several of its valuable computer programs. The employee allegedly used a password that had been assigned to him to enter the company's computer from a remote terminal; in less than ten minutes, he is said to have erased all the programs dealing with the firm's latest products.

Destructive acts directed against computers and their components are on the upswing. Many of these involve alienated employees; some are connected to labor–management disputes. A growing number—particularly overseas—involve political malcontents. Guns, screwdrivers, gasoline bombs, water, acid, and a variety of other devices have been used to damage or immobilize computer systems. The more sophisticated attacks are electronic intrusions with the object of destroying data or programs. Although political and financial considerations (especially when a competitor is involved) play a role, most of these cases involve angry and dissatisfied employees.

Data Abuses

A scandal erupted in the Dallas Municipal Court when an attorney informed one of the judges that a defendant had paid court officials to erase his computerized arrest record. In Atlanta, the FBI arrested a systems analyst after it received a tip that he had stolen two computer tapes containing data valued at $420,000 from his employer.

Inexpensive and powerful computer devices are increasingly making it possible to stockpile and access large volumes of data. For example, the data storage capacity of desktop computers will soon be sufficient to keep tabs on the entire Canadian population. The potential for the abuse of data likewise grows. For example, a retailer in Missouri is said to have supplied a collection agency with the confidential access code to the data banks of the Credit Bureau of Greater Kansas City. And students at the University of California are said to have uncovered a simple technique for accessing most of the nation's computer systems. It is feared that if the technique is made public, business and government agencies would be forced to spend large sums of money on computer security.

According to *Computerworld*, "Data ranks among the most critical of all corporate resources." The unauthorized alteration, creation, or destruction of data could cripple most organizations. If the key records of a Fortune 500 corporation were destroyed, most experts agree that it would cease to be operational within three to four weeks.

Theft and Counterfeiting of Hardware

The high-tech black market is a multibillion dollar annual business. In Massachusetts, the police charged seven persons with the theft of over $700,000 worth of semiconductor chips from Wang Laboratories. In federal court in Atlanta, a San Diego man pleaded guilty to impersonating a General Dynamics executive for the purpose of stealing a Vector Graphics microcomputer system. And prosecutors in San Francisco filed criminal charges against two individuals who attempted to sell counterfeit Apple computers.

The theft and counterfeiting of computer hardware is well-orchestrated. Many of the thefts are carried out by industrial spies; U.S. Senator Charles Mathias, Jr., called them "computer pirates." Specialized fencing networks are also involved. Since few of these cases result in criminal prosecution, nobody really knows the full scope of the problem. Some industry sources place the annual losses in the hundreds of millions of dollars. But few business executives have shown any inclination to assist prosecutors; sadly, the business community comprises much of the market for stolen and counterfeited computer hardware.

Software Pirating

In Ohio, a man was arrested for tapping into a General Tire Corporation computer and making a copy of the program used to operate the tire-press machines. A Purdue University student was charged with attempting to sell a pirated copy of his former employer's software, valued at between $50,000 and $1 million, to a West Coast company. And Nestar Systems is trying to apprehend whoever is selling unauthorized copies of its software in Europe.

Software is to computers what gasoline is to cars. For every ten dollars a user spends on hardware, another three are spent on software. Software sales now exceed $2 billion annually; they are projected to exceed $12 billion by 1990. Losses to software pirating are likewise on the increase. According to *PC Week*, a respected industry publication, "millions, possibly billions, of dollars are being lost." Industry sources place the annual losses at over $1 billion; they fear that this figure could exceed $5 billion by 1988. And there is growing concern that these losses could affect the long-term financial viability of the software industry.

Financial Thefts

Unfortunately, the computer is an ideal vehicle for white-collar crimes—especially financial thefts. A claim supervisor for an insurance company stole

$500,000 from his unsuspecting employer. He used a terminal to add his accomplices' names to the eligibility file, and the computer than generated checks payable to his cohorts. And officials at the University of Maryland Hospital were shocked to learn that one of their more trusted computer operators—'a good, solid, professional worker'—had been implicated in a $140,000 computer fraud.

Unauthorized Use

Several employees at the U.S. Department of Energy data processing center in Germantown, Maryland, are alleged to have used the department's computers to play games. Some 200 individuals are charged with defrauding the University of Toronto of $15,000 worth of computer time; nearly 3,500 computer jobs were illegally billed to the university.

A member of the computer department of the California State Polytechnic University observed that, "If someone were to conduct an audit of some of the large computing installations in Southern California and elsewhere, I suspect you'd find a lot of processing time that couldn't be really accounted for." In many states, the absence of legislation specifically prohibiting this conduct makes prosecution difficult, if not impossible. Nor has the Congress enacted any federal legislation to address the problem. Yet experts agree that annual losses to businesses and government run in the millions of dollars.

The computer has had a profound impact on crime, altering the way many criminals steal, and making it possible for them to steal more. But the computer criminal, like the hacker, is an ordinary person. Very few computer thieves are electronic geniuses, and the majority have not previously broken the law. Although this may change as more professional criminals enter the arena, the overwhelming number of computer thieves are trusted but dishonest insiders. There are no supercriminals; there is merely a technology that has given ordinary men and women the tools with which to steal a king's ransom with relative impunity.

5

Organized Crime Goes Electronic

We are bigger than U.S. Steel.

— Meyer Lansky

T HE Russians were among the first to discover the high-tech gold of California's Silicon Valley. So when Monolithic Memories lost more than $3 million worth of advanced memory circuits to a gang of thieves, everyone pointed at the KGB. But they were wrong. The thieves were in the pay of a different master: the mob. Organized crime is also interested in "hot chips."

When a combined task force of New York and New Jersey police officials cracked a multimillion-dollar mob-controlled bookmaking operation, the press paid scant attention at first. But when the police disclosed that the bookmakers had gone high tech, the press took note: floppy disks, modems, and the latest personal computers had replaced the bookies' slips. The mob had used computers to calculate betting odds and determine how to lay bets; computers were also used to keep track of customers and communicate with associates in other parts of the country. And the mob's programmers had even developed customized software for the operation.

It's bigger than IBM, Texas Instruments, Apple, and the entire high-tech industry combined. According to *Forbes* magazine, its annual take is estimated to exceed $300 billion; much of that is tax-free profit. It is the biggest money-maker in America. But its stock is not listed in any of the nation's papers; nor is its stock traded on any of the exchanges.

What exactly *is* "it"? The answer depends on who you talk to. In the Midwest, they call it the Outfit or the Syndicate; in the West, it's the Mob, and in the Northeast it's the Arm. To most Americans, it's organized crime: a loose confederation of racial, ethnic, and regional criminal groups that are bound by economic, social, and political ties. It can aptly be called an invisible enterprise.

But organized crime is both big and sophisticated. Law enforcement officials believe that it has funneled more than $20 billion into as many as 15,000 to 50,000 businesses; the annual take from these businesses reportedly exceeds $50 billion. Its business investments, according to the U.S. Senate Permanent Subcommittee on Investigations, include "banks, brokerage houses, and pension funds."

Organized crime has been quick to see the value of high technology. According to the Illinois Bureau of Investigation, it is using computers in many of its illicit operations. Mob-connected thieves are also using computers to commit sophisticated frauds. The FBI warns that electronic payment systems are especially vulnerable to mob-engineered heists. To quote a U.S. Department of Justice source, "If they streamline their operations with computers, we're really in trouble."

The Electronic Mafiosi

Although nobody knows the exact size or composition of organized crime in America, we do know it has an uncanny ability to stay abreast of high technology. Like any other large and complex organization, organized crime employs an array of lawyers, accountants, and other professionals to help it run its vast business holdings. And like any modern organization, it is interested in the tools of modern technology. An investigation by *Computerworld* uncovered evidence that the mob is moving into the twenty-first century with a growing army of mainframes, printers, disk drives, and personal computers at its disposal.

Today's mobster views himself as a businessman. To quote *Computerworld*, "mob operations are much like those of any other business. The greatest profits accrue to those with the lowest costs." For the modern mob, computers are ideal for helping keep track of its vast legal and illegal business holdings; making it easier to prey on legitimate businesses; and keeping tabs on law enforcement intelligence activities. In addition, computers are ideal for storing damaging evidence, since they can be programmed to erase or manipulate all of a system's files in the event of a police raid. In fact, computers are increasingly used in most of organized crime's traditional acitivities.

Gambling

The mob's annual take from its illegal gambling operations is said to exceed $40 billion, which is more than the combined gross income of IBM's domestic and international operations. The Internal Revenue Service estimates that illegal gambling provides the mob with over $1 million in untaxed profits each hour of the day.

Traditional mob operators kept track of their gambling bets and customers in ledger books and on flash paper (which is easy to destroy if the police stage a raid), but the modern bookmaker has gone high tech. With $40 billion at stake, he needs to. Gambling information is increasingly stored on computer tapes and disks. And programs are also being specially prepared by bookmakers to keep track of the win–lose histories of their clients, the bets placed, odds, and money paid out.

There is also evidence that the mob is using computers to administer its sprawling gambling empire. For example, a nationwide gambling ring was found to be using a mainframe, connected by microcomputers to its branch offices around the country, to keep track of its bets and clients. At the end of each day, the branch offices used microcomputers to feed their betting information to the mainframe. And in Tulsa, Oklahoma, a police raid uncovered evidence that local bookmakers were keeping coded files on their clients; the computer was also equipped with a "raid button" designed to destroy the program in case of a police raid.

Traditionally, the mob has had little or no difficulty recruiting professionals to assist in its operations. Nor is it encountering any problems in recruiting data processing professionals. For example, a systems analyst at the Sandia National Laboratories in Albuquerque, New Mexico, used the lab's computer to prepare a sports betting program for local bookmakers; the program was designed for easy entry of point spreads, odds, bets, and profits. The analyst owed gambling debts to local mobsters, and wrote the program to repay the debts. But someone tipped off the authorities and he was arrested just as he was about to deliver the program to the bookmaker. The Sandia lab is engaged in highly sensitive nuclear weapons research work; the analyst had a security clearance at the time of his arrest.

According to Jack Bologna, a computer expert and a former federal investigator, computers are ideally suited to the mob's gambling operations. Computers eliminate the need for large numbers of runners, collectors, and other personnel. Computerization reduces overhead costs, and even the mob wants to trim its operations.

Prostitution

When police officials in Santa Ana, California arrested the head of a prostitution ring, they were startled to find that he had stored records on more than 4,000 customers in a personal computer. The files included billing information as well as the sexual tastes of his customers. A Northeastern prostitution ring used a sophisticated, centralized computer system to keep track of its business; its files included such information as the aliases used by the prostitutes, their criminal records, their current home addresses, and the likes and dislikes of their customers. The system was also used to dispatch the women from city to city on a moment's notice.

Prostitution is a multibillion dollar annual business. Many of the larger prostitution rings, according to law enforcement officials, easily lend themselves to computerization. Criminals have been quick to see this. To quote a police source, "Computers are increasingly being used in more sophisticated operations."

Pornography

Both the movie industry and our mass circulation magazines and journals live by computers. But when the police cracked a Florida mob-controlled pornography operation, they were taken aback to find that organized crime was using computers to distribute pornographic material. In fact, mobsters employed a highly sophisticated computerized system to keep track of their customers, profits, payroll, and marketing operations.

The mob is also using computers to distribute its films. For example, Joseph Peraino, a soldier in the Colombo Mafia family, produced his first movie in 1972 in southern Florida. This low-budget film, *Deep Throat*, eventually made more than $50 million for the Colombo-Gambino Mafia families. But computers helped the mob market to distribute the movie to cinemas around the country. According to U.S. Senate investigators, the mob is also using computers and bulletin boards to distribute pornographic literature and assist in its marketing efforts.

Pornography has grown into a $6 billion annual industry in the United States. Pornographers employ thousands of people, have developed a distribution network that rivals those of the large national magazine chains, and retain the services of all types of experts and professionals—including computer programmers and operators. Without the increased use of automation, the system would simply dwindle into a cottage industry.

Drugs

When the Massachusetts police raided a mob-run drug operation, they also confiscated two personal computers. They later discovered that the mob used the computers to keep track of its statewide drug distribution network. When federal agents raided a motel room near the Miami International Airport, they didn't realize they had stumbled onto an international multimillion-dollar drug-smuggling ring. The agents seized eight pounds of cocaine, nine guns, $30,000 in cash, and a slip of paper listing the names of two individuals. As it turned out, the two were IBM employees who had been hired by the gang to help it computerize its smuggling operations.

Unfortunately, cocaine has become the drug of choice for many American addicts; their ranks include many professionals. When the police arrested two former Intel Corporation employees, they found that the two were part of a national "coke for chips" ring: cocaine was exchanged for stolen memory chips. The police theorized that the ring was part of a larger, more complex mob-controlled network that specialized in swapping drugs for high tech gear.

The drug trade in the United States is big business. It's said to make $80 billion a year—profits that reportedly exceed the combined incomes of America's 500 largest corporations. Drug traffickers are also turning to high technology to keep track of their businesses and evade the authorities. A police source observed, "they can easily run and keep track of their operations simply with a computer terminal."

Fencing

The mob has been active in the multibillion-dollar fencing industry for many years. Mob-connected fences, or middlemen, buy and sell everything from guns to stolen auto parts. A California gang specialized in just that: it ran a national stolen auto parts business. Customers used their terminals or microcomputers to access the gang's mainframe in California and place their orders; if a part was not in stock, the gang stole it and then shipped it to the buyer. The computer also helped the gang identify markets with a high demand for stolen auto parts.

Mathew De Filippo worked for E.R. Squibb & Sons as a computer operator in the company's distribution center in Burlington, Massachusetts. Little did his employer and his fellow workers suspect that De Filippo was using the company's computer to divert more than $1 million in drugs from the company to the mob. To cover his tracks, he altered the computerized records to show that the missing drugs had been given away as samples. The scheme continued undetected for five years.

If you ever decide to buy railroad cars, the mob can assist you. They do it by computer. That's exactly how the mob diverted 230 railroad cars belonging to the Penn Central railroad to a yard in the Chicago area. The cars were painted and given a "face lift." It took the police several months to locate the stolen cars; they have yet to apprehend the culprits.

Fencing is a multibillion dollar annual business, and fences come in all sizes and levels of sophistication. The largest fences are often mob-connected. They serve an important role: bringing buyers and sellers together. Computers are ideally equipped to keep track of wares, customers, and suppliers; they also make it easy for fences to erase their records within minutes in the event of a police raid.

Pilferage

Four individuals with ties to the New England Patriarca Mafia family were charged with stealing high-speed modems, multiplexers, and data entry terminals valued at more than $1 million from the Codex Corporation in Mansfield, Massachusetts. The police speculated that "there is a lot more of it going on." In a separate case, over 115 boxes of chips belonging to Wang Laboratories were hauled away by mob-connected thieves; the stolen semiconductor components were valued at $750,000. In Sunnyvale, California, a mob-connected thief was arrested for the theft of $40,000 worth of chips.

Pilferage is a $4 billion-a-year business. According to the U.S. Chamber of Commerce, mob associates have both funded and planned some of the more complex heists, especially in the high-tech area. *Computerworld* writes that the New York mob is especially interested in the growing multimillion-dollar stolen microchip market.

Through its wide network of contacts, organized crime has had little difficulty finding a market for its high-tech loot. For example, a mob fence is said to have been behind the theft of 10,000 chips from a Silicon Valley manufacturer. The fence had planned to sell the loot to a West German firm. There is also concern that the mob may be selling stolen high-tech equipment to foreign agents.

Money Laundering

Federal prosecutors have charged that the Sunshine State Bank of Miami was controlled by organized crime and used to launder more than $250 million in drug money. Police officials say it is merely the tip of the iceberg. In Washington, D.C., prosecutors charged a congressional lobbyist and former vice president of the Riggs National Bank with laundering at least $1 million. And in Australia, authorities charged that a defunct Sydney bank had been merely a "shell" for the laundering of narcotic profits.

Mobsters still remember that Al Capone was jailed in 1931 not for murder, but for tax evasion. Other criminals and tax cheats engage in money-laundering operations, but the mob has perfected the technique. Colombian mobsters alone are said to launder more than $10 billion in drug money annually through U.S., Caribbean, and Central American banks. For assistance, gangsters employ the best professionals that money can buy, as well as the most advanced technology currently available. According to the *Wall Street Journal*, computers and electronic banking are increasingly playing an important role in the mob's money-laundering efforts.

In a traditional mob laundering operation, the money—in the form of cash—is first flown out of the country by a trusted courier to a safe tax haven; there it is deposited in a secret account with a licensed bank or other financial institution. The funds are then transferred by wire from the bank to a mob-controlled company (shell) in another country. Finally, the funds are returned to the United States in the form of a loan or investment to a mob-controlled company. The source of the funds remains anonymous, and no taxes are paid on the profits.

Electronic banking is fast changing this technique. The mob can now use its computers to keep track of its money as it moves from various domestic and foreign accounts and to instruct a bank's computer to wire funds to a Caribbean account. With hundreds of billions of dollars being wired in and out of the United States daily, it is almost impossible for the authorities to distinguish a mob wire transfer from a legitimate one. As banking at home by computer continues to increase, international wire transfers could be easily carried out from the comfort of the home or office. This development would enable bookmakers and other mob associates to launder money at the press of a button.

That's exactly what Anthony Giacalone, a soldier in the Genovese Mafia family, did before he was arrested. With the assistance of a dishonest Citibank employee, and through the use of an account at the bank, he laundered more than $3 million. The scheme worked as follows: On instructions from Giacalone, the money was wired from his Citibank account in New York to banks in the Caribbean; the funds were channeled through several Panamanian corporate shells and then returned to Giacalone's Citibank account.

Giacalone then simply withdrew the laundered funds from the account. According to a security officer at Citibank, the scheme covered three continents. The funds were transferred electronically with the assistance of computers.

The mob is also adept at using the banks and brokerage firms it controls to wire its profits to overseas accounts. For example, a mob-controlled bank could easily use the Fed Wire (a massive electronic pipeline belonging to the Federal Reserve) to transfer its profits to overseas banks. Policing the Fed Wire is not a simple matter for the authorities; although banks are required under the Bank Secrecy Act to report all cash deposits and withdrawals in excess of $10,000, wire transfers are not covered. Efforts by the U.S. Treasury to require banks to report wire transactions in excess of $50,000 have met with opposition from the banking community, on the grounds that reporting is "unnecessary and intrusive." According to Treasury sources, a majority of the nation's banks do not even comply with the present reporting requirements of the Bank Secrecy Act.

Loansharking

A programmer who fell behind in his payments to a mob-connected loanshark was pressured into stealing valuable software from his employer. An operator, who also fell behind on her mob loan, was forced to embezzle more than $80,000. And a bank clerk stole over $1 million in order to pay a loanshark for his gambling debts.

Loansharking consists of lending money at extortionate (illegal) interest rates, which can range between 250 and 1,000 percent a year. Profits for the mob are often enormous—billions of dollars annually. For example, a $100,000 loan can easily bring in millions of dollars in profits for the loanshark (often referred to as a Shylock). Personal computers are being used by loansharks to keep track of clients and compute interest on the loans. Loansharks and bookmakers have been known to pressure programmers, operators, systems analysts, and other data processing professionals to steal money, data, and other valuables.

The evidence suggests that the mob is increasingly turning to high tech to streamline its traditional illegal activities and also to screen them from the authorities. Likewise, the computer age presents organized crime with new opportunities to steal; drugs-for-chips schemes and other thefts are on the increase.

Preying on Business and Government—High-Tech Style

Police wiretaps in New York and West Germany disclosed that associates of organized crime were planning to counterfeit more than $900 million in securities. Among the companies targeted were the Chrysler Corporation, Pan American World Airways, and General Motors. In Chicago, federal investigators linked members of the mob to several Las Vegas casinos. And the founder of a large conglomerate listed on the New York Stock Exchange is said have been a secret associate of such gangsters as Meyer Lansky, Benjamin (Bugsy) Siegel, and Gus Greenbaum.

Preying on business and government has been a mob pastime since the turn of the century. Traditionally, the mob has made its presence felt in the coal and trucking industries, the waste-disposal business, entertainment, the garment industry, casinos and restaurants, and labor unions. According to the U.S. Department of Justice, more than 300 local labor unions are presently under the mob's tight control. But the syndicate is shifting gears. The theft and pirating of software, the manipulation of automated payment systems, and high-tech espionage are fast gaining its attention. And unlike the petty thief, the gangster brings with him a criminal organization with vast experience and resources at its command. The modern mobster understands business; this makes him a dangerous protagonist.

Money Cards

Alfonse Confesore was thirty years old when he went into partnership with organized crime. As a repairman for the Dashew Business Machine Corporation of New York, Al knew he was in demand. The mob likes money cards and Dashew handled the embossing of credit card plastics for some of the nation's largest retailers and financial institutions. But the partnership was short-lived: Al was found shot in the head near a Long Island railroad depot in Queens, New York. Nevertheless, he had been useful to the mob. He counterfeited thousands of cards, which ultimately caused more than $600,000 in losses to the credit card companies.

A money card weighs less than an ounce and costs less than fifty cents to produce, yet it's worth its weight in gold. With it, you can pay for magazines, airline tickets, gasoline, telephone calls, and food, and carry out a multitude of other financial transactions. You can also use it to access and transfer funds from your bank account. Today's money cards are multifunctional—largely as a result of the computer revolution.

According to the *Nilson Report*, a credit card industry publication, there are now more than 700 million credit and debit cards in the United States. And card-carrying Americans now spend over $300 billion annually. Like other cards, money cards are now loaded with numerous options. For example,

VISA offers an electronic card that allows you to withdraw—both in the United States and overseas—cash from more than 8,000 automated teller machines located in over a dozen countries. American Express, Plus Systems, and dozens of other financial institutions are well on their way to constructing international financial networks. JCPenney, Woodward & Lothrop, and other retailers are offering point-of-sale transactions that make use of electronic debit cards. MasterCard customers can now use their cards at teller machines belonging to such networks as Ginny, Most, and Master Teller.

But frauds and the counterfeiting of money cards are also on the increase. According to the American Bankers Association, they account for more than $200 million in annual losses; some industry sources go as high as $1 billion. For example, VISA alone has said it lost more than $50 million in 1982. MasterCard reported losses of over $20 million in 1983—a substantial increase over the $200,000 it lost in 1979. And according to the Senate Judiciary Committee, "Card fraud operations appear to coincide with locations of major known organized crime families."

The mob has been quick to see opportunities created by the exploding money card industry. A New York mob-connected ring, for example, counterfeited more than 20,000 cards, which were then sold along with phony drivers licenses. And a Chicago mob was reportedly behind a massive credit card fraud scheme that may have cost credit card companies millions of dollars. Employees of 80 New York businesses, ranging from national chain stores to neighborhood shops, knowingly accepted credit cards that were stolen or counterfeit. Another 104 merchants cooperated with members of the Gambino Mafia family in a multimillion-dollar credit card counterfeiting operation. The Senate Judiciary Committee has found evidence that the mob's profits from credit card counterfeiting are being channeled into its drug trafficking operations.

And according to security experts, half-hearted efforts to deter organized crime will prove ineffective. It has both the requisite resources and technical know-how to counterfeit almost any money card. Given enough time, it can find the experts needed to help it counterfeit even the so-called counterfeit-proof money cards. The mob, some industry sources fear, may have a bright future in the electronic banking environment.

Chips and Counterfeits

A Los Angeles gang known as the Israeli Mafia was behind the theft of 10,000 microcomputer chips from Intel Corporation. Comprised largely of Israeli-

Americans, the gang specializes in insurance frauds and the theft of microchips. The Israeli Mafia is also suspected in several murders in Silicon Valley. The One Eye Jack gang, also based on the West Coast, is suspected of having masterminded the counterfeiting of more than 100,000 chips. And on the East Coast, the Gennano-Anguillo gang in Massachusetts is reputed to have run a multimillion-dollar stolen chip operation.

The theft and counterfeiting of computer microchips is big business in America. Their high value, the business demand, and their compact size makes them ideally suited for theft. For example, because stolen integrated circuits can sell for as much as $1,000 a piece, a thief can make several thousand dollars by simply stuffing his or her pockets, socks, or shirt with a handful of chips.

The mob has had little or no difficulty in making its way into the high-tech industry. Counterfeit computers are also a big and growing business for the mob. In many parts of the world, especially Asia, they are said to out-sell the real thing. In one catch alone, the U.S. Customs Service seized $9 million in counterfeit computers. Counterfeit computers are such a lucrative business that criminal groups in Hong Kong, Taiwan, Singapore, Malaysia, and South Korea have increasingly become involved in this black market. Police officials suspect that the Four Seas Gang—a powerful Taiwanese criminal syndicate whose membership includes both business and government officials—and some of the Asian Triad syndicates are involved in this black market.

The mob is also busily employed in drugs-for-chips schemes. To quote a California police official, "security is worthless in most high-tech firms." As for the private security guards, "some are junkies." And the engineers and other high-tech professionals "pop pills and snort coke." Mob loansharks and bookmakers are taking chips in exchange for gambling debts, while mob fences are actively buying and selling the high-tech loot.

Data Bases

It is estimated that the pirating (copying and altering) of data bases costs American businesses more than $1 billion annually; some experts place the losses as high as $3 billion. The mob has also taken interest in this area. For example, a federal grand jury in Los Angeles has found that individuals with ties to organized crime were behind the manipulation of several credit data banks, including those of TRW Data Systems, which stores information on more than 50 million persons. The gang sold "A-1" credit ratings to businessmen, lawyers, and other persons with bad credit histories, for fees ranging between $175 and $1,500. More than 100 persons received positive credit ratings. American Express and several other companies reportedly lost over $1 million because of the fraud.

Government data bases have also been mob targets. Like any good businessman, the mobster wants to know what his opponents (the police) have up their sleeves. For example, a computer printout belonging to the Drug Enforcement Administration (DEA) made its way into the hands of a mob-operated drug ring. A DEA computer operator is suspected of having been the source. In Florida a former employee of the Dade County State Attorney's Office is alleged to have attempted to erase criminal records from the county's Criminal Justice Information System in return for fees of up to $2,500. And a former Los Angeles county deputy sheriff is suspected of having unlawfully accessed the police data center. The U.S. Treasury Department's Enforcement Communication System, which stores information on drug trafficking, stolen vehicles, and other criminal activities, is also alleged to have been accessed by persons with ties to the mob.

Electronic Catalogs

Shopping machines resembling arcade video consoles are being installed in stores around the country. To shop, a customer merely calls one of the electronic catalogs; a video disk allows him or her to choose among some 60,000 brand-name items. Once the customer selects a product, he or she then runs a credit card through a reader, which is connected to the catalog; the product is later mailed to the customer's home.

The purpose of electronic catalogs is to make shopping more convenient. As an inducement, customers are offered discounts (often 50 percent below the suggested manufacturer's retail price). Although the system is still in its infancy, law enforcement officials fear that the mob may be able to manipulate it through the use of phony credit cards. Catalog-related frauds already account for millions of dollars in annual losses.

High-Tech Food Stamps

Uncle Sam's food stamp program is a multibillion-dollar annual business. The program's printing and distribution costs reportedly exceed $100 million annually, while processing costs are rapidly approaching $1 billion. And food stamp fraud now costs the government more than $1 billion in annual losses. Many of these rip-offs involve recipients who sell their coupons or receive double benefits for claiming that their stamps were lost or stolen.

And according to John Graziano, a former inspector general for the U.S. Department of Agriculture (USDA), organized crime is also heavily involved, especially in the counterfeiting of stamps. Food stamps are being used by crimnals to purchase drugs, weapons, and stolen cars, and even to pay off gambling debts. The General Accounting Office states that food stamps have become a second currency.

But the government plans to change all of this. It has awarded a $2.2 million contract to the Planning Research Corporation of McLean, Virginia, to develop an electronic benefits transfer (EBT) system, which would replace paper food stamps with electronic blips. The principle is the same as that currently used in many point-of-sale transactions. Food stamp recipients would be given plastic, magnetic-striped cards with their photographs on them, an account number, and a PIN (personal identification number). The government's computers would record the monthly amount allocated to the recipient; when the recipient shops at a grocery store, instead of paying for the groceries with food stamps, he or she would pay with the USDA card.

The system's operation is simple. The retailer inserts the card into a terminal by the ckeckout stand; the recipient then presses his identification number. If the number on the terminal matches the one given by the recipient, the transaction goes through. The recipient's account is debited by computer, while the retailer's account is credited for the same amount. A recipient can also check the balance of his food stamp account by simply dialing the computer with a touch-tone telephone.

But critics of the EBT system warn that electronic food stamps will not solve the problem of fraud, because there is little to stop a dishonest recipient from selling his or her card and secret identification number to a thief. They observe that this has already happened with automated teller machine cards.

There is also the problem of organized crime, which has demonstrated an uncanny ability to counterfeit paper food stamps and plastic money cards. Even USDA officials acknowledge that the mob will have little difficulty in doing the same with EBT cards. The Inspector General's office at USDA has serious reservations about the new system. "The mob," said one official, "will merely go electronic." And, "the cure may be worse than the present state." Since the program is still experimental, a high-tech food stamp system could offer the mob new opportunities to steal unless it's made secure from the outset.

High-Tech Recruits

James Lemay was serving a ninety-nine-year prison term in Tennessee for murder when he decided to take a computer course offered by the state's work release program. Trained as a computer operator, he was put to work in the comptroller's office. He was so good at his job that the governor commuted his sentence to thirty years. But Lemay grew tired of prison life and escaped. He had good reason, because soon after his escape the state's auditors discovered that he had used the comptroller's computer to embezzle more than $18,000 in funds earmarked for a tax rebate program.

While serving a one-year sentence in Santa Clara, California, Scott Robinson is suspected of using the prison's computer to expedite his release date. Prison officials are also investigating the possibility that Robinson may have accessed more than 1,000 other prison release records, including the files of the state's Criminal Justice Information Center in Sacramento. But Robinson denies all of the allegations and has said that he plans to take more computer courses.

According to the U.S. Department of Justice, there are over 450,000 persons serving prison terms in the United States; half of these are in prison for nonviolent crimes. Prisons in four states—California, Texas, Florida, and New York—contain one third of all prison inmates. In addition, an estimated 210,000 people are doing time in local jails, while awaiting their trials. The cost to the taxpayer is $10 billion annually, or $16,000 per inmate. Many of them are recidivists (convicted of at least two crimes), and once released, will eventually find their way back to prison.

Efforts are underway to provide prisoners with up-to-date skills to prepare them for the outside world. For example, since 1967 the state of Massachusetts, assisted by such firms as Honeywell, has given computer training to some of its inmates. The program has paid off; inmates have used their new-found computer skills to start prison industries. Inmates at the Framingham State Prison initiated Con'puter Systems Programming in 1967; the program handled some of the electronic data processing (EDP) work for such state agencies as the Department of Corrections, the Department of Public Health, and the Department of Taxation and Incorporation.

Minnesota has likewise taken steps to train inmates for the high-tech sector. At its Stillwater Correctional Facility, Stillwater Data Processing Systems, Inc.—staffed by inmates—supplies software to such firms as 3M and Control Data. And a program is proposed to train inmates to assemble computers. More than twenty states are planning similar programs.

Computer training is quickly gaining acceptance in the federal penal system as well. One of the largest programs is based in Leavenworth, Kansas. An inmate graduate of that program has said of it, "The DP training we receive here allows us to acquire [a marketable] skill."

But these programs have been criticized. In 1977 the Senate Committee on Government Operations warned that unless properly supervised, these programs could be training criminals in computer crime. The committee was particularly disturbed by the fact that almost 50 percent of those enrolled in the Leavenworth program had been convicted of such property crimes as fraud, embezzlement, forgery, larceny, theft of securities, and burglary. In addition, the overwhelming majority were recidivists. The average computer trainee at Leavenworth had been arrested 9.04 times and convicted 5.66 times.

The committee also documented that several of the trainees had ties to organized crime, and at least one released prisoner who had found work in the EDP field had been convicted of a computer crime. Further, the committee found that some of the trainees may have used their new-found knowledge to circumvent IRS computers and file some 600 false tax returns, which allegedly generated refunds of about $6 million.

The committee's concerns have been reiterated in the law enforcement community. It would be foolhardy not to acknowledge that the prison computer training programs have had their share of problems. For example, a Virginia man who is said to have learned about computers in prison accessed the computer of various credit bureaus. And in Massachusetts, state troopers had to break up a computerized drug and gambling ring at Framingham State Prison. The authorities confiscated handguns, heroin, and betting slips. Several inmates had used the prison's computers to run extensive drug and gambling rackets; some of the inmates were reportedly connected to organized crime.

Computer training for inmates is extensive, especially in the federal penal system. Inmates receive training in computer languages, programming, and assembling computer equipment. Graduates of some of these programs have gone on to take advanced college courses.

Organized crime has already tapped the skills of criminals with computer training. Two associates of the Gambino Mafia family, for example, are said to have attempted a multimillion-dollar computer heist that involved several U.S. and European banks. They were assisted by insiders with past criminal records and some computer training. With the assistance of dishonest insiders, gangs like the Harris and Turner-Curtis groups have ripped-off credit bureaus and banks in multimillion-dollar computer heists. And mobsters in Chicago are said to have used dishonest insiders in computer-assisted frauds that may have cost financial institutions more than $1 million.

There is thus ample basis for concern that organized crime may tap this new pool of prisoners trained in computer technology. As this training expands, convicted embezzlers, stock fraud artists, an array of con men, and even members of organized crime will be trained under these programs. We would do well to implement safeguards to ensure that these valuable programs serve inmates who truly merit the training, and who will use their new skills to function as constructive individuals once released from prison. We should exclude those who would undermine and abuse these programs.

Organized crime is big business in America, and it grows daily in size and sophistication. The computer revolution has offered the mob new opportunities for committing crimes. This underscores the need for law enforcement agents to be trained to combat illegal high-tech activities.

6

From Russia with Love

It's all part of the electronic underworld.

— FBI Official

N EIGHBORS refer to it as the "place where all the beautiful people party." The villa has an indoor pool, and on weekends you can see a long procession of expensive cars dropping off passengers dressed in Europe's latest fashions. But this is not Paris, London, or Rome. It's Moscow, and the beautiful people are the sons and daughters of the Soviet elite. The host is a Middle Eastern entrepreneur, Babreck Be (a pseudonym). Socialite by night, by day he is a high-tech consultant to the Soviet Union's powerful Military Industrial Commission (VPK). Each year the VPK issues its high-tech shopping list to its agents, and Babreck Be helps them smuggle the loot back to the Soviet Union.

A Soviet-bound American shipment was seized by West German customs agents. The catch: a computer system with military applications, valued at more than $1 million. The shipment had originated in Boston. A West German official was quoted as saying, "Computers are very actively sought by the Eastern bloc. They're willing to pay a lot." This haul was only a drop in the bucket, however, because the annual Soviet theft and diversion of American high technology exceeds $1 billion.

In Los Angeles, a high-tech firm signed a contract with the National Aeronautics and Space Administration (NASA) to construct a ground station that can eavesdrop on satellite communications. But the company forgot to tell NASA that it was under investigation by the FBI for allegedly trying to smuggle high-tech equipment to the Soviet bloc.

Have you heard of Japscam? It was an Abscam-style FBI operation, in which more than a dozen U.S.-based employees of several Japanese computer firms were arrested. The Poles, Libyans, Pakistanis, Chinese, and Russians have also been busy searching for better silicon chips, the brains of the computer. Power and technology are interchangeable, and the Russians fully understand the value of high technology in the global power game. High tech, in the parlance of industrial espionage, means more than simply computers. The term includes microelectronics, programs, structural metals, semiconductors, lasers, optics, robotics, and a host of other new technologies.

Everywhere, Soviet agents are looking for high technology. CIA Director William J. Casey warned a group of Silicon Valley executives that Soviet agents have established a "sophisticated international [high-tech] diversion operation." Its purpose is to steal and divert the West's computers and microelectronics. Its primary targets are more than 11,000 American high-tech firms. The modus operandi is through a high-tech pipeline consisting of more than 300 firms operating out of 30 countries. FBI Director William Webster has described these Soviet activities as a "serious problem because of the damage [they] can do to our national security."

Yet there are skeptics in business and government who downplay the Soviet threat. One business leader has described efforts to control the flow of American high technology to the Soviet bloc as "questionable." And a member of Congress has warned that they constitute an effort to "recreate the House un-American Activities Committee." Even though the debate continues, there is no escaping the conclusion: According to a study by the U.S. Senate Permanent Subcommittee on Investigations, the Soviets owe much to our high technology for their "giant strides in military strength." The Soviets take their work very seriously. According to Western intelligence sources, the KGB (Committee for State Security) employs more than 20,000 full-time agents; over 1,000 of the more than 3,000 East European diplomats in the United States are known to be intelligence officers. Many of them are engaged in the far-reaching Soviet efforts to steal the West's high technology. The CIA has described these efforts as being "massive, well-planned, and well-managed." To quote a FBI source, "It's from Russia with love."

Of Spies and Chips

The theft of industrial secrets is not new. The ancient Chinese, eager to safeguard their silk-making monopoly, made it a capital offense to reveal the secret process to outsiders. The Venetians, whose survival depended on commerce, developed one of the most sophisticated industrial spy networks in Europe. And the English made it a crime to export manufacturing secrets.

Stealing high technology pays off. It saves the Soviet bloc more than $1 billion in research and development costs every year; it also enhances their economic and military muscle. "Military technologies have also civilian application," an executive with a high-tech firm warned. According to the American Society for Industrial Security, the theft of America's high technology not only undermines our national defense, but also our ability to compete in the global markets. Power in the computer age rests with the chip.

But the theft of high technology is not unique to the Soviets. High-tech theft is big business, and all countries do it—enemies and friends alike. For example:

Japan. The Cabinet Research Office specializes in economic and industrial intelligence.

China. Badly in need of high technology, the General Administration of Intelligence agency has been known to spy on the West's high-tech secrets.

Israel. A tiny country whose survival is tied to exports, Israel's Mossad has a well-deserved reputation for dedication and the ability to peep into other nations' high-tech bags of tricks.

East Germany. More than $25 million annually is spent on high-tech espionage by the GDR. Its target is the West's computer industry, especially IBM, Texas Instruments, and Control Data Corporation.

Poland. Polish intelligence services are closely tied to the KGB. One Polish intelligence officer, while employed as a representative of the Polish American Machinery Corporation, paid an American engineer $90,000 for secrets concerning a highly advanced radar system and other high-tech equipment.

Unlike the Cold War spies, high-tech pirates steal for profit. Ideology does not figure into their business. A former high-tech pirate put it best: "The East-West trade for us is not a matter of politics. It's simply a way to bankroll our extravagant life-styles. We're hustlers." And they will steal for anyone. For example:

An American high-tech thief was caught at Kennedy Airport trying to smuggle 5,000 pounds of zirconium to Pakistan. Zirconium is used to construct nuclear reactors.

Libya is said to have paid more than $40 million to a group of high-tech pirates in return for computers, weaponsighting devices, and guided missile components.

American and British high-tech suppliers are said to have smuggled over $5 million in computers and related equipment from the United States. The buyers included communist and noncommunist nations. One supplier said, "My loyalty was to my customers who needed the equipment."

Japanese high-tech thieves have been implicated in an international scheme to bilk secret data on computers from several American companies.

High-tech pirates used a half-dozen Austrian and Swiss corporations to smuggle sophisticated computers, microchips, and fiber optics out of the United States.

Few nations can match the Soviet Union's history of stealing the West's technology. It started with the czars. Peter the Great felt that stealing technology was easier than inventing it. In 1917 the Bolsheviks picked up where the czars left off—and they did it better. First came the CHEKA, then the GPU, OGPU, GUCB/NKVD, MGB, and finally the KGB. Part of the job of Soviet intelligence agencies has always been to spy on Western technology. The Soviets have traditionally done well by their thefts. Consider the following:

Much of the microcircuitry used in Soviet jet fighters has its origins in U.S. laboratories.

Laser optical mirrors and high-speed computers—used in the development of nuclear weapons and missiles—originated in San Francisco's Silicon Valley and Boston's Route 128.

A top-secret microwave receiver developed for the U.S. Navy made its way into the Soviet navy.

Ball-bearing guiders obtained from the United States made it possible for the Soviets to develop sophisticated intercontinental missiles that can reach any city in the United States.

Soviet laser equipment for space warfare came from the United States, as did plans for the TOW antitank missile.

The Soviet bloc is hooked on the West's high technology. So dependent are they that Moscow's telephone system would not operate for long without

U.S. computers. A West Germany survey classified over 70 percent of all exports to the Soviet bloc as "research intensive." There is no doubt that the Soviets intend to keep their high-tech pipeline open—even if they have to steal.

The Pipeline to Moscow

Albert Franz Kessler, thirty-nine, was a typical Swiss businessman. He traveled frequently to the United States. Smartly dressed and polished looking, he made a very good impression on his American business associates. And he had a knack for high tech. Kessler traveled often to southern California. But things changed on May 28, 1981. As he was waiting at the Los Angeles airport to board a TWA 747 jetliner destined for London, U.S. Customs Service agents arrested him. From his luggage they confiscated more than $200,000 in military electronic equipment. Kessler had planned to smuggle it to Europe. Soon after Kessler's arrest, federal authorities caught two of his associates, a West German businessman and a California high-tech consultant. Kessler and his partners were part of a high-tech smuggling operation that extended from Silicon Valley to the Eastern bloc.

Kessler's electronic underground is merely the tip of a giant iceberg: just a small fraction of the high-tech smuggling that encompasses several continents and billions of dollars. Transfer points in this international operation are located in Sweden, Austria, West Germany, Switzerland, and South Africa. A vast and complex network of corporate fronts is used to funnel the loot to the Soviet Union. For example:

> One of Britain's largest computer manufacturers, 41 percent of which is owned by Control Data Corporation, has been the target of searches by customs agents in both Britain and the United States. Agents sought evidence of high-tech diversions (primarily computers) to the East.

> The U.S. Department of Commerce fined a leading computer company, Digital Equipment Corporation, $1.5 million for export law violations that may have enabled the Soviets to obtain at least one of its high-powered minicomputers. This computer was allegedly a general-purpose super-mini, which can be used in missile tracking systems.

> According to the department, Digital had been doing business with a West German firm, Deutsche Integrated Time, which reportedly buys sensitive military technology from the United States and resells it to the Soviets. The owner of Deutsche, Richard Mueller, had already had a brush

with the authorities. He was indicted in 1979 by a California federal grand jury in connection with the shipment of semiconductor manufacturing equipment to the Soviet bloc.

The owner of a high-tech firm in California was charged with conspiring to ship more than $700,000 worth of computer disk manufacturing equipment to Bulgaria. It is alleged that he acted as a go-between for the Bulgarian government and an American high-tech firm, and that he planned to funnel the equipment through a company in Holland. According to U.S. Department of Justice sources, "The Bulgarians were very interested in and willing to pay top dollar for [the equipment]."

A $50,000-a-year California engineer boasted to his associates that he had "an open invitation to visit Poland." Little did they know that he was telling the truth. James Durward Harper, Jr., visited Poland, Switzerland, Austria, and Mexico. His Polish employers had given him a high-tech shopping list and $250,000; in return, Harper provided them with valuable military high-tech secrets.

Between 1979 and 1980, Massachusetts businessman Paul Carlson shipped computer equipment to a British businessman, Brian Muller-Butcher. Carlson had been looking for overseas markets for his high-tech wares. Muller-Butcher said that he could provide a buyer: the Soviet government. Carlson went on to become a part of high-tech history: he was the first Massachusetts businessman to be convicted a a result of Operation Exodus. The U.S. Customs Service launched Operation Exodus in 1980 to crackdown on the export of American high technology.

The Boston metropolitan area has been called Silicon-East. And the Soviets have long enjoyed shopping in New England. So when seven men and five corporations (based in Switzerland, Canada, and the United States) were charged with smuggling computers to the Soviet bloc, few eyebrows were raised. One Massachusetts businessman remarked, "we were surprised that the feds waited this long to act."

Even former spies have gotten into the high-tech act. Three businessmen (one an ex-CIA spymaster) were indicted by a federal grand jury in Virginia on conspiracy to smuggle more than $5 million in high-tech equipment to the Soviets. The defendants had been dealing with a Paris-based company without realizing that it was part of a U.S. Customs Service sting operation.

Lenin's Heirs

A Soviet engineer visits an American laboratory where his host invites him to try their latest desktop computer. Sitting down to the keyboard, the engineer proceeds to enter a series of mathematical equations; the computer responds. The engineer shakes his head, "you Americans are lucky." The Soviet Union, although well stocked in brain power (it has more than 1,500 science centers and 1.5 million scientists), lags behind the United States in high technology—particularly in cybernetics, which underlies much of our computer science. A considerable part of their technology is in dire need of improvement and modernization.

The Soviets are very aware that they're behind us in high technology—especially computers—and openly admit it. To quote a Soviet scientist, "We need to move from theory to applied technology." What he means is that they're forced to steal from the West what they don't have at home. But you may wonder why a nation with so much intellectual power is so backward in high technology. The answer is simple: bureaucracy, politics, and Marxist-Leninist ideology all hobble the physical sciences.

The Soviet Academy of Sciences is one of the oldest scientific bodies in the world. Russian scientists Mikhail Lomonosov, Dmitri Mendeleyev, and Ivan Pavlov have all left their mark on history. But none of them had to deal with the miles of red tape that seriously impede the progress of an idea from the laboratory to the plant in the Soviet Union today.

Then there are the politicians. From early on, communist politicians have viewed scientists with suspicion and occasionally disdain. Under the dictatorship of Stalin (1924–1953), science was looked on as a Western aberration, a necessary evil that had to be controlled by the Party. Many scientists are thought to have been among the millions of men and women who were killed or sent to concentration camps during Stalin's mass purges.

The Stalinist legacy lives on, and Soviet scientists have good memories. They know that scientific change must conform to Marxist-Leninist ideology; it must not pose a threat to the Party's grip on Soviet society. Unfortunately for Soviet science, the Party's leadership has traditionally viewed the West's ideas—including its scientific advances—with suspicion. This outlook may make for good politics, but it makes for bad science. Such thinking has hindered Soviet achievmenet in the high-tech area.

But necessity breeds change, and Soviet leaders if somewhat disdainful, have been quick to see the value of Western science. In 1921, in his *State Papers*, Lenin wrote: "The Capitalists will supply us with the materials and the technology we lack. They will restore our defense industry." A KGB training manual reiterates this theme: "The average American soberly regards money as the sole means of ensuring personal freedom and independence, . . . this attitude toward money engenders an indifference to the means by which it is obtained." The KGB has traditionally had little trouble finding high-tech pirates in the West.

The Russians are paranoid when it comes to national defense. They remember only too well that the West has invaded their country several times in this century. During World War I, the Germans occupied much of western Russia. Then the West tried to topple Lenin's regime in 1919–1920. Neither have the Russians forgotten World War II; they suffered more than 20 million casualties. For the Soviets, high technology and a strong military are one and the same; they know that high-tech weaponry can often make the difference between independence and subjugation. Thus, defense of the revolution and the motherland is in large part behind the Soviet effort to pilfer the West's technology. And the powerful Military Industrial Commission (VPK) in Moscow is responsible for compiling an annual high-tech shopping list; an army of high-tech mercenaries stand ready to do its bidding.

The VPK's Shopping List

Acting on a tip, the U.S. Customs Service alerted the West German and Swedish governments about several crates containing computers destined for the Soviet Union. On November 9, 1983, as the ship carrying the cargo was about to sail from Hamburg, West German officials moved in and seized the cargo. Several more crates were seized in Malmo by the Swedish police. This time, the Russians had failed.

It all started in New York. A computer manufacturer struck a deal with an exporter. "The computers," the exporter told the company, "are for a South African firm." It seemed to be a normal transaction; just one of many the manufacturer makes every year. And the U.S. Department of Commerce saw nothing wrong: it approved the export license. As it turned out, however, the South African company was a front, part of an elaborate international smuggling network headed by a group of European businessmen. And this was only one of their many deals with the KGB. Had the transfer succeeded, the computers would have been used to construct a plant for high-speed integrated circuits.

The VKP is primarily interested in high technologies with military applications; consumer needs matter little. They will go to any length to accomplish their objective. Moscow's high-tech shopping list is assembled for and by the military. According to Western intelligence sources, their main target areas are electronics, missile systems, and metallurgy.

Electronics. The U.S. military leads the Soviets' in most basic areas—for example, computers, microelectronics, robotics, communication systems, radar sensors, and telecommunications. But the Soviets are quickly catching up. The West no longer enjoys the lead in lasers, night vision systems, and ground combat equipment. They are also closing the gap in computers, microelectronics, and the manufacture of silicon chips, semiconductors, software (including artificial intelligence), and electro-optical sensors. For example, many Soviet computers use the same components as those manufactured in the West; Soviet terrain-hugging cruise missiles use the same computer-controlled radar guidance system as their American counterparts. Integrated circuitry and microcomputers are being manufactured in Soviet plants that closely replicate U.S. plants.

Missile Systems. The Atoll missile used by the Soviets to shoot down the South Korean 747 jetliner is an exact duplicate of the American sidewinder; the SAM-7 surface-to-air missile is a copy of our Redeye. And Soviet submarine cruise missiles are so similar to the American Tomahawk missile that they have been dubbed the "Tomahawksis." The silos of their SS-13s are exactly like those used to house our Minuteman missiles.

Metallurgy. Soviet titanium-hulled submarines can dive to greater depths than their American counterparts; lightweight materials are used in many of their modern jet fighters. Soviet heavy-duty metallurgy receives high grades from experts in the West. Soviet metallurgical breakthroughs have enabled them to construct the strong alloys used in their latest aircraft. But they borrow as much as they can from the United States, to reduce the likelihood of poor design choices.

During the early 1970s, in the spirit of détente, many of the West's high-tech wares were readily available to the Soviets (legally and illegally). When the Reagan administration began its crackdown on high-tech exports in 1980, the KGB simply modified its modus operandi. Soviet techniques have become more sophisticated and refined; now they just have to dig deeper for Silicon gold.

In the Service of the KGB and the GRU

In Belgium the director-general of a Soviet-Belgian company was asked to leave the country. The authorities suspected that he was a KGB agent engaged in industrial espionage. A Soviet diplomat in Denmark was likewise asked to depart. The Danes believed that he was the head of the Copenhagen "Line X"—a field section of the Chief Intelligence Directorate of the Soviet General Staff (GRU) responsible for science and technology. In France, more than forty Russians were expelled; the French charged that they were involved in widespread scientific and technological espionage. Italy, Holland, West Germany, and Spain have also expelled KGB industrial spies. And the Japanese suspect that more than 100 officials at the Soviet embassy in Tokyo may be involved in some form of industrial spying.

The KGB is busy these days. Known in the Soviet Union as the Komitet Gosudarstvennoi Bezopasnosti (State Security Committee), it combines the functions of the FBI, CIA, and Secret Service. Headquartered in Moscow, the KGB consists of four chief directorates, seven independent directorates, and several independent departments. Some intelligence sources place the KGB's annual budget at over $10 billion. But nobody really knows how much it is—probably not even the Kremlin.

The expansion and growth of the KGB into a highly professional organization must be credited to its former chief, the late Yuri V. Andropov, who headed it for fifteen years. With Andropov's ascension to leader of the Communist Party, however, the KGB's power grew even more. But no one is really sure how large the agency is. The *New York Times* has placed the number of its agents at more than 1 million.

As for the KGB's operation, each of the directorates and departments has a specific task. For example:

> The First Chief Directorate, with more than 7,000 agents, is responsible for "disinformation" (purposely false information) and stealing high technology. Spying in the United States and Canada is the job of its First Department; smuggling high tech is the primary responsibility of its Service T.

> The Second Chief Directorate is responsible for recruiting and monitoring agents for the KGB. It specifically targets American diplomats, academicians, journalists, students, and visitors to the Soviet Union.

> The Fifth Chief Directorate is in charge of internal security in the Soviet Union. More than 50 percent of all KGB agents are said to be assigned to it.

> The Eighth Directorate handles all KGB eavesdropping activities at Soviet installations in the United States and Canada.

The Third Department is responsible for intelligence activities in Great Britain.

The Thirteenth Department has been dubbed the KGB's "contract killers." Its job is to "neutralize" the enemies of the Soviet state, and assassinations are part of its program. Agents from this unit are assigned to various embassies around the world. Their job is to sabotage key installations, depots, communication centers, computer networks, water supply systems, and fuel depots in the event of a war.

The KGB's efforts in the United States have been increasing for the last twenty years and are known to be extensive. FBI director William Webster has commented, "I do not think there's been another time in our history when our country has been under such a sophisticated espionage assault." There is basis for concern:

More than 30 percent of all Soviet officials in the United States are said to be KGB or GRU agents. In turn, they can call on the assistance of more than 3,000 Eastern bloc officials.

Contrary to public perception, the FBI has limited resources. It has committed more than 2,000 agents to full-time counterintelligence operations, but keeping the more than 200 Soviet bloc offices in the United States under close surveillance is a problem—especially since they can call on thousands of U.S. high-tech spies for assistance.

The Soviet consulate in San Francisco sits on one of the city's highest hills. Its antennas target Silicon Valley, and its computers are programmed to intercept intelligence communications. The scene is repeated in Washington, D.C., where antennas from the Soviet embassy are aimed at the State Department and the Pentagon. It's all part of an effort to intercept intelligence communications. The Russians are also busy in Havana, Cuba, where giant antennas are poised to intercept America's satellite communications.

The KGB has been setting up corporate shells throughout the United States, as well as in Canada, Switzerland, Austria, and Sweden. These fronts serve as conduits for smuggled technology.

Although the KGB has been getting much of the credit for stealing the West's technology, the GRU has been equally busy. It has well-earned a reputation for tenacity, and many intelligence experts rank it higher then the CIA and at least equal to the KGB; its budget is said to be larger than that of the KGB. In intelligence circles it's called Military Department 44388. Until the diaries of Colonel Oleg Penkovsky (a double agent for the GRU and CIA) were published in the late 1960s, little was known about it.

The GRU, like the KGB, is based in Moscow. But unlike the KGB, it is part of the Soviet military structure and falls under the umbrella—while remaining largely autonomous—of the Ministry of Defense. Its chief has traditionally come from the upper ranks of the KGB. Selecting a KGB officer to head the GRU ensures that the generals will not be able to turn that powerful body (since the KGB and the military are often at odds with one another) against the civilian leadership at the Kremlin.

However, the GRU is far from under the thumb of the KGB. It has its own school for spies, the Military Department 35576 (also known as the Military-Diplomatic Academy of the Soviet Army). Its chief sits on the powerful Military Industrial Commission, along with the chief of the Soviet General Staff, the KGB chief, and the heads of the other ministries. GRU insiders keep an eye on their KGB boss to make sure that he doesn't get out of line. While the KGB is not reluctant to draft minority members, such as Jews and Lithuanians (as long as they are loyal to the Soviet government), into its ranks, the GRU is suspicious of minorities and is said to almost have a caste system. Only the Party faithful are allowed into its ranks.

The GRU has a record that is second to none; many say even better than that of the KGB. For example, it was the GRU that masterminded the theft of America's atomic bomb secrets, that was behind the theft of classified satellite data from TRW, and that almost made off with the plans for the French Mirage-2000 fighter plane.

The GRU prides itself on efficiency. It has little or no love for the KGB. Rivalry between the two runs deep. But like the KGB, it devotes sizable resources to stealing Western high technology. Because it is the main supplier of technology to the military, its budget for industrial espionage activities is said to be almost unlimited.

We know very little about the GRU's organization because of the veil of secrecy surrounding it. But we do know that:

> Its agents in the West assume a variety of covers—as diplomats, United Nations employees, students, scientists, and employees of various Soviet corporations doing business in the West.

The Soviet airliner Aeroflot is a favorite GRU front. A GRU general is assigned to Aeroflot's Moscow offices to coordinate GRU's operations with the Aeroflot civilian staff.

The Second Direction of the GRU specializes in terrorism, sabotage, and assassination; its Line X specializes in the theft of high technology.

Trade shows, universities, and foreign corporations are favorite recruiting places for its agents.

The GRU is particularly interested in French high technology, especially in the area of telecommunications and computers.

Together with the KGB, the GRU is said to run more covert operations than all of the West's intelligence agencies combined.

We also know that the GRU (like its rival the KGB) is busy buying—and stealing if necessary—the West's high-tech wares. It is very good at its job, and at times extremely ingenious. For example, GRU agents were part of a Soviet delegation that visited plane factories in the United States. They were especially interested in seeing how Lockheed's L-1011 commercial wide-body jet was constructed. When they did, some were wearing shoes with adhesive soles. Nobody noticed. The soles picked up metal particles, which were later analyzed by GRU experts in Moscow. Enough was learned about the metal's composition to enable the Soviets to construct a plane similar to the L-1011.

During the era of détente, many in the West—blinded by technological arrogance and the profit motive—were reluctant to acknowledge that Moscow was pilfering the best of our technologies. And the efforts of the KGB and GRU have been so effective that, according to Washington's Institute of Strategic Trade, the West has subsidized Soviet research and development costs to the tune of more than $100 billion.

Industrial Espionage—Russian Style

The CIA claims that the Soviets spend more than 15 percent of their gross national product on defense (the Soviets say it's only 4 percent). Decisions on military matters start with the Defense Council, which consists of the most senior civilian and military leaders in the Soviet Union. Once policy decisions are made by the council, the nuts and bolts are left to the State Planning Agency (Gosplan). It's the job of the Military Industrial Commission to compile and issue an annual "requirement book," a military shopping list about

500 pages long. Upon receiving the shopping list, the KGB and GRU search for the required technology.

If samples are not available in the open market, then there is always the black market where everything is for sale. And there are also the pirates. A defense analyst has described security in the high-tech sector as "deplorable . . . they hardly do any background checks, or security checks." The FBI agrees: "All these companies are lax. That's the problem."

If it's available on the open market, the Soviets will pay the going price. The plans and equipment for their Kana Truck Plant were purchased on the open market; the Soviets paid American and West European companies more than $1 billion. But the sale of controlled technologies—those with military applications—to the Soviet bloc is prohibited by law. The Export Administration Act empowers the president to restrict exports that would "make a significant contribution to the military potential of any other country . . . detrimental to the national security of the United States." The Department of Commerce is required to compile a list of prohibited technologies (the *Commodity Control List*), as is the Department of Defense (the *Militarily Critical Technologies List*).

But that's no problem for the Soviets. Plenty of American and foreign business people are ready—if the price is right—to sell to anyone. In a secret report compiled by the Pentagon for Congress, more than a dozen techniques used by the Soviets to obtain American technology were identified. Some of these are outlined in the following paragraphs.

Complete plant sales. The Soviets have been known to purchase, both lawfully and unlawfully, entire plants and then reassemble them back home.

Public sources. Patent applications and licenses contain a wealth of technical information, as do scientific and technical journals, professional conferences, trade shows, and exhibits. All of these avenues have been used successfully by the Soviets to acquire Western technical know-how.

Soliciting bids. By asking Western companies to submit bid proposals for an assortment of projects, the Russians have picked the West's brains.

Intelligence sources. The feats of the KBG and GRU are the stuff that makes movies. Bribes, drugs, blackmail, and even extortion have been used with success to gain access to the West's secrets. For example, a CIA clerk was bribed by a Soviet agent to sell a copy of the secret KH-11 spy satellite manual.

Industrial spies. These people are recruited for the right price by the Soviets to assist them in stealing or diverting valuable technologies. Some are professional criminals, while others are simply dishonest employees. Greed, not ideology, is what motivates both types. For example, the former general manager of a West German firm, Deutsche Beryllium, was convicted of selling confidential technical data to Soviet agents. The manager had gotten the data from the Defense Marketing Services Corporation of Greenwich, Connecticut. And Belgian businessman Marc Andre DeGeyter was prosecuted in a scheme to purchase a computer trade secret with military applications for $500,000. He later confessed that he was trying to purchase it for the Soviet foreign trading firm, Techmashimport, headquartered in Moscow. DeGeyter described himself as an "honest businessman, who made a mistake."

Arms dealers. Arms merchants have flourished since antiquity. They care little about legalities and have been quick to exploit the high-tech underworld. One such group, headed by an American businessman, is said to have sold the Libyans and Soviet bloc countries more than $40 million in high-tech wares.

Third parties. The Soviets have also proved adept at acquiring American secrets through third (allied and neutral) countries, which are either not aware or don't care that the equipment is in transit to the Soviet bloc. Anatole Maluta is said to have run a $10 million high-tech smuggling operation from Austria and Switzerland—both neutral countries. And Werner Bruchhausen used a network of over a dozen corporate fronts to run an $8 million high-tech smuggling operation. Some of these firms were based in West Germany and Austria; Bruchhausen's caper fell through only when American authorities moved in. Although these corporate fronts had identical directorships and worked out of the same offices, none of the foreign governments took notice.

Dual-use technologies. Such technologies have both military and civilian applications. For example, when American companies sold ballbearing grinders to the Soviet Union they did not suspect that they would be used to produce ball bearings for the guidance systems of Soviet SS-18 missiles. The accuracy of the SS-18 led the United States to embark on the multibillion-dollar MX missile system.

Foreign investments. Foreign companies—some private and others government-owned—have invested in and formed joint ventures with American firms, especially those in the high-tech sector. An American high-tech firm, Chipex, is said to be owned by a Hong Kong company, which is a joint venture between two other Hong Kong firms. And one of these is owned by the People's Republic of China.

And the French, Spanish, Indians, Japanese and others have few qualms about trading with the Eastern bloc. A congressional subcommittee reported that some of our high technology may be getting to the Soviet bloc in this way. The report warned that we are in need of a "prudent policy on foreign direct investments in the United States."

A Tunnel without End

Selling high technology is big business for the Japanese. Fanuc, one of the world's largest manufacturers of computer numerical controls, has few misgivings about selling its robots and other high-tech goods to the Soviets. And the ministries of Foreign Affairs and International Trade have made little effort to stem the diversion of Japanese high technology to the Soviet bloc—even technologies with direct military applications. Japan's National Police and Public Security Investigative Agency—both charged with safeguarding high-tech goods from the KGB and GRU—have likewise proven lukewarm about prosecuting for export control violations.

Few of our European or Asian allies have been willing to limit high-tech exports to the Russians. The French and West Germans enjoy a thriving business with the Soviets; Austria, Sweden, Switzerland, and Liechtenstein have become willing conduits for the high-tech pipeline to Moscow. And although our NATO allies and Japan have joined the United States to form the Coordinating Committee for Multilateral Export Controls (Cocom) to coordinate high-tech export controls, efforts have been more cosmetic than substantive. Cocom has rightly been called a gentleman's club, because it lacks enforcement mechanisms and fails to penalize violators. Even though Cocom maintains an export control list for dual-use technologies, its members have resisted the United States' efforts to expand it. Cocom has been aptly labeled a paper tiger.

But Americans themselves disagree over the value of export controls. Although Defense Secretary Caspar Weinberger has warned against selling to the "Soviets the rope to hang us," the U.S. Chamber of Commerce, Business Roundtable, and other business groups have publicly come out against efforts to export controls. Some business sources say that such efforts are "simply suicidal." The Semiconductor Industry Association, a spokesgroup for the high-tech industry, warns that "things are very tough right now" for the industry. And a study by the Rand Corporation (prepared for the Department of Defense) warns that, in the long run, export restrictions could do more harm than good to our economy.

The National Academy of Sciences concedes that America has a "substantial and serious" high-tech leakage problem and that "70 percent of the military significant technology acquired by the Soviet Union has been acquired through . . . intelligence organizations." Yet the academy has failed to support export controls. Former New York congressman Jonathan Bingham, who helped shape the Export Administration Act, has been quoted as saying that "by refusing to export, we do not eliminate uncertainty; we only opt out of the game." With growing competition from the Europeans and Japanese, America's business community has justifiable reasons for concern. On the verge of losing its global high-tech monopoly, business will continue—through its friends in Congress and government—to oppose tighter export controls.

The Executive Branch under several presidents has likewise been half-hearted and inept in efforts to address the problem. For example:

From 1980 to 1982, the Department of Commerce (an important federal agency in the war against high-tech smuggling) spent less than $30 annually to train each agent in this area—even though U.S. Senator Sam Nunn has publicly stated that Department of Commerce staff has little law enforcement expertise in high-tech smuggling.

Although the Customs Service began more than 450 investigations during 1981–1983, these resulted in only thirteen arrests. U.S. Senate staffers have described the service's efforts as "ineffective." Out of 1,785 seizures made by Customs agents of export cargo valued at over $90 million, more than 90 percent of this cargo was later relicensed. To quote a Senate source, "The investigations were bungled."

Operation Exodus, the heralded attempt to block the export of secret technologies to the Soviets, did not gather momentum until late 1981. The stress is not on arrests, but on slowing down exports. This approach has only served to make the business community nervous, while the criminals continue stealing with impunity.

Feuding among the federal executive agencies (Commerce, Customs, Justice, and the Department of Energy) has hampered investigative efforts. For example, Customs officials complain that Commerce officials will not allow them ready access to the license application information they keep.

The U.S. Department of Justice has shied away from prosecutions for high-tech smuggling because, in part, these cases can be complex and time consuming. Justice sources also complain that the investigators at Commerce and other agencies are not well trained in this area, and that the cases they refer to Justice for prosecution are often poorly investigated and of little value. And the FBI complains that Commerce has been unwilling to work with its agents on cases.

Red tape within the agencies has further stymied efforts. The Department of Commerce, for example, has a backlog of several thousand cases. By the time these cases are finally referred to the Department of Justice for prosecution, the thieves have long flown the coop.

But there are remedies to the situation. Both congressional and private groups have called for a new approach. For example, the American Society for Industrial Security has recommended:

Large fines and mandatory prison terms for high-tech smugglers.

More training for law enforcement officials in the detection and investigation of these crimes.

Better coordination between the private and public sectors.

Improved cooperation among the various federal agencies responsible for enforcing existing controls.

Tightening controls on exports to countries suspected of being shipment points to the Soviet bloc.

Some changes are afoot. Federal regulators are trying to better coordinate their efforts. The FBI is assuming a larger role—especially in the area of counterintelligence—and bringing its criminal investigative expertise to bear. And President Reagan has authorized the Department of Defense to review high-tech exports to Austria, Sweden, Switzerland, Hong Kong, Singapore, India, South Africa, and Liechtenstein. The exports covered include: computers equipped with CRT (cathode ray tube) terminals; electronic computers and data communications switching gear; electronic calibrating equipment; and machinery and equipment for manufacturing electronic equipment, components, and materials.

Those who favor greater controls charge that too little is being done too late. Those opposed to controls warn that we may be playing into the hands of our competitors: if we don't sell the goods to the Soviet bloc, others will. And the bureaucrats? They continue to squabble. The whole area of export controls has appropriately been called a political quagmire.

A Balancing Act

Few disagree that the Soviets are diverting—by both lawful and unlawful means—America's high-tech secrets and goods. Nor would anyone dispute that these technologies have enhanced the Soviet Union's military muscle. Now that technology is no longer an American monopoly, the Europeans and Japanese are rapidly becoming tough competitors in the high-tech arena. They would like to increase trade with the Soviet bloc. Technology knows no boundaries.

Efforts to control high-tech exports in this day and age must be balanced with reality; otherwise they will prove ludicrous and impossible to enforce. Not only are the Europeans and Japanese willing to sell high technology to the Soviets, but emerging high-tech firms in Southeast Asia are also able and willing to fill the void. The high-tech merchants of Hong Kong, Taiwan, South Korea, Malaysia, and Singapore, in need of foreign markets, care little about global politics.

There is no denying that high-tech export controls are a double-edged sword; if applied too harshly, they could undermine the ability of American companies to compete effectively in global markets. Foreign competition grows daily. And the high-tech hemorrhage to the Soviet Union continues. The long-term political consequences could prove dangerous; yet the needs of commerce must be balanced with political necessity.

Jose Louis Llovio Menendez, a high-level Cuban defector, has said that American embargoes have "no weight," since high-tech goods are readily available from Europe and Japan. The Soviets know this only too well. And given the present global reality, the best one can hope for is to limit the quantity and quality of high-tech goods with military applications that make their way to the Soviets. At best, we can only slow the hemorrhage; to expect more is to delude ourselves. But to expect less is to undermine our national security. The KGB plays a good game of high-tech roulette.

7

Ripping Off James Bond Is Easy

The billions of bytes of free computer capacity in federal computers invites the dishonest to tap into them for personal gain.

— Federal Official

I T's not often that the federal government hands out $10 million in gifts. But miracles do happen; especially with a little help from high tech. Up to 2,000 Americans received checks averaging $5,000 from the Social Security Administration (SSA). Some tried to return the money; one recipient even walked into the SSA offices to return the money. "I think there's been a mistake," he told an SSA official. But nobody listened. After all, the SSA's computers cannot even account for $69 billion in worker earnings. So why worry about a small computer error?

Morale is high in the U.S. Army. Recruitments are up, and the quality of enlisted personnel has improved dramatically. The military is doing well. If you don't believe it, take the case of James Smith, Jr., a graduate of St. John's College, a multilingual nominee for a Rhodes Scholarship. But Smith is nowhere to be found: he's a phantom recruit. It seems that, under pressure to meet their weekly quotas, some recruiters fed phony names and data into the army's computers.

If you think only the private sector has problems with computer crime, then you should talk to Washington's bureaucrats. A General Accounting Office (GAO) study of federal computer systems found disturbing evidence of fraud and abuse. For example, a Department of Transportation clerk used a computer to steal $800,000; IRS employees entered phony returns into the agency's computer to collect tax refunds; and Department of Agriculture employees sold confidential data to outside sources and used its computers to perform outside consulting work.

There are more than 127,000 mainframes and desktop computers in the federal government. According to the General Services Administration (GSA), their number could reach anywhere between 500,000 and 1 million by 1991. Washington lives by its computers. Without them, the government would find it nearly impossible to support and administer a multitude of programs in such areas as national defense, intelligence, air traffic control, health and social welfare, and finances. And the government spends over $25 billion annually to maintain, manage, and upgrade its computers; these expenditures are expected to grow by as much as 20 percent annually.

But the consensus appears to be that the federal government's computer systems are in trouble. A U.S. Senate committee has warned that data and program errors cost the government billions of dollars a year. These problems also impede the efficiency of many government agencies. For example, improper payments by the Social Security Administration's computers in a two-year period cost taxpayers $60 million; a computer error at the navy's supply system in Norfolk, Virginia, cost the government over $300 million in lost supplies; and the Pentagon's computers made more than $3.5 million in overpayments to 262 survivors of deceased veterans. The General Accounting Office, a congressional watchdog agency, warns that the government's computers are highly vulnerable to sabotage and fraud. For example, a former employee of the National Aeronautics and Space Administration (NASA) is said to have copied over 100 valuable programs for personal use; and the U.S. Army's computers have been used by South Korean gangsters to divert more than $10 million in food and supplies. Not all is well with Uncle Sam's computers. A Washington source has aptly described the situation as the "high-tech Dark Ages."

Snafus—Washington Style

Life in America was simpler at the turn of the century. Washington exercised much less influence on American citizens. Then came the New Deal, World War II, the Great Society, and computers. The federal bureaucracy now numbers some 3 million persons; federal spending now accounts for more than 20 percent of our gross national product.

With this growth in bureaucracy also came computer dependency. Military and intelligence agencies used them first; then came the FBI and IRS. Now every agency in Washington has its own army of computers. For example, the number of large computers more than doubled between 1980 and 1985, from 11,000 to 27,000. The number of terminals connected into these computers more than quadrupled during the same period, and the number of desktop computers now exceeds 100,000.

The gargantuan federal edifice has continuously been bogged down by red tape, waste, and fraud. The Department of Defense (DoD) has led the parade. Computerization was going to change all this: it was supposed to streamline the government, making it more efficient and responsive to the public. To ensure that computerization worked, Congress allocated money for training and hiring 200,000 full-time computer science personnel.

To further ensure the security of the government's computers, Congress enacted laws. For example, the Budget and Accounting Procedures Act requires the federal agencies to establish internal controls to safeguard their systems. The U.S. Comptroller General—in conjunction with the Office of Management and Budget (OMB) and the Treasury—has likewise developed guidelines (published in the *Comptroller General's Manual for Guidance of Federal Agencies*) to ensure that the government's computers function properly and efficiently. To ensure coordination, Congress passed the Paperwork Reduction Act; thus, responsibility for purchasing all government computer systems now rests with the GSA. The National Bureau of Standards was directed to provide technical advice and guidance.

Yet none of this seems to have helped. Government records are still lost, billions of dollars are squandered with little or no accountability, waste and inefficiency are the rule, and frauds and thefts continue unabated. Nor have the federal agencies taken any steps to remedy the problem. According to the Office of Technology Assessment (OTA), a research arm of Congress, 40 percent of the agencies have never tested the vulnerability of their computer systems; 60 percent have no contingency plans in the event that their systems are disabled.

The National Telecommunications and Information Security Committee (NTISC), a special government-wide organization created in 1984, has questioned the accuracy, manageability, and security of the federal government's computer systems. The NTISC has reported that the existing situation is "poor and rapidly getting worse." The daily news out of Washington confirms this. For example:

> Between 1982 and 1985, the Immigration and Naturalization Service investigated more than 100 computer tampering cases involving its employees.

A Social Security Administration computer erroneously forwarded more than 150,000 checks to the wrong addresses; another computer foul-up was responsible for over $140 million in welfare overpayments.

Slipshod computer record-keeping caused 248 tons of federal surplus food to spoil in warehouses, while several thousand people waited to be fed in overcrowded soup kitchens.

Computers at the Department of Health and Human Services grind out more than $1 billion in overpayments each year; some of it goes to persons who have been dead for over fifteen years.

Because of a computer software problem, the air force junked more than $500 million in usable spare parts; the Pentagon's computers paid out more than $700 million to military reservists for exercises they had never attended.

Computer errors caused the Department of Defense to pick up the tab for over $1 billion in foreign arms sales, which should have been paid for by overseas customers.

The Pentagon accepted delivery of more than 4,000 faulty microcircuits (used in high-tech weapon systems) without ever testing them; its computers cannot identify the systems in which they were installed.

But Washington's answer is simple: spend more money and enact new laws and regulations. For example, thirteen major federal departments and twenty independent agencies spent more than $35 million in 1985 to improve the accuracy and security of their computers and communication devices; this was four times what they spent in 1980. And the GSA has set up a Quality of Workplace Commission to improve the efficiency and accuracy of federal computer systems; the OMB has issued a multitude of guidelines (for example, *Circular A-71* and *Transmittal Memorandum No. 1*) to improve the reliability and security of federal computers. Then there are the millions of dollars spent annually by the many federal departments and independent regulatory agencies to identify and remedy the problems plaguing their computer systems.

But even after the multimillion-dollar studies, reports, guidelines, and directives, the computer foul-ups persist. The mere mention of Uncle Sam's computers provokes jokes among experts; yet the computer horrors are real, and institutionalized by a gargantuan bureaucracy that opposes reform. The existing federal computer systems have been aptly described as bordering on self-destruction. The problems are very severe and directly affect the government's ability to provide services to the American public.

The snafus and frauds continue unabated. Take the Pentagon's "fast payment" system. Its computers are programmed to make advance payments to contractors who give the Pentagon discounts on purchases. At least on the surface, the fast payment system makes sense: the DoD saves the taxpayer money, and contractors do not have to wait months or years to get paid for goods and services.

But the Pentagon's Inspector General's Office has found serious flaws with the system. For example, an audit disclosed that the system's computers paid $24 million for goods and services that cannot be accounted for. In response to recommendations to abandon the fast payment system, Pentagon officials are likely to tell you, "If 'fast payments' are prohibited, we anticipate adverse impacts."

Waste, theft, and fraud appear to be endemic to the federal bureaucracy. Computer and manual snafus are responsible for over $30 billion in annual losses. The causes are no secret; among them are thefts and abuses by employees, natural disasters, mismanagement, weak audit controls, technical flaws, poor planning, and lax (and sometimes nonexistent) computer security. The list goes on. If a corporate computer errs, a business stands to go bankrupt. But when the government's computers fail, millions of persons can suffer irreparable harm. Computerization has not made the federal government more efficient; rather, it has merely magnified the impact of its snafus.

Ripping-Off the Feds

The Social Security Administration's computers issue over $1 billion in disability payments each month to 5 million workers and their dependents. With the assistance of its computers, twenty-nine-year-old Janet Blair, an SSA clerk, pulled off a half-million-dollar theft. Blair is said to have fed the names of phony beneficiaries into the SSA computers; since controls were lax, this was an easy matter. Each month, the computers forwarded checks to the addresses Blair listed. She and two associates picked up the checks at the addresses they were mailed to, and cashed them through several bank accounts. The fraud surfaced by accident, when a bank official became suspicious and called the Secret Service. It took the agents more than eighteen months to unravel the theft.

Apparently the SSA did not learn very much from the Blair case. Todd Skinner, a thirty-four-year-old claims representative with the SSA's district office in Riverside, California, used the same scheme to steal $104,500. Skinner used his computer terminal to access the SSA's national computer in Baltimore, Maryland and add six fictitious beneficiaries to the disability benefits program list. The prosecutors who worked on this case later remarked that the SSA's computers were "totally vulnerable to fraud by lower-level employees bent on stealing."

The Pentagon's more than 3,000 computers disburse $25 billion annually, which makes it easy to conceal thefts. If you have any doubts, simply ask Albert W. Coachman. To his friends and neighbors Coachman was a devoted family man; his coworkers at the DoD described him as a nice guy. When agents of the U.S. Secret Service arrested him, his supervisors thought it was a mistake. But it was no mistake. Albert W. Coachman had committed an almost perfect computer heist. With the assistance of the Pentagon's computers, he added more than a dozen ghost employees to the payroll of the Defense Intelligence Agency (one of the Pentagons superspy agencies). Coachman pocketed over $40,000 in wages.

Federal computers handle trillions of dollars every year. For example, the SSA computers issue—with little or no human intervention—more than $170 billion in disability payments annually. The potential for fraud has been described as staggering. The Secret Service alone is investigating more than 250,000 questionable computer transactions. And a GAO survey of sixty-nine computer crime cases in nine agencies found that over 60 percent of them involved low-level employees. The average take exceeded $40,000, and the schemes often involved payments to phony employees and fictitious firms. The GAO reported that the overwhelming number of computer heists in the federal government go unreported.

Further, a survey by the President's Council on Integrity and Efficiency of 172 known computer crime cases involving thirteen agencies found that most government computer crimes involved the diversion of assets. More than 75 percent of the heists involved unauthorized payroll payments or fictitious benefit claims. Four out of five of the crimes were committed by low-level employees; three fourths of the perpetrators were nonsupervisory personnel. Most of the crimes involved in-house facilities and occurred during normal processing. The council also reported that over 50 percent of these frauds were detected by accident, not by internal system controls. The Office of Technology Assessment likewise reports that existing computer safeguards in the federal government have proven largely ineffective.

Increasingly, financial transactions in the federal government are being handled by fewer people; computers are being programmed to issue payments, transfer assets, and handle an array of routine transactions, with little or no human intervention. Experts warn that this accords dishonest insiders an opportunity to use computer systems to create armies of ghost employees and beneficiaries; they also warn that more than 80 percent of the cases that are discovered are not reported to the authorities for prosecution.

A study by the Merit Systems Protection Board supports this assessment. It found that the majority of federal officials sweep computer frauds under the rug because they believe that the prosecutors will not act. Unfortunately, in part, they are correct; the U.S. Department of Justice has shown little interest in prosecuting computer heists by federal employees.

Scope and Modus Operandi

Stealing from the federal government is a way of life in Washington's sprawling bureaucracy. Thefts against the Pentagon alone are said to exceed $15 billion annually; more than 30 percent of these are committed by insiders. The daily headlines bear this out: "Military Reservists Pocket Almost $1 Billion in Overpayments," "Pentagon Loses $400 Million in Equipment," "Army Pays $470,000 to Dead Veterans."

As if that were not enough, the Inspector General's Office at the Department of Defense uncovered over 17,000 cases of fraud and waste by dishonest insiders in one year. Equally disturbing is a congressional survey that documented over 77,000 cases of fraud involving twenty-one federal agencies. Many of the cases involved computer thefts by insiders; the Department of Justice declined to prosecute over 95 percent of these cases.

The federal government is the world's largest computer user. As in the private sector, automation has its price: increased dependency on computerization has spawned the growth of high-tech frauds and abuses. However, unlike the private sector, the opportunity for computer frauds appears to be greater in government and must be attributed, in large part, to two factors: the large volumes of computerized financial transactions that federal agencies conduct daily, and the hundreds of thousands of government employees with access to Uncle Sam's data bases. Sadly, when it comes to computer security, the private and public sectors can be said to lag equally.

This is not to say, however, that computer-assisted crimes in government differ much in form from those in the private sector. For example, according to a congressional survey, government employees, like their private counterparts, have used computers to divert assets, steal computer time, copy programs, and alter data bases.

However, because the function—in terms of services and objectives—of government agencies differs from private businesses, the frequency and targets of computer frauds and abuses do differ. In addition, since the dollar value of the average government transaction is often smaller than its counterpart in the private sector, government computer heists often have a smaller dollar value per incident. According to a GAO study, the average computer heist in the private sector can average as high as $400,000, in government it often averages $50,000. Thus, although the opportunity to steal from government is greater, the take per incident is on average smaller.

Fraudulent Records

The most common type of computer thefts and abuses in the federal government involves the fabrication of agency records. These often take the form of phony unemployment benefits, disability and social security payments, food stamps, authorizations, and other related problems. Such thefts pose a serious and growing threat to the ability of government to deliver services to the public.

For example, in one case, several Rhode Island hospital officials diverted more than $2 million in medicare funds to their accounts by altering the computerized payment records. And five employees of the Department of Health and Human Services diverted over $40,000 of the agency's money to their accounts by adding ghost employees to its payroll. An enlisted man in the army did the same thing by feeding a fictitious captain's name into the Pentagon's computerized payroll; he received more than $4,000 in payroll checks.

System Abuses

System abuses often involve insiders who use government terminals, computers, programs, and files for personal profit. For example, U.S. Department of Agriculture (USDA) employees were found to have tapped more than 6,000 times into government computers that contained secret crop forecasts, military research information, and confidential Census Bureau data. One employee used the USDA's computers to run an outside consulting firm; another allowed his children to use a remote terminal to play computer games; and two others are known to have copied a valuable program. An investigation by the Inspector General's Office later disclosed that USDA officials had failed to use passwords to protect their computer files. Further, computer programmers with access to highly sensitive data had not been properly screened.

Although most studies have found that government computer frauds and abuses are mainly the work of insiders, occasional attacks involve outsiders. For example, several computer enthusiasts are said to have gained access to two of the NASA computer systems at its Marshall Flight Center in Huntsville, Alabama; other enthusiasts are known to have penetrated the computer systems of the Naval Ocean Systems Center in San Diego, the Naval Research Laboratory in Washington, D.C., and the DoD's Advanced Research Projects Agency Network. The last system links various governments, agencies, and universities in the United States and in Europe.

Processing Alterations

By evading existing controls, a thief can alter, modify, or delete files or programs that affect promotions, job assignments, or salaries and benefits. For example, a surprise inspection by GSA auditors of two federal computer centers in Washington, D.C., found that: employees were allowed unrestricted access to media libraries; terminals lacked sign-off capabilities; and the computer center was open to anyone who simply walked in. The increased use of time-sharing and networking by the federal agencies has also increased the vulnerability of their computer systems. Unauthorized access through remote terminals and consoles has become a serious problem.

Theft of Output

Such acts as the theft of returned checks, the alteration and destruction of output data, and the filing of bogus claims are output thefts. For example, when SSA's computers erroneously mailed several thousand checks to people who had been dead for several years, many of the checks were cashed by their relatives and friends. When the GAO sent the USDA ten bogus vouchers for payments to be made to a Mr. George A. Orwell, the USDA promptly complied and mailed the checks. And on a sudden inspection visit to a district office in California, SSA auditors were startled to find more than $14,000 in checks on the desk of an absent employee.

Most computer heists involving governmental systems have been carried out by amateurs; many of these individuals have financial problems. Employees have also been found stealing to support their drug habits. Many of these offenses can be traced directly to two causes: lax system controls, and failure by administrators to upgrade the security of their systems. Young computer enthusiasts have demonstrated the ease with which the government computer systems can be penetrated—in some cases just to browse, in others to copy valuable data and programs.

Blame It on High Tech

Arlene Smith's daughter had been receiving monthly benefit checks from the SSA since her father died. When she got married, her mother wrote to the SSA: "Please don't send any more checks. She's married now." But the checks kept coming anyway. When Mrs. Smith returned them, the computer wrote back: "Please accept payment." Melvin Rostow had been making social security payments for more than thirty years, only to find when he retired that the government's computers had no record of it. Angry and frustrated, he remarked, "I can't believe it. They kicked it through the computer, and nothing came out." It is the norm in Washington to look for scapegoats. Increasingly, fingers are being pointed at the computer. Whenever waste, fraud, and theft pop up, the bureaucrats say the computer fouled up. But is this really true? Not if you listen to the experts; they will tell you that the problem is not the computers, but rather those who manage the government's computer systems. Many of the government's problems can be directly attributed to management's failure to plan and coordinate its efforts, to institute and ensure compliance with existing controls, and to upgrade the system's safeguards.

Planning and Coordination

More than thirty years ago the federal government's computer systems were considered the best in the world—the state of the art. But today it can take a government agency up to ten years to discover a computer error, and another eighteen months to remedy it. And the government uses over 300 different computer languages; coordinating its computer systems has thus become almost impossible. In fact, the Pentagon has taken more than ten years to develop a standard language for its computers; many agencies still keep their records on archaic magnetic tapes. The SSA needs over 2,000 employees just to move its daily supply of 14,000 reels.

The government is also plagued with hardware problems. Many agencies are often forced to cannibalize old mainframes for spare parts, since many of the computers in use in government are no longer manufactured. And data processing backlogs are a continual problem; some agencies have backlogs of as much as 15,000 hours. Much of the software used by the government dates from the 1950s, and many of the agencies have no blueprints for how their systems operate. It's not unusual for an agency to retain a former employee as a consultant to show its new employees how the system works.

Federal computer systems have been aptly described as a mess—the result of inadequate planning and coordination. Central direction is the exception rather than the rule, and confusion appears to reign. Systems and equipment are rarely purchased with the future in mind. Red tape hampers efforts to avoid duplication and contain costs; waste and fraud are the norm. This mess can be laid at the door of government's top management.

Lax Controls

Thieves used the government's computers to divert more than $500,000 in goods and merchandise to a fictitious government warehouse. A retired clerk was startled to find that Washington had increased her monthly benefits from $181 to $9,281; the proper increase should have been $32.

According to the Department of Justice, 10 percent of all frauds against the government exceed $1 million; increasingly, many of these are computer-assisted. Such frauds are largely the result of inadequate controls. Computer controls are designed to ensure the effectiveness and accuracy of a system; they are often built into the system itself. However, this is often not the case in government systems, where controls are frequently either lax or nonexistent.

A GAO study discovered that nine out of nineteen federal agencies lack adequate computer controls; these nineteen agencies account for over 90 percent of all federal computer systems. The study also found that many of the government's control systems can easily be overridden to compute benefits of up to $2,000; other systems lack consistent instructions to remedy inaccurate data. In addition, field office personnel were found to be able to override some system controls; suspect transactions were often not investigated.

In many government computer systems, errors go uncorrected and frauds are never detected. Experts say the blame rests with top management, which neither understands nor appreciates the value of controls.

Security Guidelines

The federal government has spent millions of dollars on security devices and guidelines; and federal computer security centers abound to develop hardware and software standards, support research in computer security, and assist in designing and implementing security systems. But nobody in top management seems to be listening or interested. The Department of Energy, which maintains seventy-four computer sites, is one of the few agencies that has implemented comprehensive computer security measures. Many of the other agencies and departments have yet to act.

The consensus seems to be that the federal bureaucracy has become a faceless entity, aloof from the public it was set up to serve. And although computers were supposed to improve bureaucratic efficiency, they have instead aggravated the chaos, waste, and fraud already pervading it. Errors have been magnified and frauds are easier to pull off now than ever before. Planning, controls, and security are often just buzzwords used to placate an angry and frustrated public. The bureaucracy appears to lack both the imagination and will to initiate the needed changes to improve the effectiveness and reliability of its computer systems. Little wonder, then, that ripping off James Bond is easy.

8

Why the Cops Can't Cope

PROSECUTOR. Will you please tell the court what a console log is.
WITNESS. It's used to check the correct operations of a computer.
JUDGE. I don't understand this . . . I'm totally confused.
— Scene from a computer crime trial

I MAGINE a thief breaking into your office in the dead of night and stealing some computer disks containing confidential information about your company. There can be little doubt that the thief, if caught, will be prosecuted for burglary. But what if he simply taps into your company's computer and copies the data stored in it? Has he committed a crime? The answer is not so simple. Maybe.

Then there is the case of the municipal employee who uses the government's computers to run his outside private business. If he is prosecuted under the general theft statute, the judge may find him innocent on the grounds that the statute does not apply. In jurisdictions without a computer crime statute on the books, the law continues to be in a state of limbo.

Or, suppose that two employees of a fast-food chain attempt to erase the inventory and payroll data on its more than 400 stores. The weapon is a logic bomb, a program timed to self-destruct once it has erased the data. They are arrested, but prosecutors are doubtful whether they have a case. Prosecuting an individual for the erasure of computer files can be difficult, because traditional criminal law does not define such intangibles as property.

But computers can also be valuable police tools. For example, the San Francisco police use a computerized laser scanner to match fingerprints; the Houston police department uses a computerized artist system to convert a witness's descriptions to a composite drawing. High tech is a double-edged sword: it can be used both to commit crimes and help apprehend criminals. But, unfortunately, the criminals seem to have the sharper edge.

On Deaf Ears

Speaking at an annual security conference, the president of a public data network told the attendees that over 25 percent of all Fortune 500 corporations had been victimized by computer crime. The average theft ranged from $2 million to $10 million. "Computer theft and abuse costs North American businesses billions of dollars annually," he said, and called on them to "band together with users and government to find an effective and just solution."

This advice must have fallen on deaf ears. The business community can play an important role in combatting computer crime (especially since the police can do little if victims won't come forth), but business has been—at best—only lukewarm toward efforts to streamline the legal system and provide training for law enforcement in this area. In fact, a *Computerworld* survey of computer industry executives found that many of them were reluctant to turn to the authorities for assistance. A Fortune 500 executive summarized their sentiments: "Computer crime is a media creature, exaggerated by politicians, security consultants, and law enforcement."

These feelings are not shared by those outside the high-tech industry. The American Bar Association, noted for its stalwart conservatism, warns that "losses sustained by American business and government organizations as a result of computer crime are . . . huge." Congressman Bill Nelson fears that, at present, law enforcement agencies find it difficult to "make effective cases against computer criminals because the . . . laws that could be applied were designed to control other kinds of criminal activity."

A study on computer crime by the Association of Chief Police Officers of England, Wales, and Northern Ireland reported concern on the part of law enforcement in Japan, West Germany, France, Switzerland, and other advanced nations. But the association noted that some members of the business community in these countries—especially those in the high-tech area—were not enthusiastic about talking openly or acknowledging that there was a problem. Further, they were unwilling to admit the apparent insecurity of their computer systems. The association went on to note that current laws do not take into account a modern computerized environment and called for cooperation between the private and public sectors in the investigation and prosecution of computer crimes. It also recommended a revamping of police priorities and the enactment of legislation specifically designed to address these offenses.

According to *USA Today*, computer criminals are merely "white-collar crooks armed with a computer and a telephone." Computer-assisted fraud appears to be the fastest growing category of white-collar crime, with an estimated cost of $200 billion annually in the United States. But we are not expending the resources needed to train and prepare law enforcement agencies in this area. To deter such crimes, particularly those by the more professional criminals, society needs an adequate legal arsenal: police and prosecutors trained to handle computer crimes, and laws specifically designed for these offenses. According to the FBI, our traditional criminal laws are inadequate. Little wonder that the cops can't cope.

Silence Is the Rule

Two Silicon Valley computer chip brokers were charged with attempting to purchase an estimated $500,000 in stolen chips; the authorities claimed that some of the chips were to be sold overseas. A former Hewlett-Packard engineer was charged with illegally copying computer tapes worth over $40,000. And a group of computer buffs is said to have used home computers to break into the TRW computers, which are estimated to hold the credit histories of more than 90 million Americans. The TRW service is used by more than 24,000 subscribers—including banks and department stores—and can be accessed from some 35,000 locations.

The American Bar Association has called technocrime the crime of the twenty-first century. Total Assets Protection, a Texas security firm, places annual losses from technocrimes at over $1.2 billion. Some experts forecast that annual losses from these offenses could reach $10 billion by 1990. And what's more, high-tech crime pays. The thieves find it easy to evade prosecution—especially since only 12 percent of all computer heists are ever reported to the police and only 18 percent of these result in convictions.

And while America's police are trying to catch up on the basic levels of technological advancement, computer thieves are rapidly becoming more sophisticated. The reasons for their successes are many. Some of the more important reasons are discussed in the following sections.

Public Perception

A textile company executive implicated in a $200 million computer-leasing fraud was sentenced by a federal court to two years of probation and a $10,000 fine; a coconspirator received a five-month prison term. And a New York judge threw out charges against a programmer who was said to have used his employer's computer for his own personal business.

Few members of the public would dispute the need to allocate more resources to combat traditional crime or to close the existing legal loopholes that allow street criminals to walk free. But the public has yet to urge its government officials to address the problem of computer crime. The FBI, for example, trains more than 160,000 law enforcement officers annually, but fewer than 1,000 local and federal agents have been trained in computer fraud investigations. And although legislation has been passed that makes prison sentences longer, increases fines for drug offenses, and provides for preventive seizure and detention of criminal assets, Congress has yet to enact legislation that would fully address the threat of computer crime.

Why has virtually nothing been done about computer crime? And why does the public stay silent about the problem? It is a matter of public perception. The average citizen does not understand either the impact or seriousness of these crimes—especially since many of them are committed from many miles away, and involve such intangibles as trade secrets, marketing plans, and electronic funds. Nor does the public view computer crime as a direct threat to its physical safety—unlike street crime. Further, the media's portrayal of the computer criminal as a high-tech Robin Hood, has downplayed the long-term threat of many of these offenses.

Also, the public is generally unsympathetic toward victims of computer crimes, many of whom are businesses and government agencies. Corporate America and bureaucrats are not held in high public esteem. Further, since these victims are often reluctant to report computer crimes, there is little or no public pressure to get tough on the electronic thief. For example, a computer programmer, testifying before a Senate subcommittee on the need for federal computer crime legislation, put it this way: "So far as I can tell, the business community, the supposed victim of the 'computer crime,' is not storming Congress demanding [computer crime legislation]." He then added, computer crime legislation "is supported instead by a few prosecutors, who, I suspect, find 'computer crime' a glamour issue." His testimony summarizes the public's perception: if the victims of computer crime are really concerned, then they should seek help.

Invisible Crimes

The public's attention span is short and has little interest in what is not visible and simple to grasp. Most computer heists simply don't fit the profile of the standard crime. Unlike a robbery or mugging, computer heists are frequently invisible. They can be committed within seconds, from thousands of miles away. Because the criminal can even program the computer to erase the evidence of the illegal act, it may take the victim many years to discover that it has been robbed. Even when discovered, it often takes years to unravel these crimes and bring the criminal to trial.

Fear of Publicity

Although most victims of street crime are quick to report an attack to the authorities, most victims of computer crime are not. This reluctance does not come from ignorance of the extent or scope of computer crime. A survey of executives in Fortune 1000 companies found that nearly half of them (46 percent) were aware of the threat. Rather, keeping computer crime skeletons in the closet has become an accepted practice. Adverse publicity is bad for public relations, so silence is the rule. For example, banks fear that going public with a computer crime may scare away their customers. The computer industry fears that publicity would undermine the public's confidence in the reliability of its products.

Meager Sanctions

Most Americans are said to have little or no confidence that our criminal justice system will deter crime and assist its victims. It can also be said that victims of computer crime share this lack of confidence. They know only too well that many of our police and prosecuting agencies are ill-equipped and poorly trained to address these offenses, that judges and juries don't understand them, and that existing laws are in many cases inadequate to provide meaningful sanctions.

Even when convicted, most computer thieves merely receive a slap on the wrist. For example, a businessman convicted of illegally exporting electronic components with military applications to the Soviet bloc was ordered to undergo two years of supervised probation and 200 hours of community service. And two Virginia men charged with grand larceny (a felony) in the theft of a bank's customer list were instead found guilty of petty larceny (a misdemeanor). The judge dismissed the grand larceny charge on the grounds that the computer list was not worth more than $200, the cutoff point between grand and petty larceny. Such meager sanctions can hardly induce victims of computer crime to come forward.

Threat of Lawsuits

Victims of computer crime (especially businesses) also know that a computer fraud can sometimes result in a lawsuit. Credit bureaus, for example, have been sued for failing to enact the necessary safeguards to protect their computers. And government officials have been reprimanded for failing to secure their agencies' computers. Government officials are particularly vulnerable in cases involving federal systems, since computer security at the federal level is sometimes mandated by law.

Similarly, businesses within regulated industries can face criminal sanctions if their computers are violated. For example, the Food and Drug Administration (FDA) has rules governing the proper operation of computers. These rules require appropriate controls to ensure that changes in records are made only by authorized personnel, that input is checked for accuracy, that back-up data is maintained, and that the data is secure from alteration, erasure, or loss. Fear of civil and/or criminal liability dissuades some victims of computer crime from reporting incidents.

Violent Crimes versus Computer Crimes

A survey by *USA Today* found that street crimes, not economic crimes, are uppermost in the public's mind. A survey by the U.S. Bureau of Justice Statistics confirmed this: the public is concerned with its physical safety. Murders, rapes, and muggings are the most feared crimes; financial crimes play a small role in public thinking, and computer crimes even less.

Thus, because elected officials (prosecutors, judges, sheriffs, mayors, and others) are responsive to the public's concerns, hackers, industrial spies, and computer embezzlers are not viewed as a threat. Because victims of computer crime know this, they often sweep their problems under the rug.

While the street tough is seen as a threat to society, computer thieves are not always looked upon as criminals. In fact, many computer felons don't view their acts as unlawful. And few judges and juries are willing to send a convicted computer thief to jail. Until the public's perception of computer crime changes, and until adequate training and resources are provided for law enforcement officials, victims will continue to stay mum—making policing even more difficult.

High-Tech Theft Pays

A computer operator with a Connecticut police department was accused of having used his employer's computer to run background checks on various persons at the request of a private investigative firm. The case was referred to the local prosecutor, who declined to take action because no laws had been violated. "What do we charge him with?" asked an assistant district attorney.

The vice president of a time-sharing service learned that in less than a week a gang of hackers had cost his firm over $500,000. They had also prevented legitimate users from accessing the system by tying up its limited number of ports. When his company finally referred the case to local prosecutors, they took no action, saying, "There's nothing we can do."

In the United States, there are more than 2,000 computerized credit bureaus holding data on over 200 million people. The federal government keeps another 4 billion files on citizens. Congressman Dan Glickman, chairman of the House Subcommittee on Science and Technology, has stated that "we have no national policy" and "no set of cohesive Federal laws" to safeguard this data. And he's right, because as federal law now stands, authorities would find it difficult to prosecute anyone who disrupts an electronic mail system, carries out an unauthorized search of computer files, alters or manipulates data, or attempts blackmail by computer.

And the number of home and office desktop computers keeps growing daily; it will exceed 80 million by the end of this decade. Because many current criminal laws often do not precisely address the computer situation, they cannot touch the computer enthusiast who tries to penetrate the security systems of major public and private computers. As a result of inadequate laws, only one in thirty-three computer crime cases referred to prosecutors results in a conviction. Of those cases that do result in convictions, more than 90 percent are the outcome of a plea bargain between the government and the defense, in which the defendant agrees to plead guilty to a lesser charge—often a misdemeanor, which carries a jail term of up to six months and a fine of up to $500. In return, the government agrees to drop the more serious charges, usually several felony counts, which can carry prison terms of up to fifty years and large fines.

The nebulous state of existing criminal law makes it difficult and time consuming to obtain a conviction in a contested computer crime case. For example:

A claims agent with a Florida insurance company used a computer to take her employer for more than $200,000 in a phony claims fraud. She probably would have escaped prosecution if Florida had not passed a computer crime law in 1978.

When it was discovered that the Wisconsin 414 group had tapped into the computers of the Memorial Sloan-Kettering Cancer Center and the Los Alamos National Laboratory, prosecutors were unable to act. Tapping into a computer system to browse or copy data is not an offense under existing law in many jurisdictions.

A hacker who broke into a government computer evaded prison and large fines by pleading guilty to making obscene telephone calls, a misdemeanor. Had he been convicted under the felony charges, he would have faced imprisonment for up to thirty years.

A former employee of a high-tech firm used a terminal in his Virginia office to access the company's computer in Maryland and made more than forty copies of a valuable program. Upon discovery, he was charged with transporting stolen property in interstate commerce. But a federal court threw out the stolen property charge on the grounds that electronic blips transmitted over telephone wires are not property.

Legal experts agree that the present wiretap statutes don't cover thieves who tap computers. The statutes cover only aural communications; they don't apply to computer language or digitized voice transmissions (many of the nation's phone systems are switching to digital transmission technology, in which voices are translated into computer language and then back to voice).

It's important to note that, for purposes of prosecution, computer-related offenses fall into one of two categories: those in which the computer is used as a tool to embezzle or defraud, and those in which it is used to copy or alter data stored in interlocking computer systems. Many of the early computer heists fell into the former category. Prosecution was certainly not easy, but some courts were willing to apply traditional criminal laws to these high-tech thefts.

But computer heists involving the copying or altering of data have proven difficult to handle because existing criminal laws don't apply to intangible property, and computer data are considered intangible. For example, when a former student of Carnegie-Mellon University in Pittsburgh used a terminal to access Columbia University's computers in New York (causing the loss of large amounts of data and forcing the school to change the passwords of several thousand users), local prosecutors declined to act. They said that existing state laws did not apply; the government would have had to prove that the defendant intended to defraud his victim of tangible property. Thus, Columbia University was forced to bring a civil lawsuit with the hope of recouping over $25,000 in damages.

The Need for New Laws

The first recorded computer heist occurred in 1967. And computer crime bills have been waiting in the wings of Congress since 1977, when former

Senator Abe Ribicoff first introduced the Federal Computer Systems Protection Act. Other bills followed. Finally the 98th Congress passed a watered-down version of Senator Ribicoff's bill in October 1984. The statute makes it a felony to gain unauthorized access to federal computers for the purpose of using the information to cause injury to the United States.

The new law has received a mixed reception. For example, a spokesman for the Information Industry Association said, "It was about time Congress took some action." The Computer Crime Committee of the Data Processing Management Association called it merely a first step; and a representative of the Electronic Funds Transfer Association was quoted as saying, "There was serious concern that Congress would not enact anything." But all of the commentators concede that the new federal law is just a compromise. It suffers from serious drawbacks, among which is the fact that it does not cover crimes involving business computers or private information systems. And many computer-related offenses are directed at private computer systems.

In another compromise gesture, Congress passed (and the president signed into law in July 1984) the Small Business Administration Act. The Small Business Administration (SBA) sponsors more than 10,000 training programs a year—none of which have dealt with computer security. The law requires the SBA to offer training to small businesses in computer security; to establish an advisory council to study the scope of computer crime; and to recommend guidelines that would help the small business community protect itself from computer crime. However, the statute provides no criminal sanctions, and it will prove of little or no value to prosecutors seeking new tools for effectively combatting computer thieves.

Both government and business are aware of the problem. A survey by the American Society for Industrial Security of 1,319 business and governmental officials found that 82 percent felt that both state and federal computer crime laws are needed. And a survey of 283 firms by the American Bar Association (ABA) found that 79 percent of those surveyed agreed that present criminal laws are inadequate to address computer crime. The ABA's Computer Crime Task Force has already reported that "comprehensive Federal computer crime legislation is long overdue." The National Association for State Information Systems has recommended a model computer fraud statute that would make it a crime to access computer systems or modify their programs.

You may well be wondering why—since business and government know that federal computer crime legislation is needed—the efforts to enact laws have met with reluctance and half-heartedness. The reasons are twofold. First, there is philosophical opposition from within and without the government to extending the powers of law enforcement agencies—especially those of the

FBI. And second, the business community in general has been lukewarm toward computer crime legislation.

Concerning the first reason, one might say that computer politics makes strange bedfellows. For example, the American Civil Liberties Union (ACLU) has joined some computer users in opposing the enactment of a comprehensive federal computer crime law. The ACLU feels that such laws can "result in extensive intrusions into citizen privacy." A computer user has written, "We give it as our fixed opinon that there is a sickness in this land . . . and that sickness is the ingrained belief that the federal government can legislate a solution to any problem." Further opposition comes from states' rights groups, which fear that a comprehensive federal computer crime law will give the FBI jurisdiction over many criminal activities that are now the province of state and local police agencies.

But the business community (especially the computer industry) could easily overcome this opposition if it publicly supported the legislation. But, far from supporting such legislation, some of its members have openly opposed any legislative efforts, calling them an overreaction to computer crime. There are also those in the business community, particularly in the high-tech industry, who see such legislation as a first step toward government regulation of their industry.

Simply put, the private sector has little to gain by going public with the problem. After all, losses to computer crime are just passed on to the consumer in the form of higher prices. Since the public picks up the final tab, why should business worry?

Training Is Needed

The objective of criminal law is to deter antisocial conduct. To do so, it must rely on an effective and efficient law enforcement edifice. Even the best laws are of little or no value if they are not backed by well-trained and properly equipped police agencies. Under our legal system, prosecutors depend on local, state, and federal police agencies to investigate criminal acts. The police bear the responsibility of investigating and compiling the evidence necessary for a successful prosecution. Presently, however, our police forces—especially local forces—are ill-trained to meet the challenge of the high-tech criminal.

Lack of money is not the problem. The U.S. Department of Justice's annual budget now exceeds $3.5 billion, a six percent increase over the previous year. The department has spent over $200 million on computer-related equipment and plans to spend another $60 million by 1986. Even localities are spending millions on high-tech equipment, and computer terminals are now common features in patrol cars.

Many top law enforcement officials agree that computer crime will continue to grow. For example, according to the FBI, hackers now cause more than $100 million in annual damages to business and governmental computer systems; of the more than 1,000 computer crimes documented to date, many average $400,000 in losses.

Yet, according to many experts, training in computer crime for law enforcement is almost nonexistent. The FBI's computer crime program is too small to meet the growing demand from federal and local police agencies. Even many of the FBI's own field offices don't have agents trained to investigate computer crimes, and they are often forced to call headquarters or the private sector for assistance.

At the local level, things aren't any better. The St. Louis police department was the first to create a computer fraud squad in 1983; the unit consisted of twelve officers who had taken the FBI's computer crime course. The district attorney's office for Santa Clara County, California, has also created a fraud unit to investigate computer crimes and high-tech smuggling. The unit consists of eighteen investigators drawn from various local police departments around the county. Each investigator is given forty hours of training in high-tech thefts and smuggling.

But little is being done in other localities. In fact, in most cities and counties, computer crimes are investigated by burglary and check fraud units, which lack the training needed to do an effective job. Computer crime investigators not only require training in handling evidence and drawing up search warrants, they also need skills to help them uncover the evidence in these cases, which is often electronic, not physical, and may be buried in a computer program or one of many data bases.

The FBI reports that only 1 percent of all computer frauds are detected. A study of these frauds by the FBI revealed that 58 percent are committed at the data entry level, 35 percent occur at the programming stage, and 7 percent involve sophisticated penetrations of the system. The FBI also reports that alterations of the input or output data are the least technically difficult schemes to investigate, and often involve the least-skilled computer thieves. More complex frauds, involving computer communications and operating systems, can prove difficult to investigate and are often committed by sophisticated computer criminals. The FBI notes that some of the so-called hackers who emerge in sophisticated computer crimes are really skilled industrial spies who shield their activities under the hacker's guise.

In response to the various types of threats, the FBI has developed three levels of training, which range from one to six weeks in duration. Law enforcement officials throughout the country (and those from police departments in countries friendly to the United States) can apply for admission. Each class averages between fifteen and twenty students. There is a two- to three-year waiting period to get in, which limits the classes' effectiveness.

The first level of training introduces students to the basics of computer crime. After an introduction to the technology, the class discusses how to investigate input and output data alterations, how to draw up a search warrant, and how to collect and safeguard high-tech evidence. The FBI's objective for this one-week course is to prepare students to investigate 58 percent of the computer fraud cases they will encounter in the field.

The second level of training concentrates on more complex computer frauds, which involve the manipulation of programs and auxiliary storage. According to the FBI, more and more cases are surfacing in which entire computer programs have been written for no other purpose than fraud. The second course lasts four weeks, and agents who complete it are expected to be able to investigate more than 90 percent of the cases they will encounter.

The third level of training, open only to specialists, lasts for six weeks. It's designed to train agents to investigate highly sophisticated penetrations of a system and the alteration or interception of communications. However, because computer technology advances daily, it is acknowledged that agents should call on the private sector for assistance with more complex computer frauds. Plainly, cooperation from the computer industry is sorely needed.

But according to the FBI, its computer fraud classes are too small and too few to train the necessary number of local law enforcement officials. And although the U.S. Secret Service has its own computer crime training program at its Washington headquarters, it is also small, and is restricted mostly to Secret Service agents. As things now stand, local police agencies have to content themselves with attending two- and three-day courses, and with calling upon the FBI and the private sector for assistance when necessary. But aid from other sources is not always forthcoming, and computer crime goes largely uncontested.

An International Problem

Four Montreal men were charged under Canada's theft of services statute with using a microcomputer program to make more than $20,000 worth of long-distance telephone calls to bulletin boards in Canada and the United

States. But some Canadian legal experts fear that the courts will be reluctant to apply traditional criminal statutes to high-tech crimes. An Alberta court has already overturned the conviction of two defendants charged under the theft of telecommunications service statute.

In England, a defendant had his burglary charge thrown out of court on the grounds that the evidence against him was a computer printout. His attorney argued that computer-generated evidence is unreliable and fraught with errors; the court agreed. An employee at the Danish postal service and the department head of a Norwegian bank likewise escaped prosecution on legal technicalities. Their attorneys convinced the courts that the traditional theft statutes did not apply to the theft of electronic blips.

Computer crime is no longer only an American problem. It's international. Electronic thefts have been documented in every industrialized nation, including Brazil, South Korea, Poland, Japan, France, and the Soviet Union. Hacker undergrounds continue to proliferate in North America, Europe, and Asia. It's a simple matter for a thief, armed solely with a terminal and the correct access code, to tap into computer networks in many parts of the world.

The ability of U.S. law enforcement agencies to detect, investigate, and deter computer thefts will depend largely on the quality and type of assistance they receive from their foreign counterparts. In an age when data flows freely from country to country, domestic forces alone will not be able to tackle thefts. Yet many foreign police agencies lack training and expertise in this area. Some, like Hong Kong and Japan, rely on American police forces for training. Our police can thus expect little international assistance.

United Kingdom

When staffers on the *London Daily Star* read that the FBI had seized a sixteen-year-old hacker's computer equipment, they invited the hacker and his parents to fly to the United Kingdom (U.K.) free of charge, to give the British a demonstration. Robert Grumbles accepted and, before an audience in a London computer store, proceeded to demonstrate his talents. But neither the press nor onlookers were prepared for what happened: Grumbles stumbled onto an active hackers' underground based in England—bulletin boards and all. One board was found to contain the access codes of more than 400 U.K. users, including those of the Barclays Bank and University of London.

Computer crime is estimated to cost British businesses over $50 million annually. The average heist yields between $64,000 and $85,000—much lower than U.S. figures. As in the United States, many of these frauds surface by accident and are followed by pleas of guilty, according to the Association of Chief Police Officers of England, Wales, and Northern Ireland. The association notes that this "should not be overlooked by those who claim no problem confronts the Police Service."

Many of the frauds in the United Kingdom occur at the input stage. They often involve the alteration of a master file (updating it with fraudulent data); many of the perpetrators prosecuted to date have been insiders in supervisory positions. Frauds involving the alteration of programs or the diversion of goods and merchandise seem to be less of a problem. However, the unauthorized use of computer time by data processing employees is on the increase.

As for the victims of computer crime in the United Kingdom, they are no more willing to come forth than their American counterparts. According to the *Guardian* of London, over 90 percent of all computer crimes go unreported. British law enforcement also faces difficulties in prosecuting these crimes. For example, British courts are reluctant to admit computer printouts or receipts from bank teller machines as evidence, on the grounds that computer-generated data is untrustworthy and unreliable; the legal jargon is "hearsay." British authorities face two additional problems. Piecing together the facts of a complex computer fraud can prove difficult, since most U.K. police officers have had no training in this area; and translating the facts into terms a lay judge and jury will grasp can prove difficult.

But ways to combat computer crime in the United Kingdom are still being developed. An English police official said, "We need ten years to catch up." U.K. police officials in need of advanced computer crime training have to be sent to the FBI Academy in Quantico, Virginia, or to the Canadian Police College in Ottowa, because much of the training within the United Kingdom consists of three-day workshops, which merely introduce students to the basics of computer technology and are hardly sufficient to handle complex computer frauds. Few dispute that the training is inadequate.

In an effort to facilitate the prosecution of computer frauds, some jurists have recommended that Parliament enact laws to address these crimes. Legal experts have also suggested that if computer-generated evidence can be shown to be reliable, accurate, and material, the courts should admit it in a trial. But neither Parliament nor the courts are convinced. Prosecuting computer crimes is still difficult. A Scotland Yard report summarized it best: "The United Kingdom is the only country in western society not yet training its police to investigate computer-related crime." American police officials will tell you the same thing about the U.S. system.

Japan

In Kyoto, a computer engineer with the Nippon Telegraph and Telephone Public Corporation (NTT) used a cassette recorder and a microcomputer-operated decoder to copy and retrieve valuable data from an on-line network that NTT had leased to a bank. In Yokohama, a salesman used a password he received from an unsuspecting university professor to access the school's computer. And in Osaka, the director of sales for a finance company conspired with several other people to transfer funds to phony accounts that they had created. The thief then attempted to alter the computer's program to erase his tracks.

A White Paper by Japan's national police has disclosed some interesting aspects of computer crime in Japan. For example, most of these crimes involve the unlawful input of data and are done by individuals employed in a supervisory capacity, usually with a financial institution. Although unlawful alterations of software and data are serious problems in America, this is not the case in Japan. But its police have uncovered cases of vandalism against computers, as well as the theft of programs. The unauthorized use of another's computer appears to be less of a problem in Japan than it is in the United States. However, the White Paper noted that computer crime in Japan is still in its "embryonic stages."

The Japanese turned serious attention to computer crime only in the late 1970s. As a result, training for their law enforcement agencies in this area lags behind that in the United States. A Study Group on Computer System Security Regulations has been looking at the problem since 1982, but its recommendations have been largely ignored.

As for the Japanese business community, its response to computer crime can best be described as benign neglect. For example, a police survey found that 69 percent of the businesses did not control access to their computer facilities, only 0.8 percent restricted access to authorized personnel, only 6.3 percent used a key or other identifying code to control access, and only 17.2 percent had instituted a computer security program.

Nevertheless, computer crime does not seem to be as serious a problem as in the United States, largely because of the culture and value system of Japan's people and workforce. The United States and Europe lag far behind in this area.

Canada

Hacking and other computer heists are not new to Canadians. The computers of hundreds of Canadian firms have been accessed by hackers and ripped off by computer thieves. To quote a Canadian source, "Although the numbers are smaller, the pattern of computer crime in Canada is similar to that in the United States." And hackers have been active for many years on both sides of the border. Consequently, Canada's law enforcement community started training some of its officers earlier than many other industrial nations. The Canadian program is second only to that of the FBI and Secret Service.

Canada's training program on computer crime is a four-week course given at the Police College in Ottawa. The program stresses hands-on experience in computer programming, case studies, and legal issues. The course, however, is limited to only twenty students per class, and it's open not only to Canadians, but to police personnel from the United States, Great Britain, and some Commonwealth countries as well. To qualify, a candidate must demonstrate that he or she is a member of an accredited police force, has some experience investigating frauds, and has training or formal education in basic accounting.

Most investigations of computer fraud in Canada are handled by the Royal Canadian Mounted Police (RCMP). Since Canada is a federation, the RCMP plays a role similar to that of the FBI. Local police forces have little experience in this area; like their American counterparts, they lack the resources and training needed to handle the more complex computer frauds. Canadian businesses are also much like American businesses: they're often reluctant to report computer heists, thus making the task of the police more difficult. A Canadian business professional said it best: "We're in it to make money and not play cops."

Australia

Australia shares a similar legal tradition and federal structure with the United States and Canada. Like North America and Europe, it is an industrialized nation, where computers are employed in growing numbers in both government and business. And computer crime is a problem, although it is not as extensive as it is in the United States and Canada.

One of the first studies of computer crime in Australia was carried out in 1979 by the Caufield Institute of Technology in Victoria. A questionnaire was circulated to more than 2,000 Australian computer users, and fifteen cases were documented. Among them were the following:

> A computer bureau with annual sales of between $1 million and $10 million and with a staff of 150 reported that an intruder had made unauthorized use of its system. The thief was never arrested, nor was the incident ever reported to the police.

A distribution and wholesale company with annual sales between $10 million and $100 million reported an unauthorized use of its system by an eighteen-year-old computer operator who had been employed by the company for two years. The incident was discovered by accident. Although losses in computer time were said to exceed $5,000, the thief was merely fired and the case never reported to the authorities.

A large retail firm with annual sales in excess of $100 million reported that a disgruntled twenty-eight-year-old systems software manager, who had been employed by the firm for more than ten years, used one of its in-house terminals to alter a program. The employee was only reprimanded. The incident was not reported to the police because "it was simply an in-house matter."

A twenty-one-year-old computer operator, employed by a government agency for two years, destroyed a master file belonging to the agency. The saboteur was not prosecuted because "proof of guilt was held to be impossible."

A computer bureau was surprised to find that one of its system managers had attempted to copy one of its programs. Although the case was reported to the police, no action was taken because "no hard evidence was available."

The institute's survey found that the documented cases were the result of "slackness in physical control of the output material, masterfiles, and program material." Poor internal audit techniques also contributed. In many cases the thief was found to be a trusted insider who had been with the victim for at least two years. The thefts ranged from the unauthorized use of a computer to the diversion of money and property.

Scandinavia

In Sweden, a bank employee transferred large sums of money to phony accounts he had created. The fraud, perpetrated by making false entries into the bank's computer, went unnoticed for five years. In Norway, a female employee defrauded her firm by adding the names of ghost employees to its computerized payroll. The caper went undetected for several years.

Computer fraud and abuse is a serious and growing problem in Scandinavia. Although unknown before 1970, it is now a common occurrence. The Swedish Ministry of Justice warns that "modern computer systems have certain weak points as regards vulnerability to . . . criminal actions." The ministry has identified several of the more common types of crime, which include unauthorized modifications of data and programs, stealing data and funds, and copying proprietary information. Especially vulnerable, the ministry reported, are the Post Office, the Telecommunications Administration, the Swedish Railway, the State Power Board, and the Civil Service Salary Circulation System.

But of the more than 200 cases that have surfaced, the majority have been the work of trusted insiders, many of whom received larger-than-average salaries. The motives have often been simple greed. Losses have exceeded "those in the case of traditional economic crime," according to the ministry. And not surprisingly, many of the thieves did not see themselves as lawbreakers; the thefts often involved computer centers and communication networks.

Denmark and Norway also have their share of computer crime, although it is a more recent phenomenon in Norway than in Denmark. For example, a Danish computer consultant used a client's computer without authorization to run his own business, and an employee of the Danish postal service swindled it by authorizing payments to phony accounts he had created.

Most of the known frauds in Scandinavia have involved the manipulation of data programs. Vandalism and sabotage, however, are reportedly on the increase. For example, someone is said to have cut off the power to the computer center for Bromma airport in Sweden, and an unknown person threatened to bomb IBM's Scandinavian offices. Especially since the Soviets have increased their high-tech theft activities, crimes like industrial espionage and the tapping of data communication lines have increased.

The small size of the Scandinavian nations, the hesitancy of many of their smaller firms to convert to computers, and the homogeneous culture in these societies have slowed down the growth of computer crime. However, this appears to be changing, largely because of the growth of transborder data transactions. Now that computers in Scandinavia are linked to those in other parts of the world, they are more vulnerable to criminal attack.

The Scandinavians have discovered that the detection and investigation of computer crimes can prove difficult. Victims are often reluctant to come forth. And although some Swedish police personnel have received training in high-tech crimes at the Police Academy in Solna, the police in Denmark and Norway lag behind. There is also a need for laws and procedures specifically designed for computer crimes. Some cases have been successfully prosecuted under old fraud laws, but this was possible only because computer criminals in Scandinavia are not as technologically advanced as their counterparts in North America. But this will change as computer literacy grows in Scandinavia.

West Germany

Unlike the other West European peoples, the West Germans consider computer crime a serious threat and train their law enforcement personnel accordingly. Because it is highly technologically advanced, West Germany's experience in this area has been very similar to North America's. Computer fraud courses are now available for specialized units of its police forces. These courses are given at the Federal Office of Criminal Investigation (Bundes-kriminalamt) in Wiesbaden and the Training College for Intermediate Ranks of the Criminal Police of North-Rhine-Westphalia (Landes-kriminalschule) in Düsseldorf.

Other Countries

The Royal Hong Kong Police acknowledge that they are faced with a growing number of computer crimes. These cases are handled by specially trained members of the colony's Fraud Squad, who are sent to the United States and Canada to learn their trade. Since Hong Kong is one of the world's key financial centers, the problem can only grow. Computer crime also concerns the authorities in Singapore, now that this small republic is emerging as the high-tech and financial center of Southeast Asia. The government knows this, and has sent some of its police officials to the United States and Canada for training.

Computer crime has yet to manifest itself in New Zealand. At least, this is the opinion of experts in New Zealand who have studied the problem. New Zealanders are not overly concerned now, but as the nation's computers are linked to networks in Australia, Asia, and other parts of the world, the situation will certainly change for the worse.

Switzerland is one of the world's most important financial centers. Geneva and Zurich are second to none in automated banking. Computers handle billions of dollars in transactions daily. Although the Swiss government has established a four-day computer crime course to train its police personnel at the Criminal Investigative Department in Zurich, the Swiss do not seem too worried. Government spokesmen will assure you that computer crime is not a problem there.

The Swiss lack of concern over computer crime can be explained in at least three ways: the Swiss, noted for their honesty and strict work ethic, simply don't steal; the police, especially at the local level (since Switzerland is a federation), are not sufficiently trained to detect and investigate these cases; or, since banking is a key industry, the problem is swept under the rug. Most experts favor the last two explanations, although the Swiss traits of honesty and hard work are also factors.

Addressing a group of bankers, a prosecutor noted, "I would like to tell you that prosecutors are waiting around for a good computer crime case. But they aren't." He could have added that prosecutors will shy away from computer-related cases whenever possible. Can you blame them? After all, why use valuable (and limited) resources to prosecute cases that judges and juries don't understand and that the victims want to sweep under the rug? The absence of computer crime laws and the lack of training for law enforcement only further complicate the situation. And a conviction usually means a mere slap on the wrist for the thief. "So what's to be gained from it?" prosecutors often ask.

The proliferation of international computer networks and data banks has only made matters worse for the police. It's now possible for a thief in Europe to access a computer system in the United States. The thief only needs a terminal and the correct access code, and pirate bulletin boards will readily supply the latter. Meanwhile, police departments around the world find themselves scrambling to catch up with the computer revolution. Computer crime will soon demand increased international cooperation; but cooperation in this area among the world's police forces continues to be the exception rather than the rule. As matters presently stand, there's no question that computer criminals the world over have a bright future.

9

High-Tech Terrorism

There we were unlucky, but remember we only have to be lucky once.
— Irish Republican Army

D URING an Easter weekend, members of a mysterious group calling itself the Committee for the Liquidation or Deterrence of Computers (CLODO) broke into the computer centers of Philips Data Systems and CII-Honeywell-Bull, in Toulouse, France, and set them on fire. In a statement justifying their attack, CLODO declared: "Computers are the favorite instrument of the powerful. They are used to classify, control and repress."

Terrorist attacks in Western Europe are old hat; they average more than 500 a year. And computers are fast replacing political and business leaders as terrorist targets. To date, terrorists have bombed more than 600 computer sites and suppliers, including those of the Frascati nuclear research laboratory near Rome. The U.S. Department of Energy fears that such high-tech terrorism could set off a nuclear catastrophe.

Terrorism is a growing industry. It has claimed more than 4,000 lives and billions of dollars in property losses. According to the U.S. Senate Subcommittee on Security and Terrorism, there have been over 2,800 bombing incidents in the United States alone since 1982, directed equally at business and government. And the State Department had identified more than 100 terrorist groups, mostly armed, funded, and supported by what it calls the League of Terror (nations such as Libya and Iran that employ terrorists as instruments of their foreign policy).

Terrorists are skilled at what they do. Their success rate exceeds 80 percent. For example, they have a 90 percent chance of escaping capture or death; a 50 percent chance of having at least some of their demands met; and a 100 percent chance of getting most of the publicity that they want. But terrorism has taken a turn. Assassinations and kidnappings now account for less than 30 percent of terrorist activities, and bombings account for more than 60 percent. Increasingly, many of these targets include computer sites. Terrorists have been quick to appreciate the dependence of modern societies on high technology.

League of Terror

Members of the East Asian Anti-Japan Armed Front made their way into the ninth-floor offices of a Japanese construction company and planted a bomb that seriously damaged the company's computer facility. In England, members of a group calling itself the Angry Brigade attempted to bomb police computers in London. And in the United States, saboteurs made four attempts to damage the computer center at the Wright-Patterson Air Force Base near Dayton, Ohio.

Terrorism is not confined to one nation or continent. Modern terrorists traverse the globe at will, armed with the best weaponry that technology has to offer. Although airplane hijackings, assassinations, and kidnappings continue to be their stock in trade, high-tech targets—telecommunications systems, computer networks, scientific laboratories, power plants, and nuclear facilities—are increasingly catching their attention.

According to the CIA, the number of hardcore terrorists is less than 4,000. But don't let the numbers fool you: terrorists have the support and assistance of numerous governments and millions of political malcontents. And terrorists are also known to pool their resources. For example, British intelligence has confirmed that the West German Red Army Faction (the Baader-Meinhof group) has worked closely with members of the Palestine Liberation Organization (PLO) and Irish Republican Army (IRA). One demand of the Arab terrorists who hijacked a Lufthansa Airlines Boeing 737 to Somalia was the release of jailed leaders of the Red Army Faction. And the Japanese Red Army is said to have carried out an attack at Lod's Airport in Israel in support of the PLO. Carlos the Jackal (Illich Ramirez-Sanchez) and his group are known to work closely with a multitude of terrorist elements.

Modern terrorists have been quick to learn that there is strength in unity. Alliances are often welded not so much out of ideological fervor as out of necessity and a hatred of the West—especially the United States. For example, diverse terrorist groups from such nations as Bolivia, Chile, Paraguay, and Uruguay met in 1974 to form the Revolutionary Coordinating Junta. Largely bankrolled by the Argentine Revolutionary Army, the purpose of the junta was to pool the resources of these various groups to augment their effectiveness against "Yankee imperialism." In 1982, at the invitation of the PLO, more than 1,000 members of various terrorist organizations met in southern Lebanon. Those present included members of the Red Brigades, Japan's Red Army, the Red Army Faction, and terrorists from Libya, Pakistan, and several Latin American countries. Their objective was to better coordinate their efforts against "imperialism."

Terrorists can also count on friendly governments for support. Libya, for example, is said to provide more than $50 million in annual assistance and to run twenty terrorist training camps. The Cubans provide terrorists with the latest modern technological weapons, such as Katusha rockets, RPG-7 antitank rockets, SAM-7 missiles, and RGD5 hand grenades. Cuba also maintains several terrorist training camps—for example, a 4,000-acre facility near Guanabacoa, and a smaller camp in Oriente. And the Soviets—through their International Department of the Central Committee of the Soviet Communist Party—are said to spend over $300 million annually in support of terrorist groups. East Germans are also busy running terrorist training camps in the South Yemen.

But terrorists don't rely solely on foreign governments for funds and assistance. They have proven to be resourceful on their own. They know that dependency on foreign governments carries with it a price tag. Thus, some groups like the PLO have invested their money wisely; the PLO's investments are said to exceed $100 million and are managed by the Arab Bank of Jordon. David Gravier, an Argentine businessman, is said to have managed the funds of various Latin American terrorist groups. The investments were funneled through two now-defunct banks, the American Bank and Trust Company of New York and the Belgian Banque Pour l'Amerique du Sud. Gravier not only invested the money, but also made sure that members of these groups were paid monthly salaries and provided with funds to bankroll their operations.

One of the traditional sources of funds for terrorists has been kidnapping. Since 1974 more than 4,000 businessmen have been kidnapped for profit by terrorists. In one case involving two wealthy Argentinian businessmen, their families paid $60 million for their return. A Cuban-backed Puerto Rican terrorist group, the Fuerzas Armadas de Liberacion Nacional (FALN), planned to kidnap President Reagan's son.

Bank robberies have likewise proven an important source of income. They are particularly favored by American terrorists. Such groups as the Islamic Guerillas of America, May 19th Communist Organization, Weather Underground, Black Liberation Army, United Freedom Front, Armed Resistance, and Revolutionary Fighting Group have all resorted to bank robberies.

Vice and extortion have also generated money for some of these groups. For example, terrorists in Italy are known to have assisted the Sicilian Mafia, the Neopolitan Camorra, and Calabrian gangsters in smuggling narcotics. Drug dealers in Latin America are said to work hand-in-hand with terrorists from Colombia, Peru, and Bolivia, as well as the Cuban intelligence service. And groups such as Omega 7 (an anti-Castro organization that has been linked to more than 100 bombings in the United States), the IRA, and the Justice Commandos of the Armenian Genocide (JCAG) are said to engage in protection rackets and contract murders. Some terrorist groups have even been connected to prostitution rackets.

But terrorists are also able to raise money for people and communities that are sympathetic to their cause. For example, sympathizers within the American Irish community have bankrolled some of the IRA's operations; members of the Armenian community have done the same for the JCAG, as have American Cubans for Omega 7. Terrorists, like organized crime, have long known that there is no shortage of funds, patrons, or weapons in today's world. One only needs the will to employ them in the service of a cause.

Anatomy of Terror

An unknown group seeking independence for the Canary Islands exploded a bomb in Gran Canaria. In the ensuing confusion, jet traffic was diverted to the airport at Tenerife; during the scramble that followed, two jumbo jets collided on the ground and killed 581 persons. Italian police thwarted an attack on the U.S. embassy in Rome; seven people—members of a Middle Eastern terrorist group—were arrested. And in Frankfurt, West Germany, a U.S. Army intelligence facility was bombed; its computer was made inoperable. A terrorist group calling itself In the Heart of the Beast took credit, proclaiming, "Death to U.S. imperialism."

Terrorism is a very old profession—perhaps as old as recorded history itself. One of the oldest and better-known of these groups was the Assassins. Founded in 1090 A.D., the Assassins reigned supreme in the Middle East for more than two centuries. Another famous group was the Jacobins in late eighteenth-century France. During this period the term "terrorism" came to signify acts of violence designed to influence the political behavior of governments and individuals. During the nineteenth century secret societies like the Carbonari, Social Revolutionaries, Black Hand, People's Will, and others, made the word terrorism part of the daily vocabulary. And we would do well to remember that World War I was sparked, in part, by the assassination of the Austrian Archduke Ferdinand and his wife at the hands of the Serbian Black Hand Society.

The strength of terrorism today lies not in numbers, but in modern technology and organization. Technology, in the form of the electronic media, enables terrorists to convey their messages throughout the world. Technology also gives terrorists awesome destructive powers. In terms of numbers, terrorists are insignificant. For example, more than 80 percent of all terrorist groups are said to number fewer than 50 persons; 8 percent number 50 to 500; and only 6 percent are said to have over 500 members. According to intelligence experts, many American terrorist groups have organized into cells of 5 to 25 members.

Likewise, many of the foreign terrorist groups are insignificant in terms of numbers. The IRA is reputed to have a core of only 300 to 400 members. These are organized into member cells of 6 to 10 people each, and are known as "active service units." The units are independent and highly self-sufficient, which makes it difficult for the authorities to penetrate them, since the members of one unit often do not know the members of their sister units. Unless called upon to join forces in a combined operation, the units operate independently.

Terrorists know only too well that they cannot defeat the modern state in conventional warfare. So, instead, they seek to intimidate the populace and undermine its confidence in the ability of government officials to protect people from terrorists. Simply put, the terrorists' objective is to bleed the state to death. For example, Japan's Red Army has frequently targeted key industries; West German terrorists have often bombed American military bases, like the U.S. Air Force's European headquarters in Ramstein. And French terrorist groups like the M5 have bombed numerous transportation facilities.

Terrorists stress discipline and regimentation; their survival often hinges on it. Those who deviate from the cause are dealt with harshly. And they are often killed. Tyron Rison, a former member of the Family, told the *Wall Street Journal* that a contract hit had been put out on him because he assisted the authorities. Ismail Darwish, a member of the PLO, was less fortunate: he was murdered near Rome's fashionable Via Veneto while traveling on a false Moroccan passport. Intelligence sources were quoted as saying, "This looks like an internal feud." The modern-day zealot, like his predecessors, associates dissent with treason.

Why do some people, mostly young, turn to terrorism? Nobody really knows. On the surface, most terrorists differ little from the average law-abiding citizen. Neighbors of captured terrorist members are always shocked to hear that such fine young men and women could be involved in such activities.

Associates often describe terrorist acquaintances as kind and quiet people who never displayed any violent tendencies. For example, members of Japan's Red Army would often distribute candy and cookies to their neighbors; the same people, in a span of one year, killed or maimed more than 300 persons.

Terrorists do differ from the average citizen, but not so much in appearance as in commitment. They are true believers, and blindly accept the precepts their movement espouses. These ideologies vary from group to group, because modern terrorists represent all shades of the political spectrum. Basque terrorists, for example, are driven by nationalism and seek political independence from the Spanish state. The PLO seeks a homeland for the Palestinians. Shiite terrorist groups seek to purify Islam of the West's corrupting effects. The Red Brigades and Red Army Faction seek to establish Marxist states. And the Italian Armed Revolutionary Nuclei and The Front seek to turn Italy into a fascist state. (The Front was responsible for the Bologna train station bombing that killed and wounded over 200 persons.)

But terrorists are also often pawns in the international power game. For example, Libya's Muammar Qaddafi is said to have paid Carlos the Jackal and his team $2 million for their successful attack on OPEC's headquarters in Vienna. And according to intelligence sources, the hijacking of a Kuwaiti airliner by Shiite terrorists to Tehran may have been prompted by Iran's intelligence service, in an effort to force Kuwait and the other oil-rich Arab states to stop supporting Iraq in its war with Iran. Further, the IRA is said to receive funds and arms from Libya, which views the British support of Israel as contrary to its own interests in the Middle East. And Soviet and Cuban assistance to Latin American terrorists is prompted by a desire to undermine the U.S. influence in that part of the world.

It would be a mistake, though, to think of terrorists as merely the creation of governments hostile to the West and its interests. Rather, terrorists often have a will of their own. They have been aptly described as "freebooters . . . in business for themselves." Although terrorists may cooperate with each other and receive assistance from various foreign countries, their primary commitment is to their own cause. What makes them dangerous is their readiness to sacrifice even their own lives in the pursuit of their cause.

High-Tech Targets Abound

Four masked persons, armed with automatic weapons, made their way into a university's computer center in Rome and set it on fire. Losses exceeded $2 million. In West Germany a group calling itself the Rote Zellen claimed responsibility for bombing the computer facility of Maschinenfabrik Ausburg-Nuernberg AG; damages exceeded $7 million. The group warned that additional attacks would follow if the company didn't cease manufacturing transport vehicles for NATO's missiles. In Eagan, Michigan, saboteurs broke into a Sperry Corporation plant and destroyed military computer equipment that was to be used for nuclear weapons guidance and control systems.

The high-tech society is a highly integrated system of diverse technologies. Although complex, our society is also a fragile structure; a disruption in any one of its critical units could cause domino-effect failures in other interdependent units. For example, the sabotage of a key computer system could leave millions of people without electricity, shut down entire transportation systems, and bring thousands of business and government computers to a grinding halt. A ninth-grader with a home computer almost did just that when he accessed the Pentagon's computers and erased some of their data.

Terrorism thrives best in a highly industrialized and urban society; such an environment offers the terrorist a multitude of targets. Destroying such targets can often prove to be a simple task. An Office of Technology Assessment (OTA) study concluded that modern society employs many fragile technologies; a major disruption in any of them could prove catastrophic.

Power Plants

The great Northeastern blackout of 1965 took the nation and much of the world by surprise; it amply demonstrated the fragility and interdependence of the fabric of our society. A faulty relay in Queenston, Ontario, knocked out the electrical power for more than 25 million persons over an 80,000-square-mile area; 800,000 people were stranded in subways, thousands of businesses went without electricity, and widespread civil disobedience took 50,000 national guardsmen to quell. It took over fifteen hours to repair the relay and restore power.

If a lesson had been learned, it was soon forgotten. In 1972 the New York region was hit by a second blackout when lightning struck transmission lines. This incident left 9 million persons without electricity for over twenty hours, and led to rampant looting, which resulted in over 3,000 arrests. A third power blackout hit in 1981. It left 52,000 persons without electricity, cost the garment industry $2.9 million a day in lost retail sales, left 3.5 million people stranded in subways, and took more than four hours to repair.

Electricity fuels modern society. It keeps our trains moving, lights and heats our skyscrapers, runs our machinery, and keeps our computers ticking. If we were without it for an extended time, society could sink back into the

Dark Ages. Yet power plants have increasingly become the targets of terrorists and other malcontents. For example, a suspicious fire at New York's Indian Point power plant caused more than $5 million in damages; the Pacifist and Ecologist Committee has taken credit for bombing one of France's most advanced nuclear power stations; and Basque terrorists are said to have carried out a rocket attack on a nuclear power plant in Bilbao, Spain.

According to the Department of Energy, there have been over 170 domestic attacks against power plants to date. The Government Accounting Office (GAO) warns that "electric power systems are . . . highly vulnerable to damage from acts of . . . terrorism," and that attacks against them could "bring our society to its knees." As an example, take the power failure that caused a computer outage at a tractor company; it cost the manufacturer more than $50,000 in lost orders for parts. And power disruptions could be catastrophic to major airline companies, which lose an average of $300,000 every time a computerized reservation system shuts down. Officials at the Federal Reserve Bank of Philadelphia acknowledge that without their computers, they would find it nearly impossible to process $7.5 billion in daily money transfers.

Fuels

Modern societies rely on a variety of fuels to meet their energy needs. Among the more widely used in the West are oils, gas, and nuclear fuel. Water, thermal, and solar energy sources provide a small portion of our needs at present. Our energy sources are also vulnerable to terrorist attacks, both during transit (while in pipelines, trucks, trains, or vessels) and while in storage. The end result of an attack on energy sources could prove disastrous.

For example, a GAO report warns that terrorist attacks against our liquified natural gas facilities could cause the death of tens of thousands of Americans. According to the GAO, the total energy of all the bombs dropped in the 1945 raid on Tokyo—which killed 83,000 people and leveled over 250,000 dwellings—equals only about 1 percent of the energy held in one large liquid energy storage tank. The natural gas explosion that destroyed a twenty-block area and killed and injured more than 2,500 people in a small suburb of Mexico City is ample evidence of the threat.

Terrorist acts against energy sources abound. In Bayton, Texas, for example, extortionists placed several explosive devices at a Gulf Oil petrochemical plant; the company was forced to shut down its plant temporarily and order more than 1,000 employees to stay home. Two of the United States' largest pipelines are said to have been attacked, and some of their pumping stations were damaged. And communist terrorists in Belgium are said to have been behind the bombing of NATO's emergency fuel pipelines, the second-largest fuel delivery system in Europe.

There is also concern that terrorists might seize a nuclear power plant and threaten to destroy it unless their demands are met. Even worse, they could threaten to contaminate a city's water or air supply with radioactive material. Plutonium 239 is said to be at least 2,000 times more toxic than the venom of a cobra snake and 1,000 times more toxic than modern nerve gas.

Seven counterterrorist experts, working for the Department of Energy and using forged credentials, have demonstrated that infiltrating most nuclear facilities is simple. During a mock raid, the "threat assessment team" had little difficulty in getting inside the government's Savannah River nuclear weapons plant in South Carolina and taking over its comuterized control facility. Likewise, it was not very difficult for the team to infiltrate the government's plutonium reactor plant at Hanford, Washington. A Pentagon official best expressed the government's concern: "The thing that really worries us most is an attack on one of these plants from a dedicated terrorist group."

Toxics

Large amounts of toxic agents are shipped daily, both here and overseas. For example, American Cyanamid is said to purchase methyl isocyanate (a highly toxic chemical used in pesticides) in quantities of 30,000 to 60,000 pounds; these are transported by truck and rail from West Virginia to various parts of the country from which freighters then take them to Brazil. Billions of pounds of this and other toxic agents are manufactured in the United States each year. The sale of many of these chemicals is not regulated, so anyone, including a terrorist, can easily purchase them in the open market. According to the FBI, one can purchase anthrax and botulism bacteria through the mail, and even the deadly T-2 toxin—the chemical the Soviets have reportedly used in Afghanistan.

Toxic agents, if misused, can be deadlier than most bombs. For example, the authorities were forced to evacuate more than 200,000 people from a small town near Toronto, Canada, when a ninety-ton freight car carrying poisonous chlorine gas was derailed. The evacuation involved a forty-square-mile area; over 400 persons had to be hospitalized. And in Bhopal, India, a leakage of deadly methyl isocyanate gas killed more than 2,000 people and may have injured another 100,000. And a California terrorist is said to have mailed toxic agents to a U.S. Supreme Court Justice; the FBI claimed that he also planned to explode a nerve gas device inside the U.S. Capitol building.

An array of toxic agents are now within the easy reach of terrorists and other malcontents. Experts warn that an entire city can be held hostage by terrorists who possess such toxic agents; society can be paralyzed. Since the chemical industry is highly computerized, terrorists could easily divert these toxic agents and erase the evidence of their act. In fact, authorities speculate that twenty-seven computer tapes at the Y-12 nuclear weapons parts plant in Oak Ridge, Tennessee, may have been deliberately erased to cover up a missing supply of uranium. And with recent developments in biotechnology, newer and ever more frightening toxic agents are coming on the scene.

Electronic Media

When lethal doses of poison were found in Tylenol painkiller capsules, millions of Americans were frightened, and the Johnson & Johnson Company was almost bankrupted. The scare illustrated that the electronic media not only accords terrorists a vehicle for their message, it can also be used to frighten entire populations. And terrorists are masterful manipulators of the electronic media. A simple bomb scare, or the threat of a fire or poisoning, can intimidate millions of Americans through the evening national news. Without meaning to, our mass electronic media can easily become accomplices after the fact to terrorists.

Communications

In Los Angeles, a group of hackers attempted to shut down the California telephone system. And a study of the nation's communication system by SRI International confirms that it is vulnerable to terrorist attack. The study warns that the loss of twenty long-distance relay facilities could cripple the nation's entire telephone system. Terrorists in Europe have amply demonstrated how simple it is to attack a communication system. The Red Brigades and the Red Army Faction have already taken credit for bombing several such facilities.

Our communication networks are the nerve centers of high-tech society. But these networks, as well as the computers that run them, are vulnerable. In England, the chief negotiator of the London Clearing Bank Employer's Federation has already warned that sabotage of key communication systems may soon replace the strike as a tool in labor–management disputes. Disgruntled employees have already demonstrated that such systems are not difficult to sabotage.

Data Centers

A terrorist attack on the computer of the Italian Ministry of Motor Vehicles was so thorough that it took the government more than two years to reconstruct its files. And a group of hackers had little difficulty in accessing the Marshall Flight Center's computers in Huntsville, Alabama, and erasing some of the data. According to the Electronic Insurance Department of Chub & Son, fewer than 7 percent of all organizations that have experienced severe damage to their data processing operations are in business five years after the loss.

Data centers are the giant electronic filing cabinets of modern society. But they, too, are vulnerable. Richard P. Kusserow, Inspector General of the U.S. Department of Health and Human Services, has told Congress, "I don't feel comfortable about the vulnerabilities we have now." The GAO warns that few of the government's data centers have contingency plans in case of a successful terrorist attack.

Factories

Automated manufacturing is here to stay. A variety of computers (mainframes, superminis, minis, and micros) are used in manufacturing; armies of robots are moving into the workforce. The automated factory lowers production costs and dramatically improves performance. But because computers are essential to the operations, automated factories pose an attractive target for terrorists. The sabotage of a main computer can bring an automated factory to a grinding halt.

Dante's Inferno Revisited

A dark blue van is parked in front of the U.S. Treasury Department building in Washington, D.C. The driver leaves the van and crosses the street to a blue station wagon, gets in, and speeds away to Maryland. One hour later a huge fireball engulfs the entire downtown area. Thousands of pedestrians are incinerated, office buildings catch fire, and a moving shock wave creates hurricane-like winds. Within minutes, the city is a shambles, a ghost town. Government buildings are ruined and their computers are in ashes. The fires rage on.

This scenario of a nuclear attack by terrorists is both probable and possible. The GAO warns that terrorists, armed with a small supply of stolen plutonium (about five pounds), could construct a homemade nuclear device. The technical know-how is available; the U.S. Senate Judiciary Committee has reported that "there is a growing body of persons, with scientific training or experience in the nuclear power industry, who could make a [nuclear] bomb." The necessary equipment to construct such a device is also available, according to the Ford Foundation, which reports that crude fusion bombs can easily be constructed by simply "using materials and equipment that could be purchased at a hardware store and from commercial suppliers of scientific equipment."

Both Congress and the Department of Energy are worried that security at many of the nation's nuclear power facilities is lax. Plutonium supplies are reportedly unprotected in many facilities, and alarm and sensor systems at facilities have often been found to be faulty. And the security guards lack the training needed to adequately protect existing nuclear facilities. Likewise, experts have warned the Nuclear Regulatory Commission (NRC) that security at university nuclear research laboratories around the country is frequently insufficient. Terrorists would have little difficulty in stealing enriched uranium from many of these laboratories.

Nuclear materials have already been diverted from some of our plants. For example, more than fourteen pounds of high-grade uranium (enough to construct an atomic bomb) went missing from a plant that processes nuclear fuels for navy submarines; several years before, the same plant reported the loss of over forty pounds of nuclear material. And sources at the NRC have disclosed that more than 200 pounds of weapons-grade uranium are missing from a Pennsylvania plant.

The FBI warns that there is a very real possibility of terrorists going nuclear, and the National Advisory Commission on Criminal Justice Standards and Goals reported several years ago that the threat of nuclear terrorism "is very real and ought to be realistically and urgently faced." Further, a consultant with BDM Corporation, a Virginia consulting firm, has told the NRC that terrorists now have the capability to make nuclear weapons with about half the destructive power of the bomb dropped on Hiroshima.

Although security at many civilian nuclear facilities is indeed lax, the government fares no better. For example, a disgruntled former employee drove his truck past guards at the Idaho National Energy Laboratory and spent half an hour inside a Navy facility that manufactures highly enriched uranium fuel for submarines. A Japanese camera crew had no difficulty in flying a helicopter over the nuclear facility at Oak Ridge, Tennessee. And the House Commerce Committee has reported that at least five government nuclear facilities suffer from serious security flaws.

There is also concern that the military's nuclear stockpile is not secure. For example, it is said that the army's 372 atomic demolition munitions (ADMs), based in West Germany, are vulnerable to theft by terrorists. A small ADM weighs a mere fifty-eight pounds and can be carried in a backpack; its explosive power is equivalent to 1,000 tons of TNT. A person can transport it in a suitcase with little difficulty. Larger ADMs, which weigh about 400 pounds, have the explosive power of the Hiroshima bomb. They, too, are vulnerable to theft and can be transported by van, helicopter, or speed boat. Terrorists armed with ADMs would have little trouble destroying important targets.

Terrorists armed with biochemical weapons can also wreak havoc on high-tech society. The chemicals needed to construct lethal weapons are readily available in the open market. For example:

Acrylonitrate—a liquid that releases cyanide when burned.

Anhydrous ammonia—a compressed gas whose caustic vapors can produce pulmonary edema.

Ammonia nitrate—a common fertilizer, used as TNT during World War II.

Chlorine gas—a deadly gas, used in water purification.

Ethylene oxide—a highly explosive and toxic gas.

Fluorine—a highly flammable and toxic gas.

Hydrogen cyanide—a highly toxic substance, available in both gaseous and liquid form, that can produce explosive fumes.

Hydrofluoric acid—a toxic corrosive chemical, available in both liquid and gaseous form.

Liquified natural gas—a highly explosive and flammable gas.

Parathion—a toxic liquid.

Tetraethyl lead—a toxic liquid whose vapors are highly explosive.

Vinyl chloride—a highly explosive gas.

There are also numerous biological agents that can be purchased in the open market. For example, an ounce of botulin toxin (botulism), if properly dispersed, can kill more than half of the American population; it is said to be deadlier than plutonium. And some nerve gases are toxic enough to kill millions of people. Fifty-three bottles of the army's VX nerve gas may have been stolen by terrorists in West Germany. The tools of terror grow daily; terrorists now have the capability to paralyze our society—business and government alike.

Terrorists are quickly learning that hijacked airplanes can easily be replaced, that embassies can be turned into armed citadels, and that kidnapped corporate and government officials are "expendable." They are fully aware that the interlocking units of our high-tech society make it vulnerable.

Few dispute that a well placed, powerful bomb could easily cripple an entire computer network—with serious consequences for our society. High technology carries a price tag: it makes us vulnerable to terrorism. And the masters of terror are fast learning that high tech is the Achilles' heel of post industrial society.

10

Tapping King Solomon's Mines

Every door is barred with gold, and opens but to golden keys.
                                                    — Tennyson

H OME banking is the wave of the future. Several national services are presently being offered by such industry giants as Chase, Citicorp, Chemical Bank, and American Express. Bankers say it's the "in" thing to do. And those sentiments were shared by a thirteen-year-old Maryland student who used his home computer and the secret identification numbers of legitimate users to access several national home banking systems. In exchange for immunity from prosecution, the student identified several dozen other students who were engaged in similar electronic heists.

Admittedly, the roof of his home in Fairfax, Virginia, looked odd with half-a-dozen antennas protruding from it, but there was little else to distinguish Richard P. Shanklin from his neighbors. To some he was a nice guy; to others, a bore. His neighbors were shocked to read that a federal grand jury in Alexandria had returned a fifteen-count indictment against Shanklin, charging him with using his home computer and a secret access code to tap into the computers of the Credit Bureau in Atlanta. Shanklin is alleged to have gained access to account numbers and credit limit information on more than eighty consumers.

Officials at Philadelphia's Family Court were surprised and embarrassed to learn that one of their most trusted juvenile court officers had been charged with an automated teller machine heist. The police charged that the accused had used a stolen electronic bank card to make several dozen withdrawals from Philadelphia Money Access teller machines.

Electronic payment systems have been growing at 20 percent annually for the last twenty years, and their annual growth rate could reach 40 percent in the near future. In the United States alone, customers now own more than 35 million electronic bank cards, and the use of automated teller machines (ATMs) exceeds that of credit cards. More than 80 percent of all bank transactions can be handled by electronic payment systems, known as electronic funds transfer (EFT) systems in the financial community. In many parts of the country, a consumer can pay bills by simply dialing his or her bank's computer.

America's cashless revolution is off and running. In an almost frantic drive to replace paper currency with "electronic blips," America's financial institutions, according to a survey by Input Inc., will triple their expenditures for computer equipment in the coming years—largely for EFT systems. By the year 1990, many electronic bank accounts will also serve as computerized mailboxes. Under instructions from a customer, merchants would transmit their bills electronically to the customer's bank, where its computers would make automatic payments.

While the world of EFT systems promises a bright future for consumers, there is mounting evidence that these electronic payment systems may be spawning new multimillion-dollar crimes. The National Commission on Electronic Fund Transfers reported in 1977 that the increased use of EFT systems could result in new and more costly types of fraud. Five years later, the Congressional Clearinghouse voiced similar concerns. And a report released by the U.S. Bureau of Justice Statistics in February 1984 warned that "[EFT systems] may create the potential or opportunity for new types of criminal activity."

Experts in the retail industry are convinced that by 1990 annual losses to credit card and EFT frauds and thefts could exceed $10 billion. A U.S. Senate Judiciary Committee report, released in March 1984, warned that organized crime and other professional criminals are making their way into the area. The report detailed how, in one such case, an international criminal organization defrauded California banks and merchants of more than $5 million. The committee's report also warned that organized crime was channeling these ill-gotten gains into its "drug trafficking activities."

Yet the financial community continues to display a cavalier attitude toward the problem. Many financial institutions, including the ten largest ones, do not encrypt their EFT data—despite their full awareness that, for the price of several hundred dollars in equipment, an amateur can tap their EFT communication lines. A Federal Reserve official best summarized the seriousness of the threat: "When one realizes that these [EFT] systems move more than $100 trillion annually, nobody would miss several billion dollars." The cashless society is a reality. The question is: How safe are King Solomon's Mines?

What Are EFT Systems?

If the EFT revolution maintains its present pace, experts predict that paper currency may become obsolete by the year 2000. The typical American living room will resemble an airplane's cockpit; customers will be able to use video screens and computers to conduct their daily financial transactions from the comfort of their homes—twenty-four hours a day, seven days a week. You and I, and millions of other Americans, are already plugged into the cashless society. If you don't believe it, then look around you:

Chase Manhattan Bank customers can make cash withdrawals from more than 2,000 automated teller machines in over forty states.

Motorists in many states can now purchase gasoline with electronic bank cards. When a purchase is made, the amount of the transaction is deducted electronically from the customer's account and credited to that of the gas company.

VISA customers will soon be able to use an all-in-one electronic card that will enable them to make purchases anywhere in the world.

Indiana National Bank customers can use a computerized system to pay their bills by telephone.

French financial institutions have started issuing a "national electronic" card that can be used by their customers at more than 300,000 European point-of-sale systems.

We have been conditioned to think of money in terms of paper. Checks merely carry information about financial transactions. Simply put, paper is the main medium for the transference of funds. In an EFT transaction, however, electronic blips replace paper as the vehicle for this transfer. Information about a financial transaction is initiated, transmitted, and recorded electronically. An EFT transaction thus differs from a paper transaction not so much in substance as in form.

As with checks and other forms of paper currency, electronic payment systems come in many forms and shapes. The cashless society should be viewed as a conglomeration of various electronic payment systems. Among the elements found in most EFT systems are:

> Access devices, which take the form of a plastic card, an account number, or a password, and which allow the user to gain entry into the system. They are used in conjunction with a personal identification number and a terminal.

> Personal identification numbers (PINs), which identify the user to the system; they basically tell the system that the person is authorized to use it.

> Terminals, linked to a central computer by communication lines, make it possible for the user to contact the computer and direct it to carry out specific transactions. Terminals are the gateways to the system.

> Computers, which are the workhorses of the cashless society. They record and transmit information on financial transactions.

Although there are more than a dozen EFT systems in use, over 80 percent of all EFT transactions are currently handled by the five types of systems listed in the following sections.

Wire Transfer (WT)

Each working day the computers of the Reserve Fund of New York handle more than $30 billion in wire transfers, an average of over 5,000 daily EFT transactions. Both government and business rely on WT systems to move funds and information at very high speeds; they are the oldest and most heavily used EFT systems, especially in the international funds transfer area. The more important WT systems are:

> Fed Wire. The largest and best-known of these systems, the Fed Wire is owned and operated by the Federal Reserve. Initially limited to the Fed's twelve member banks, their branches, and member commercial banks, Fed Wire was opened in 1981 on a fee basis to all financial institutions. Used by more than 800 banks, it handles more than $360 billion in daily transactions.

> Clearing House Interbank Service (CHIPS). Based in New York, CHIPS serves more than ninety banks, fifty-six of which are branches of foreign financial institutions. It processes more than $120 billion daily—over 10 percent of all international dollar transactions.

Bank Wire (BW). A pioneer in the EFT revolution, BW is owned and operated by more than 250 member banks in over seventy-five cities.

Automated Teller Machine (ATM)

The Citizens & Southern National Bank of Atlanta instituted one of the first ATMs in 1971; a national network has since evolved, and it includes more than 1,000 banks in over forty-five states. A dozen similar systems are in various stages of implementation—such as the Exchange EDP Network, with more than 530 banks in thirty-seven states; Cirrus Systems, with 930 banks in forty-one states; and NATIONE, with 3,300 banks in twenty-five states. VISA has joined a nationwide ATM network that will include more than 8,000 teller machines by 1990. And Southland Corporation plans to install ATMs in all of the 7,000 stores it owns or franchises.

The ATM revolution is in full swing. There are more than 40,000 ATMs in use in the United States; by 1990 their number should exceed 200,000. The number of ATMs in use worldwide now exceeds 75,000, and their annual growth rate is expected to reach twenty-five percent. ATMs are quickly gaining consumer confidence and acceptance.

What makes ATMs especially attractive is that they are simple to operate. A customer merely uses a magnetically encoded access card and a secret PIN—known only to the user and the financial institution—to make deposits, withdrawals, interaccount transfers, or account balance inquiries.

Point-of-Sale (POS)

The First Federal Savings & Loan Bank of Lincoln, Nebraska, pioneered one of the first POS systems in 1974. The Glendale Federal Savings & Loan Association followed suit in 1975 with a more complex system that included 137 POS terminals in twenty southern California supermarkets.

POS systems are fast gaining international consumer acceptance. For example, Scotland's Clydesdale Bank was one of the first European pioneers. In 1982, Clydesdale's Aberdeen customers were given EFT-POS (electronic funds transfer at point-of-sale) cards that they could use to pay for their parking at British Petroleum (BP) garages. To operate the system, the customer inserts the EFT-POS card into the terminal at the garage, which is hooked up to the bank's computers, and punches in a secret identification number. Once the information reaches the computer, it transfers funds from the customer's account to that of the BP garage. The committee of London Clearing Banks has recommended that fully operational national POS systems be established in England by 1990.

Considered one of the more sophisticated EFT systems, the POS signals the beginning of a truly cashless society. Experts predict that by 1990, the majority of the nation's supermarkets and retailers will be linked to some type of POS system.

Telephone Bill Paying (TBP)

More than 400 banks, savings and loan associations, and credit unions now offer some type of TBP service. New York's Chase Manhattan Bank plans to offer an "intelligent phone" system. This system, which resembles a hand-held calculator, will allow a consumer to transmit bill-paying information directly to the bank's computers.

TBP systems are easy and economical to use, and often require only a touch-tone phone. The bill-paying information is transmitted to the bank's computer by pushing the buttons on the phone that correspond to the customer's account number, transaction information, and security code; the computer than debits the customer's account and credits that of the merchant. The major drawback of TBP is that a thief, armed with a customer's secret account and identification numbers, can easily manipulate the system.

Home Banking (HB)

Home banking systems promise to revolutionize the way we bank and shop. Customers of the Chemical Bank of New York can now use an HB system to pay their bills. Bank of America has extended its HB system to more than 1,000 of its branches. Available seven days a week, the service can be used to pay more than 600 types of bills. With more than 800,000 home computers in California alone—and the California market is said to be growing by as much as 60 percent annually—Bank of America's system is off to a good start.

HB systems can be used to carry out a number of transactions, such as transferring funds between accounts, making account balance inquiries, reviewing outstanding transactions, and rescheduling payments. Since home computers can be programmed to trade securities, review certificates of deposits, and handle a multitude of other financial transactions, HB systems could also be used in the not-too-distant future to carry out international financial transactions—all from the comfort of the consumer's home. Payees range from hospitals and department stores to insurance companies. The customer pays a monthly bank charge for using the system, which is automatically debited by the bank from the customer's account.

Although presently not as popular as other EFT systems, HB has a promising future as home computers increasingly become household fixtures. Experts predict that by 1990 five to seven percent of American households will be hooked up to an HB system, and the number could reach 80 percent by 2005.

As little as five years ago, many prominent forecasters were skeptical that we stood on the brink of an international cashless society. In recent years, however, the swift progress of cashless systems has forced such forecasters to change their stance. Both conservative Americans and Europeans are going cashless daily. Yet in our frantic drive to embrace EFT systems, we need to pause and give serious consideration to the threat of crimes and abuses involving cashless systems.

Jesse James Goes Electronic

One weekend in 1965 a gang of safecrackers used a seventy-millimeter antitank gun to blast their way into a Brink's vault in Syracuse, New York. They made away with more than $300,000. The leader of the gang was Herbert F. Wilson, a former Baptist minister who had become bored with his career. Wilson, now a Hollywood legend, worked the hard way.

Today's successful safecracker has gone electronic. As vaults give way to EFT systems, security experts are concerned that EFT thefts could run into the trillions of dollars. A bank security officer once remarked that "it's something that really scares us. It's frightening."

EFT makes police and banking officials nervous—and with reason. More than $2 trillion moves daily through global EFT networks. ATMs alone handle more than 3 billion transactions that involve $250 billion annually. But the Interbank Card Association—which represents the MasterCharge system—and other banking groups fear that ATMs are vulnerable to theft. The U.S. Department of Justice has already identified four areas in which EFT systems are vulnerable: unauthorized use of access devices; frauds by authorized users; internal manipulations by dishonest employees; and sabotage. The federal government, the biggest user of these systems, is particularly concerned with the manipulation of EFT systems by dishonest insiders.

Magnitude of the Problem

In Switzerland a gang of electronic thieves intercepted an EFT transmission and diverted the funds to their own accounts. In Japan a communications engineer with the Nippon Telephone and Telegraph Company tapped a bank's EFT lines and gained access to the account numbers of its cash card customers. With these codes and counterfeit cards, he took the bank for more than 170 million yen before being discovered. In the United States a bank data entry clerk stole more than $25,000 in a two-month period by manipulating the automated central information files to access customer accounts through the bank's ATMs.

According to the American Bankers Association, more than 60 percent of 225 banks that it surveyed had been the victim, at least once, of an EFT fraud; many of the offenses had been committed by dishonest insiders. A series of hearings on EFT systems by the U.S. House Banking Committee came up with these findings:

> "Remote muggings" involving ATMs were becoming a problem. Thieves were finding it lucrative to rob people who had just withdrawn money from ATMS.
>
> The theft of EFT cards and codes had become commonplace.
>
> Dishonest customers were making withdrawals while claiming they had lost their EFT cards.

Although there is mounting evidence that EFT crimes are on the increase, there is not yet a consensus on what exactly constitutes an EFT crime or on the scope of the problem. Even the American Bar Association's 1984 report on computer crime barely mentions EFT frauds. But these crimes can perhaps best be defined as unlawful acts directed at, or making use of, one or more EFT systems. As for the scope of the problem, annual losses attributed to EFT crimes are said to range anywhere from $100 million to several billion dollars, depending on the source.

In part, the lack of valid data in this area must be blamed on the financial industry. Fearful that revelations of EFT crimes might scare away existing or potential EFT customers, the industry has often swept the problem under the rug. As with computer crime, lack of confidence in the ability of the criminal justice system to address these offenses has only reinforced the financial industry's reluctance to identify these offenses. When frauds surface, the industry's practice is often to refer them to the in-house security staff for disposition; the wide variety of definitions and procedures used by banks to record these frauds makes them easy to mask. We need to determine both the prevalence and the characteristics of these crimes to deal with the problem. Without this information, the task of developing safeguards and laws to address EFT crime could prove difficult, if not futile.

Forms of EFT Crime

Computer crime has been in the limelight of criminology in recent years, and EFT thefts and frauds in particular have recently come under the scrutiny of such groups as the American Bankers Association and various law enforcement and congressional committees. From these sources on the crimes that have surfaced, we find that EFT offenses can take the following forms:

Physical attacks directed at EFT systems or any of their components.

Robberies, thefts, and other attacks directed at users of these systems.

Unauthorized use of access devices, such as cards, plates, codes, account numbers, passwords, or any other device used to gain access to an account.

Fraud and thefts by authorized users, in which, for example, the user falsely claims that a third party used his access device to make withdrawals from his account.

Frauds and thefts by dishonest insiders; armed with a customer's card and PIN, they carry out unauthorized withdrawals and transfers.

Thefts based on errors—that is, in which a dishonest customer accepts funds erroneously deposited in his or her account.

Unauthorized transactions by outsiders, often carried out with the assistance of dishonest employees.

Blackmail, especially where the account holder occupies a sensitive political position.

Manipulation of data, often involving internal manipulation of the system's software or hardware.

Extortion, especially when terrorists and other political extremists are involved.

Electronic interceptions, often directed at a system's communication lines.

Counterfeiting access devices, a carry-over from the credit card counterfeiting.

Physical Attacks. In July 1983, thieves bombed two branches of the Marine Midland Bank in New York and got away with $10,000. In both cases, the thieves broke into the bank and used explosives against the ATM vaults. Two months later, an irate bank customer in St. Petersburg, Florida, fired six rounds from a .32-caliber pistol at one of the bank's ATMs. Apparently the ATM had swallowed the customer's card. "I got a little upset," the customer later told the police.

Most physical attacks on EFT systems have so far involved ATMs. Since ATMs do not contain large sums of money, and since the Bank Protection Act requires that they weigh at least 750 pounds when empty or be securely anchored to a base, the majority of these cases have involved irate customers, malcontents, and petty thieves. The more sophisticated criminals have turned to other, more lucrative EFT crimes.

Attacking Users. While leaving her home in Washington, D.C., a woman was abducted by three masked men. They drove her to a local ATM and forced her to use her money card to withdraw funds from her account. On a late evening in Arlington, Virginia, a twenty-two-year-old man was approached at a Money Exchange (ATM) machine by armed robbers who demanded his money. They fled with fifty dollars in cash and the keys to his car.

Local police departments around the country are becoming increasingly concerned because muggers and robbers are devising new schemes directed at ATM users. The police have found that criminals are staking out ATMs, waiting to rob late-night bank customers in need of cash. According to a Virginia robbery squad detective, "It's a growing problem." Some police officers have gone so far as to call the ATM the "alternative theft machine."

Unauthorized Use. The robbery began around 11:30 A.M., when John Smith (a pseudonym) received an unexpected guest at his New York City apartment. The stranger said that he was a security officer with Smith's local bank and produced what appeared to be legitimate credentials. To alleviate Smith's concerns, the stranger gave him a telephone number and said, "Call this number to check me out." Caught off guard, Smith hesitated. "Never mind," he said, somewhat embarrassed, "What do you want?" "We're testing our ATMs," the stranger replied, "and I'll need your card and PIN." After hesitating, Smith complied. Two weeks later Smith discovered that the so-called bank officer had used his ATM card to make several withdrawals; luckily for Smith, the police arrested the thief before he could escape. The thief had pulled off the same scheme on more than forty other bank customers, and had pocketed over $20,000.

On December 16, 1982, Assistant United States Attorney General William S. Block wrote to Leslie Fein, a Washington, D.C., attorney: "As I indicated to you at that time, the government is willing to accept a plea of guilty to a one-count felony information from Mr. Langevin charging him with a violation of the wire fraud statute." Block was referring to the case of Theode Charles Langevin, a Federal Reserve Board employee who, on November 22, 1982, at approximately 5:58 P.M., tapped into the board's computer files; these contain key financial information on the nation's money supply. The information is an important factor in determining the Fed's actions and is of great value to investors and brokers in predicting interest rates and stock prices.

On the surface, there was nothing unusual about Theode Charles Langevin. Born in Boston on November 14, 1948, he had a bachelor's degree in economics from the George Washington University. Langevin was hired by the Federal Reserve Board in February 1976 and worked there until he resigned on November 19, 1982, to join E.F. Hutton as a money market economist.

For approximately eighteen months before leaving the board, Langevin worked as a money supply projector. He was familiar with the computer files dealing with the Fed's money supply projections, and also knew the procedures necessary to gain access to those files, as well as the passwords used by other employees at his unit. Such knowledge, the FBI later discovered, was common among many of the employees in the unit.

Langevin's life took a turn on November 22 when, sitting in his office on the eleventh floor of the Hutton Building at One Battery Park Plaza, New York, he decided to tap the board's computers in Washington, D.C. The information, he felt, would help him make projections on the money supply. Armed with an Anderson-Jacobson terminal, a handset modem, and the name and password of Wayne Smith, a former colleague at the board, Langevin had little difficulty in gaining access to the files.

When Langevin tapped the board's computers a second time, on November 29, the staff became suspicious. His former supervisor alerted his superiors and the FBI when he discovered that the computer had recorded Wayne Smith as having used it on a day that Smith was absent from work. FBI agents traced subsequent efforts to tap the computer to the New York offices of E.F. Hutton. On December 3, the agents interviewed Langevin; after initially denying any involvement, he provided the agents with a signed confession. On January 4, 1983, he was charged with wire fraud in federal court in Washington, D.C., and on January 11 pleaded guilty. The Langevin case amply demonstrates that even the Fed's seemingly secure EFT network was open to unauthorized access. The lesson was painful and embarrassing to the financial community.

The most important function of any EFT system is to identify and permit access only to authorized users. Thus, the system's ability to identify authorized users is the key to its survival. Many existing EFT systems do this through the use of cards, access codes, account numbers, and passwords. But as the above cases illustrate, EFT systems are especially vulnerable to unauthorized use.

Frauds by Customers. Someone purporting to be a customer telephoned a large bank and instructed it to transfer $4 million to an account at a bank in another city. He gave the correct authorization code, and since the bank's staff saw nothing unusual about the request, the transfer was completed as directed. The customer later denied ever having issued such instructions, and the bank was unable to retrieve its money.

Many EFT-connected losses result from negligence on the part of the authorized user. For example, customers have been known to give their access codes to callers over the telephone, throw away EFT receipts that list their PINs, and lose wallets containing their EFT card and their PIN written on a piece of paper. However, not all such losses are due to negligence. Banking experts note that over 20 percent of all EFT losses are the direct result of customer fraud. A Japanese *Police Department White Paper* released in 1983 reported that the incidences of frauds involving ATMs in Japan had increased by 60 percent during 1982; dishonest customers were often the perpetrators.

In an effort to curtail frauds by customers, banks are using hidden cameras at their ATM locations to photograph transactions. This technique has met with some success. However, safeguarding EFT systems that use account numbers or passwords against customer frauds has proven more difficult. Present federal laws also facilitate these frauds; for example, under the Electronic Funds Transfer Act, an EFT customer who reports the loss of an access device within two business days can only be held liable for the first fifty dollars in losses. Since the financial institution bears the burden of proving a fraud—which is often no easy task—a dishonest customer stands to lose little by insisting that an imposter carried out the transaction.

Frauds by Insiders. On May 16, 1984, Abdulkadir Mohammed Hussein, a native of Somalia and a former clerk at the Navy Federal Credit Union, pleaded guilty in federal court in Alexandria, Virginia, to conspiracy to defraud and embezzle $106,000 from his former employer. Hussein's troubles started in November 1982 when, without authorization, he wired more than $106,000 from various customer accounts at the credit union to the account of an Ali M. Omar at the First National State Bank in Newark, New Jersey.

On December 1, 1982, Omar withdrew $101,350 from the First National account. Three days later Hussein quit his job at the credit union and opened an account in Zurich. Soon after, Omar wired him the money he had withdrawn from the First National account. Hussein then left Zurich and, by way of Somalia, made his way to Canada; on March 16, 1983, he was arrested by the Canadian authorities in Ottowa, at the request of the FBI. His coconspirators (the FBI suspects that several other Somalian citizens besides Omar may have been involved in the fraud) are free and believed to be living in Somalia. Since the United States and Somalia do not have an extradition treaty, their future seems assured.

On August 3, 1982, the U.S. Securities and Exchange Commission publicly censured the First Variable Rate Fund for Government Income—Washington, D.C.'s biggest money market fund, with assets of more than $800 million—for lax controls for the period of "March 1st to June 1st of 1981." This seemed, on the surface, to be just more hot air from the regulators. Yet those familiar with First Variable knew that the censure was caused by one of the largest EFT heists involving a money market fund. It appears that a dishonest clerk at First Variable had wired $1.55 million to her boyfriend, who deposited the money in a Swiss account.

Vera Campos and Andre L. Prestes seemed to be average people. They had come to the United States in 1978 from Brazil on a tourist visa and had tried numerous get-rich-quick schemes—but to no avail. They had talked about smuggling diamonds from Latin America, and they opened a Georgetown boutique that never panned out. Prestes took a course in computer programming at the Control Data Institute in Washington, D.C., but nothing had come out of that either. Fearing deportation by the Immigration and Naturalization Service, Prestes even considered paying an American woman to marry him. The couple's fortune took a turn, however, when Campos, using a phony resume, was employed by First Variable in early 1981. Her superiors at the shareholder transfer accounting department considered her a good employee.

May 5 was an important day in the lives of the couple. Campos's supervisor had notified Riggs National Bank that a messenger would bring them thirteen wire orders to authorize fund transfers from the First Variable trust account to those of some of its shareholders. Prestes had already opened an account with First Variable in April; he had also opened an account at Virginia National Bank in early September 1980.

Campos took a bold step that day. She typed instructions on a blank transfer order form that read: "Virginia National Bank, account number 43348351, Andre L. Prestes, $1,550,000." When the messenger delivered the wire orders to Riggs, there were fourteen, not thirteen; included was an order to wire $1.55 million to Prestes's Virginia bank account. Since Prestes already had an account with First Variable, no one questioned the transaction; when a Riggs employee called to confirm the fourteen wire orders, Campos told him it was okay. It was not until early June—a month later—that officials at First Variable noticed their loss.

On May 7, Prestes withdrew $50,000 from his Virginia account and transferred the remaining money to an account at the Union Bank of Switzerland. The next day Campos quit her job at the Fund, and the couple left the United States. If the lawyers for First Variable had not located the Swiss account and frozen the funds, Campos and Prestes would have pulled off a perfect EFT caper. But luck had let them down again. From his home in Belo Horizonte, Brazil, Prestes later told the press that the transfer was the result of an error. The Brazilian police interviewed the couple, but no formal charges have been brought to date. They are both free in Brazil: the United States and Brazil have no extradition treaty. But in the EFT world, national boundaries are invisible.

In 1977 the Office of Management of the Federal Deposit Insurance Corporation (FDIC) released a report warning that EFT systems were vulnerable to criminal attack. Of special concern to the FDIC were "dishonest personnel, either bank employees or vendor installation and service engineers." A 1980 study by the Norwegian Research Center for Computers and Law at the University of Oslo found that financial institutions were especially vulnerable to insider frauds involving automated payment systems. The study cited the case of a Norwegian bank employee who periodically transferred funds from customer accounts to his own; the fraud went undetected for almost ten years.

A 1983 survey by the U.S. Bureau of Justice Statistics found that dishonest insiders posed the greatest threat to EFT systems. The bureau's survey also found that insiders were responsible for:

Stealing EFT cards from mailrooms.

Sending EFT cards to incorrect or outdated customer addresses and stealing them when the post office returned them to the bank.

Stealing cash from ATMs.

Altering software.

Creating bogus accounts.

The survey concluded that as EFT systems grow in size and complexity, the threat of fraud by insiders will grow proportionately.

Crime by Error. The account of a California man was erroneously credited $4.4 million by his bank's computer; his $1.17 balance soon grew to $4,444,455.55. It is alleged that the customer then withdrew $2,079.63 from his enlarged account. He was later arrested when the bank finally discovered the error. His defense was simple: "My prayers were answered."

An Ohio man instructed his bank to transfer $774.75 to a new account he had at another bank. When the funds were transferred, a misplaced decimal credited the new account with $774,750.00. By the time the bank discovered its error, it was too late. The man had left town, and only $32,000 remained in his new account. In Phoenix, a customer who used her ATM to withdraw $40, was instead given $5,140. Fighting temptation, she later notified the bank and returned the money.

Errors involving EFT systems have become daily occurrences. An April 1983 survey of households by the Federal Reserve found that six percent of all the respondents complained that their banks had made an EFT error in the past years. For the police, EFT errors pose an additional problem: prosecuting a customer who withdraws money that was erroneously deposited in his or her account can prove both difficult and unpopular. Few juries are sympathetic to banks that "invite fraud." Prosecution also poses a problem for the bank: when the new-found millionaire spends the money, getting it back is often difficult. Crime by error is a serious problem, and is often the result of the victim's own negligence.

Unauthorized Transactions. On August 9, 1983, boxing promoter Harrold Rossfields Smith—who had been convicted eighteen months previously of conspiracy to embezzle more than $20 million from the Wells Fargo Bank—surrendered to authorities to begin serving a ten-year prison term at Terminal Island. A codefendant, Sonnie Marshall, was sentenced to three years in prison. Ben Lewis, a former operations officer at Wells Fargo, had already been sentenced to five years. The scam, called the biggest electronic bank heist in history, had been described as "brilliantly simple." It took Lewis only ten minutes every fifth working day to carry it out.

The scheme surfaced on the morning of January 23, 1981, when Lewis was questioned by his supervisors at Wells Fargo about what appeared to be falsified records. He was told to meet with the bank's internal auditors that afternoon. Lewis now knew that the road was at an end. As the operations officer of the Wells Fargo branch on Beverly Drive, he realized only too well what would happen when the auditors started digging. Rather than face them, he disappeared. The fraud was soon unraveled.

The scheme had involved three men: Lewis, the inside man and a board member of Muhammad Ali Professional Sports (MAPS); Marshall, president of MAPS and a former Wells Fargo employee; and Smith, chairman of MAPS. The fraud took shape in mid-1979. MAPS needed money. Its boxing match promotions were losing money and Smith's lifestyle was extravagant. The answer: find a banker.

The scheme involved thirteen MAPS accounts in the Santa Monica and Beverly Hills Wells Fargo branches. It was simple. Lewis created phony deposits at one branch and then credited them to an account at the other branch. He then wrote a phony credit ticket to cover the deposit. By transferring the funds electronically from one phony account to the other, he kept the swindle going for nearly two years. The roof fell in when he accidentally used the wrong bank form to record a routine entry into one of the phony accounts. Lewis had been able to circumvent the system's safeguards by keeping all of the transactions at about $900,000. The system's computers had been programmed to flag down any transaction in excess of $1 million.

The lesson from the Wells Fargo caper was slow in coming to the banking community. Several years later, a Chase Manhattan Bank executive took his employer for more than $800,000. He did it by creating phony debit and credit tickets; these caused the bank's money transfer department to wire funds to an account the thief had set up at Chemical Bank. The fraud continued undetected for four years.

Unauthorized EFT transactions often revolve around a person who understands the operations of the system and knows how to initiate transfers and other transactions. Once inside the system, the thief introduces phony payment instructions. Complex frauds may also call for someone with substantial computer knowledge. For example, a programmer can modify an EFT system's program to siphon small amounts of money from several thousand accounts and deposit the funds into his or her own account. Since the programmer can also instruct the computer to automatically balance the books, the fraud could go undetected for many years. When outsiders are involved, it is usually someone with knowledge of the system—often assisted by an insider, who usually works at the wire room. Large fund transfers are made to an account that the thief controls; these accounts are usually located at banks in other cities. By the time the bank discovers the fraud, the thief has made off with the money.

Blackmail. In a cashless society, where computers record every payment we make—the social and political groups we contribute to, where and with whom we travel, and other confidential data—the potential for blackmail is very great. A 1979 survey by the University of Illinois found that banks are not overly concerned with safeguarding the privacy of customers' accounts; the situation still prevails.

Manipulation of Data. Armed guards roamed the corridors of the Security Pacific National Bank headquarters in Los Angeles, as hidden cameras photographed customers making deposits. With some justification, management felt that it had little to fear from criminals. Their vaults were safe, they thought. But the bank's management and the public were startled to learn in November 1978 that Security Pacific had been robbed of more than $10 million—not by armed thieves, but electronically. One of the largest EFT heists in American history had been pulled off by a balding, congenial thirty-two-year-old computer consultant named Stanley Mark Rifkin.

When news broke out, those who knew Rifkin were shocked. One of his former professors described him as always being "five years ahead of anything else going on." But there was nothing to single him out as a thief. Rifkin lived in a three-bedroom, $400-a-month apartment in San Fernando Valley; one of his clients was a firm that serviced Security Pacific's EFT operation. Twice married, his joy was computers.

Rifkin's heist began in June 1978, when he approached Lou Stein, a Los Angeles diamond dealer. Rifkin informed Stein that he was a representative of Coast Diamond Distributors, and was looking to buy $10 million worth of diamonds. They spoke several times after that; in early October they agreed that Stein would contact Russalmaz, a Russian company based in Geneva that had been set up in 1976 to sell diamonds.

On October 25, 1978, Rifkin made his move. He went to Security Pacific's headquarters in Los Angeles and took an elevator to the wire room: Operations Unit One on Level D. The wire room handled between $2 billion and $4 billion in EFT transactions daily. Having been a consultant for the bank, Rifkin was known and liked by the headquarter's staff. He was met at the entrance to the wire room by Rosemary Hansen, a bank employee, who inquired about his presence there; Rifkin replied that he was working on a study to determine if the bank's wire operations were working efficiently.

To authorize a wire transfer, all one needed was a secret authorization code. Its numbers were changed daily for security purposes, but this was not a problem for Rifkin. He knew where to look; he found the code typed on a piece of paper and posted on a wall inside the wire room. After jotting down the numbers, he went to a nearby pay phone and called the wire room. Rifkin identified himself as Mike Hansen, an employee of the bank's international department. He then gave the code and directed that $10.2 million be transferred to an account at Irving Trust Company in New York. Rifkin later transferred these funds to the Wozchod Handels Bank in Zurich.

On October 26, Stein flew to Geneva and selected the diamonds at the Russalmaz offices. He ordered 43,200 carats, costing $8.145 million. Two days later, the Russalmaz account was credited and the deal closed. On October 29, Rifkin flew back to Los Angeles with the diamonds.

Rifkin's heist started to fall apart on October 30, when he met with his attorney Gary Goodgame at the Hermitage Hotel in Beverly Hills. Acting as if he wanted to get caught, Rifkin told him that he had robbed the Pacific National Bank; to prove it, Rifkin filled an ashtray with diamonds. Goodgame met with the FBI the next day and relayed Rifkin's story. With the FBI on his heels, Rifkin flew to Rochester. Meanwhile, the bank's unsuspecting officials were stunned when the FBI told how Rifkin had robbed $10.2 million from the bank. In Rochester, Rifkin had hoped that a former business associate would help him sell the diamonds; instead, the associate tipped off the FBI. Rifkin flew to San Diego where, on November 5, the FBI arrested him at a friend's home. They also seized a suitcase filled with several dozen packets of diamonds and $12,000 in cash. While awaiting trial in February 1979, Rifkin hatched plans to steal $50 million from the Union Bank in Los Angeles. The plan feel through when it turned out that one of his coconspirators was an FBI agent.

Although perhaps not as dramatic as the Rifkin case, several other frauds involving the manipulation of data have surfaced. In one, a programmer used his terminal to alter the software of a bank's cash management service. As a result, the computer wired funds to a special account the thief had set up. More than a dozen wire transfers netted the thief over $500,000. The bank detected the fraud only when one of the transfers caused overdrafts in the other accounts. In a similar case, a programmer altered the software so that the computer would transfer funds from inactive accounts to phony ones he had set up. To cover his tracks, he also altered the cycle codes to ensure that the monthly EFT statements would not be mailed to the unsuspecting customers until the thief had time to replace them with phony statements. The fraud involved as many as 100 accounts and continued undetected for more than one year.

As these cases illustrate, both the hardware and software of EFT systems are open to criminal manipulation. It is not difficult for a dishonest programmer to construct traps in the system that will enable him to circumvent its safeguards. Better screening of employees and consultants could help prevent the manipulation of data.

Extortion. In 1977, twenty-five-year-old Rodney Cox was employed as a computer programmer in charge of one of the shifts at the ICI data processing center in Rozenburg, The Netherlands. ICI, formerly known as Imperial Chemical Industries, is a giant European conglomerate with annual sales in excess of $6 billion. Cox cared little about ICI's fortunes; he was more concerned with his promotion. On several occasions he had grumbled these concerns to his boss, Geoffrey Cowlin; but instead of promoting him, Cowlin fired him.

Angry and bitter, Cox took matters into his own hands. He planned to leave ICI with a big bonus. With the aid of his brother-in-law, Rhys Jenkins, Cox hatched plans to steal ICI's computerized financial records—the very soul of the company. Cox decided to strike while the iron was still hot. Over the weekend, he drove to the company's computer center in Rozenburg; he knew the security staff, and with their assistance, he loaded more than 1,000 computer tapes into his station wagon. Worth a king's ransom to an ICI competitor, the tapes contained detailed records—such as capital investment plans, sales targets, new products, and research—of the entire ICI European operation for the next five years. Cox then proceeded to the company's offices in Rotterdam; to ensure that he held all the cards, he planned to steal the company's back-up tapes. Once again the security staff helped him load his station wagon. Cox now held all the cards.

Cox telephoned Cowlin the next day with an ultimatum: If ICI wanted the tapes back, it would have to pay him $400,000; otherwise, he was prepared to sell them to a competitor. Cowlin contacted headquarters, and the Dutch police were notified. Cox then contacted Cowlin again, telling him to go to ICI's offices in London and await further instructions. The Dutch police called on Interpol and the Scotland Yard for assistance. Upon arriving in London, Cowlin received a third call from Cox, who told him to meet him on Oxford Street with the ransom money. When Cox and his brother-in-law arrived at the meeting place to collect the ransom, the police closed in and the tapes were recovered. Had the tapes not been recovered, it would have taken many months and cost millions of dollars for ICI to reconstruct its records.

In a more recent case, the New York District Attorney's office announced on September 12, 1984, that a community organizer had been charged with putting glue into more than sixty ATMs belonging to Citibank. It is alleged that the man tried to pressure the bank into making grants to various community groups. He is quoted as having told Citibank officials to "make the grants or else." The ATMs were inoperable for two days.

EFT systems are vulnerable to extortion demands that can come from disgruntled employees, hackers, criminal elements, terrorists, malcontents, and others. By threatening to damage or destroy an EFT system or any of its components, thieves can succeed in forcing an organization to comply with their demands.

Interception. In an article published in 1983, the French weekly *Le Canard Enchaine* wrote that French customs officials had used military computers and cryptographers to crack the coded customer lists of several Swiss banks. The article went on to say that the officials had been able to identify some 5,000 French citizens who had secret Swiss accounts. *Le Monde* carried similar reports. If these allegations are true, then even the computers of the impenetrable Swiss banks are open to electronic interception.

For less than $1,500 worth of electronic equipment, which can easily be purchased at any local Radio Shack store, even a twelve-year-old can tap into most EFT systems. A thief merely needs a wireless microphone ($35), an AM/FM radio ($25), a modem ($200), and a computer terminal ($800)—a total cost of $1,060. One of the more simple taps involves ATM lines. By attaching a wireless microphone to the telephone lines that link an ATM to the bank's computer, the tapper can record the signals that emanate from the lines whenever an unsuspecting customer uses the ATM. By playing the recording back to the robot teller, the thief can instruct it to release funds from the customer's account.

Since most financial institutions do not encrypt their data, a thief can use a tap to discover customer access codes and related account information, even in complex EFT systems. Armed with this information, the thief can then zero in on any account.

More complex taps may be carried out using the following technique. The thief first locates the main telephone lines, often under the floors. To locate the EFT lines, a wireless microphone is attached to the telephone lines and a radio is set to the same frequency. The microphone is used to monitor the telephone circuits, while the data coming over the tapped lines is broadcasted over the radio. When the circuit produces a very high-pitched sound, the tapper knows that he or she has picked up EFT signals. The thief then records the high-pitched sound on the cassette. By connecting the radio-recorder to the modem, the thief can convert the telephone signals to digital impulses. A record of the wire transfers will then appear on his or her terminal. A professional thief can identify the secret code that authorizes wire transfers by analyzing the recorded transfers on the terminal. Once the code is broken, the thief can program his or her computer to create phony transfers. By retapping the EFT lines and mixing phony messages with the authentic ones, the thief can instruct the bank's computer to transfer funds to his or her account.

The thief's job is further facilitated by the fact that existing federal wiretap laws do not apply to EFT transmissions. For example, while Title III of the Omnibus Crime Control and Safe Streets Act makes it a crime to willfully intercept wire or oral communications, it does not cover information in the form of a computer language. Its objective is to safeguard "aural communications." The interception problem could be solved, however, if bankers encrypted their data.

Counterfeiting. According to the American Bankers Association, losses resulting from the counterfeiting of VISA and MasterCard credit cards increased almost 150-fold between 1978 and 1982. Losses to VISA and MasterCard exceeded $125 million in 1982; this figure does not reflect losses from private bank cards, retail and travel cards, or EFT access devices. Account number alterations for VISA alone grew by more than 50 percent between 1981 and 1982. U.S. Senator Paula Hawkins warns that "credit card fraud is sapping the economy of $1 billion a year."

To render EFT cards less susceptible to counterfeiting, the financial industry is looking at a number of safeguards. Among the possibilities are incorporating heat or pressure-sensitive materials, or nonlethal radioactive isotopes into the card. Such safeguards would make it more difficult to counterfeit EFT cards, but they would also add substantially to the cost of producing the cards.

Making EFT Systems Secure

The financial community does recognize the threat of EFT crime. Efforts are underway to educate EFT users on the need for security and to enact federal and state laws that would facilitate the prosecution of EFT criminals. Several bills currently before the U.S. Congress would make it a federal crime to misuse access devices.

New security devices are also hitting the market. For example, plans are afoot to improve access security through the use of fingerprint scanners. A scanner would compare the user's fingerprints to those stored in digital form in the bank's computer. Depending on whether the prints matched, the computer would either permit or deny access to the system. Chemical Bank, First Interstate, and Wells Fargo are exploring the possible use of this technique.

There are also plans to replace present-day EFT cards with smart cards: "plastic money that talks." First test marketed in Europe, the card contains a micromemory and a microcomputer in a silicon chip the size of a small coin. The microchip contains the customer's account number and credit limit; data can be encoded on the chip for up to 180 separate accounts. But the smart card is not without drawbacks. It is costly to produce—more than fifteen dollars, as compared with sixty-five cents for the type of card currently used. Also under consideration are other safeguards such as voice identification, hand pattern identification, and signature identification. All of these techniques are costly and only protect entry into the system, not the total system. They must be viewed as merely the beginning of an extended process to make EFT systems secure.

Proponents of a cashless society say that it will serve to curtail crime; by that, they mean traditional crime. Yet, the cashless society has already spawned new and more costly crimes. Difficult to detect and guard against, these crimes threaten the viability of the financial sector and pose a challenge yet to be addressed. As with computer crime, security is an important first step in safeguarding EFT systems. But of even greater importance is the need to carefully scrutinize the cashless revolution. Its implications for our society are too great to be left solely in the hands of the financial community.

11

The Orwellian Specter

You had to live . . . in the assumption that every sound you made was overheard, and except in darkness, every movement scrutinized.

— George Orwell

T HE West German Federal Criminal Office (BKA) has a giant computer network that stores over 10 million files; these contain an assortment of data on individuals who are suspected of being "political undesirables." For example, the network contains records of people's handwriting characteristics, fingerprints, and identifying ear contours, and even whether they pay their utility bills by cash. The system is connected to the computers of other European police agencies. And an even more elaborate system is being planned.

A high-ranking Western military officer has suggested a novel method for defeating urban terrorism. Under his plan, all individuals living in a "suspect area" would be issued identification cards bearing their photographs and finger-prints. The authorities would then use a complex network of computers pro-grammed to keep track of people's daily movements and record information on their social and political affiliations.

Although the year 1984 has come and gone, and Big Brother continues to be only a figment of Orwell's vivid imagination, the technological apparatus needed to give life to Big Brother is available and in place. Orwell's telescreens and hidden microphones now seem primitive when compared to modern spy-in-the-sky satellites, microwave antennas, laser beams, and giant computer banks that can place millions of persons under twenty-four-hour surveillance. The preceding examples should convince even the skeptics.

Perhaps Orwell said it best, when responding to critics of his book: "I do not believe that the kind of society I describe [in *1984*] necessarily will

arrive, but . . . something resembling [it] could arrive." In *1984* Orwell raised
an important issue that goes to the core of modern Western thought: Can
privacy and freedom survive the onslaught of modern technology, or is the
individual destined to become merely a soulless automaton? Therein lies the
Orwellian challenge. And, as the high-tech revolution continues to permeate
every facet of our lives, it is a challenge that we would do well to take seriously.

Police Automation Is Threatening

Whether or not by design, computers have dramatically enhanced the repressive
powers of the police. But most government officials are not concerned. If
asked why the police need their massive computer networks, they would re-
ply that today's highly mobile society requires computers to track down
criminals and other social malcontents.

In part, this assertion is correct. Computers have proven to be valuable investigative tools. For example:

> A twenty-nine-year-old man from Washington, D.C., who had spent six-
> teen months in jail on a first-degree murder charge, was released and charges
> against him were dropped when information from a police computer
> showed that he was nineteen blocks away from the scene of the crime
> at the time it was committed.

> A $500,000 welfare fraud ring (one of biggest in California's history) was
> uncovered during a cross-check of Los Angeles County computer records.

> Computers belonging to the Grumman Aerospace Corporation were used
> by the New York City police to single out a notorious cop killer from
> a pool of 2,000 suspects.

> With the assistance of computers, Massachusetts police officials were able
> to identify and crack a nine-person ring that had stolen more than $20,000
> worth of electricity from the Boston Edison Company.

> More than 1 million children are reported missing every year. Between
> 2,500 and 4,000 of these are murdered, making homicide one of the
> five leading causes of death among youngsters between the ages of one
> and seventeen. But computers are now being used successfully to locate
> missing children and identify their captors.

> Serial killers, violent individuals who crisscross the country and kill for
> no apparent reason, are said to be behind some 4,000 homicides a year.

With growing success, the FBI is now using its computers to track down these killers. For instance, Geraldo Stone, a crazed computer operator who confessed to killing at least forty women, was discovered with the help of computers; and Arthur Bishop, convicted in Utah for the murder of five boys, has been linked to other cases by the FBI's computers.

But police agencies are also busy constructing giant data banks that will enable them to collect and store large volumes of data on hundreds of millions of persons and will make it possible to exchange information with other police agencies inside and outside the United States.

Federal Bureau of Investigation (FBI)

Some 60,000 police agencies in the United States are now linked by more than 19,000 computer terminals to the FBI's giant National Crime Information Center (NCI) in Washington, D.C. Each day the NCI is tapped more than 400,000 times for information on everything from stolen property to criminal histories. The amount of information stored in the NCI data banks is enormous and grows daily. For example, it contains the names of over 200,000 fugitives; data on more than 1 million stolen vehicles; more than 2 million criminal files; and billions of other items of police information.

The FBI plans to further expand its computer power. Its 1984 budget for computer equipment was $62.8 million—more than three times the $18.5 million spent in 1983. The FBI's computer capacity has likewise grown dramatically from 100 units in 1979 to over 1,000 units in 1984.

U.S. Customs Service

The Customs Service has turned to computers to police America's borders. For example, an experimental computerized passport reader system, which is now being devised, will help agents identify drug traffickers, terrorists, and known criminals as they pass through customs. The passport readers will be connected by terminals to the Treasury Department's Enforcement Communication System (TECS) data banks in San Diego; these in turn will be linked to the FBI's NCI computers, enabling the two systems to exchange valuable police data. The Treasury Department also plans to link TECS to the computers of friendly foreign police agencies.

Internal Revenue Service (IRS)

The IRS was one of the first federal agencies to use computer power. Its computers are programmed to identify tax cheats, and plans are underway to create an Intelligence Office whose computers would be connected to those of the FBI, the Treasury Department, and the Drug Enforcement Administration. The IRS justifies this expansion of computer power by arguing that it is needed to successfully identify large narcotics transactions.

Intelligence Agencies

The Central Intelligence Agency (CIA), the National Security Agency (NSA), the State Department, and various military intelligence agencies have also been expanding their computer systems. These systems are primarily used to monitor the activities of foreign spies, terrorists, and others who may pose a threat to U.S. foreign interests. The NSA, for example, uses a giant computer system to eavesdrop on international telegrams, telex messages, and telephone calls; the military intelligence services use computers to collect and analyze data gathered by spy satellites.

General Services Administration (GSA)

Under pressure from federal agencies, Uncle Sam's purchasing agent, GSA, now plans to contract with commercial credit bureaus for twenty-four-hour access to their extensive data banks. This will create a giant national computer network that combines both government and private computer systems. When the plan goes through, every bureaucrat in Washington, D.C., who can use a desktop computer or terminal will have instant access to bank and credit information on more than 150 million Americans.

Local and State Police

As though taking a cue from the federal government, many local and state police agencies have turned to computers to identify suspects, fugitives, and welfare cheats. For example, Knox County, Tennessee, is using computers to upgrade its criminal justice system; its computers store information on more than 75,000 county residents.

Minnesota is also rapidly installing computers at all of its police departments; once in place, the system will enable local and state police agencies to exchange intelligence data in a matter of minutes. The San Francisco police are now using a computerized fingerprint system (Automated Fingerprint

Indexing System) to match prints found at the scene of a crime with those of suspects. And the Los Angeles police have been using computers with great success to zero in on suspects. Their computers had little difficulty in identifying the "Remorseful Rapist" (a University of California student who had committed a number of rapes in Los Angeles).

Few would dispute that much of the work of police computers is both useful and legitimate. However, there is concern that these powerful information systems could also be used to suppress political dissent. Many observers fear that as these systems grow in size and complexity, so will the problem of computer error—resulting in the inadvertent arrest of innocent members of the public. And legal experts worry that existing legal safeguards may not extend to these highly automated police systems.

Additional Concerns

An increasing number of individuals are concerned that the growing police data banks could be abused not so much by present-day political and police leadership, but rather by what could one day replace it. For example, a recent Louis Harris poll on the impact of computers on society found that 69 percent of the general public believed that Orwell's police state of Oceania was "at least somewhat close"; while 58 percent of those in leadership positions (in academia, government, and business) believed that a government takeover of the existing data banks, if combined with other modes of electronic surveillance, could result in a totalitarian regime in the United States.

Democracies are fragile political institutions. In a less-tolerant political environment than the current one, unethical political leaders could mobilize the vast power of police computers to monitor and repress their opponents. Further, since there is little legal precedent for applying existing constitutional safeguards to computerized police information systems, the legal safeguards that have effectively curtailed past police abuses may fail to cover highly automated police systems.

Of equal concern is the sheer size and magnitude of the computer networks now under the government's control. For example, Uncle Sam's computers presently store more than 3.5 billion files that deal with every facet of our lives. This figure averages out to fifteen files for every man, woman, and child in the United States, and it does not include the billions of files maintained by state and local governments and the corporate sector. Not only do these gargantuan networks grow daily, but there are also plans to develop expert computer systems that will initiate investigations on their own, independent of human intervention.

As in the private sector, police computer snafus abound. However, while private sector errors can result in the unjustified denial of credit or a lawsuit, in the police sector the result can be false arrest or imprisonment. For example, as a result of a computer error, Shirley Jones of New Orleans was charged by the authorities with theft and forgery. A California man was identified by police computers as being AWOL (absent without leave) from the Marine Corps; he spent five painful months in jail before the error was discovered. And Sheila Jackson of Virginia was detained by agents of the U.S. Customs Service when a computer check erroneously recorded that a warrant had been issued for her arrest. William Jones of Los Angeles likewise learned that a police computer error can prove costly and painful. While driving to a local grocery store for milk, he was stopped by the police for a minor traffic violation; a computer check showed that there were several outstanding warrants for his arrest. Despite his protestations, Jones was arrested and jailed for two weeks. He was then cleared, but not before he was fired by his employer.

The Need for Legal Safeguards

The U.S. Constitution has rightly been called the guardian of our liberties and freedoms. Almost two centuries old, it has adapted well to the nation's transformation from a predominantly rural, agrarian society to one that is highly urbanized and industrialized. The Constitution has also served us well by curbing government abuses, and it is the harness that restrains our police agencies.

But constitutional experts are concerned, because little legal precedent exists for applying our constitutional safeguards to police computer systems. The courts and our legislatures have only just begun to address some of these important legal questions.

The First Amendment has long been considered the guarantor of our free marketplace of ideas: our freedom of speech, religion, assembly, and press. But some civil libertarians now fear that computerized information services (for example, telecommunication networks, electronic message systems, and electronic banking) could be tapped by the police to obtain accurate profiles on millions of Americans. The implicit threat posed by potential police abuses could, in the long run, have a chilling effect on our First Amendment freedoms.

There is also growing concern over the possible use of high technology by the government to control our thoughts and behavior. For example, government scientists are presently experimenting with genetic engineering. In the not too distant future it may be possible for the government to engineer a biological caste system of individuals with safe, acceptable political views. As the First Amendment now stands, it could not curb such conduct; nor could it prevent government efforts to mold human behavior by altering and/or fabricating data stored in its computers and those of the business sector.

The Fourth Amendment was specifically designed to safeguard an individual's person, house, papers, and effects from unreasonable searches and seizures by the government. But many people fear that the Fourth Amendment may be ill-equipped to adequately safeguard us against abuses of our computer and communication systems. For example, the amendment as it now reads does not: make it unlawful for the authorities to use personal and statistical data as justification for searches and seizures; prohibit the seizure or alteration (through a tap) of property that is in electronic form; or prevent the use of police or other government computers to search public and corporate data banks without a search warrant.

There is also concern that the police could circumvent the requirement that they first obtain a court order for wiretaps, since existing wiretap laws do not cover computer and digitized transmissions. In addition, because Fourth Amendment safeguards against unreasonable searches and seizures do not apply to the corporate sector, private snooping on behalf of the police would not be prohibted either.

Further, the Fourth Amendment's safeguards only extend to papers and effects in the possession of an individual. There is serious doubt that the safeguards apply to data about an individual that is collected and stored by a third party; some recent court decisions appear to say that they do not. Such judicial reasoning, if not altered by legislation, could leave a serious void in the constitutional protection of personal records.

The Fifth Amendment prevents the government from compelling a person to be a witness against himself; nor can the government deprive an individual of life, liberty, or property without due process of law. But government computers are increasingly making decisions that affect all facets of our daily lives. For example, government bureaucrats use computers daily to identify tax and welfare cheats, zero in on criminal suspects, gather and screen evidence, and even decide whether an individual qualifies for a social program. The Fifth Amendment's safeguards appear to be of little value in this area. And because the amendment applies only to government actions, corporate abuses are outside its province.

The Sixth Amendment provides for a speedy and public trial by an impartial tribunal. But the growing use of computerized models by government prosecutors to select jurors threatens the whole concept of a fair and impartial jury. This procedure may soon mean that only the government and wealthy defendants will be able to enjoy the safeguards of the Sixth Amendment.

The Fourteenth Amendment establishes that no state may deprive an individual of life, liberty, or property without due process of law; nor may a state deny a person within its jurisdiction equal protection of the law. But the growing use of computerized models by the police and other government agencies to predict criminal behavior and screen prospective employees could deny the Fourteenth Amendment rights to an individual.

Whether for good or for bad, the use of computers by the police is on the increase at all levels of our federal system. However, there is no evidence that the widespread use of computers by the government will lead to a dictatorship. Even with abuses and errors by police computers, our freedoms are safe as long as our democracy stays healthy and vibrant.

Furthermore, we have not yet reached a stage in our political evolution in which a person can be imprisoned simply because a computer model has identified him or her as a potential criminal. Probable cause must still exist before the authorities can monitor a person's activities or invade his or her privacy. To date, however, little legal precedent exists for applying constitutional safeguards to some of the issues raised by our information society. This situation will probably change as the courts begin to tackle some of these important questions. Some computer-related issues will lend themselves to traditional legal interpretations, while others will need legislative intervention. Although the threat posed by government computers is real, if we begin to address it now, it need not fully materialize.

The Potential for Corporate Abuse

Like government, the corporate community has enormous data banks. For example, the insurance industry stores information on more than 12 million Americans; these files include everything from medical reports and patient claims to details on why a person was denied insurance coverage. Each day, TRW provides thousands of its customers with information on over 90 million persons; telephone companies keep detailed records of the more than 500 million calls made daily in the United States; and credit bureaus compile over 30 million consumer reports annually, which are distributed to various businesses. It would be nearly impossible to maintain such voluminous data if done manually.

Some corporations are using computers to keep their workers under surveillance. Computer monitoring is now used, for example, by hotels to keep a log of how fast their maids tidy hotel rooms, by telephone companies to clock the speed of their operators, and by supermarkets to see how quickly cashiers process shoppers. Like government, the corporate sector has turned to computerization to meet what it perceives as its needs. At present, no large corporation could successfully serve a highly mobile population for too long without the assistance of computers.

However, as with government, the potential for computer abuse and error is both real and growing. For example, an employee of Equifax told federal officials that he had fabricated some of the consumer information stored in his company's computers. And TRW officials estimate that of the more than 1 million persons who request to see their credit files every year, an average of 350,000 people challenge their accuracy, and TRW makes corrections in about 100,000 cases. A physician at the University of Chicago's Billings Hospital reports that, on average, at least seventy hospital employees have legitimate access to patient files.

Although no evidence suggests that most companies misuse or abuse the enormous amount of data stored in their computers on more than 130 million Americans, there is nevertheless little doubt that the potential for abuse and misuse has had a chilling effect on the public. For example, a recent poll found that 51 percent of the general public believe that corporate computers pose a threat to their privacy; the poll also found that 50 percent of experienced computer users also believe that computers threaten their privacy.

The threat to privacy from corporate computers can be directly attributed to four factors: the lack of a national policy on privacy, the growth of new technologies, the secondary use of data, and the development of increasingly sophisticated surveillance techniques.

Lack of a National Privacy Policy

In 1977 the U.S. Privacy Commission warned that the "needs for collection of information multiply the dangers of . . . abuse." Since then, few privacy experts have disputed that the threat to privacy has greatly increased, especially with the proliferation of personal and desktop computers. According to some experts, corporate computers pose as great a threat as government computers, because many of the constitutional and statutory legal safeguards do not apply to them.

Although a member of Congress will occasionally voice concern about privacy abuses by the corporate sector, neither Congress nor the states are doing much to address the problem. And except for the Electronic Funds

Transfer Act of 1980, much of the privacy legislation enacted in the last twenty years (such as the Privacy Act of 1974) is primarily directed at government. Apart from abiding by the Federal Trade Commission's regulations, the corporate sector operates largely in a legal void when it comes to privacy.

The United States continues to be one of a handful of industrialized nations that have not enacted data protection laws. Although the federal Computer Fraud and Abuse Act of 1984 constitutes a half-hearted effort to safeguard the privacy of data stored in government computers, similar legislation does not exist for data stored in corporate computers. And at the state level, much of the privacy legislation deals with manual rather than automated records.

Spread of New Technologies

Not only have corporate data banks grown dramatically in the last several years, but other new technologies are entering the marketplace daily. The electronic office, in-home information services, smart cards (which store large amounts of data on machine-readable computer chips), automated securities exchanges, electronic funds transfer systems, and genetic screening techniques (over 10 percent of all American corporations are considering such tests) are only a few of these new technologies. They have all increased the threat to privacy. Given the absence of adequate legal privacy safeguards for corporate computers, there is little doubt that these new technologies may further strip us of our privacy.

Secondary Use of Data

Every day, corporate computers collect, store, and disseminate information on American citizens—and most of it occurs without our knowledge or consent. Since very little legislation deals with the ownership or disposition of such data by corporate sources, the potential for abuse is real and serious.

Surveillance

A wide variety of computer and communication devices are now available in the open market; they make it very easy for private sources to monitor our activities without our knowledge or consent. For example, for as little as thirty dollars one can purchase a microphone the size of a match head that can monitor conversations from far away; and computer chips that act as a permanent electronic fingerprint can now be implanted by a syringe under a person's skin.

Yet except for the wiretap laws, which make it illegal to intercept oral communications over the telephone lines, there are few legal safeguards against surveillance by private sources. Although at present two dozen states have made it illegal to intercept private computer communications without authorization, and some states have laws that safeguard the privacy of information transmitted on cable television systems, no such safeguards exist at the federal level.

In addition, even in cases in which there are clear violations of the law, prosecutions are few and far between; prosecutors will tell you that privacy violations are not priority cases. For example, one private investigator told federal officials that he had installed more than 5,000 wiretaps for private clients. When asked if he feared prosecution, he merely chuckled.

According to a report by the Center for Philosophy and Public Policy at the University of Maryland, "privacy protects freedom. . . . the freedom to do anything that we would be inhibited in doing by the presence of external observation." Privacy and freedom are so intertwined that one cannot long survive without the other. A society in which the individual's every movement is monitored (whether by the government or the private sector) is in danger of losing both privacy and freedom.

In the precomputer age, even dictators like Stalin and Hitler found it difficult to monitor the movements of millions of persons. But the high-tech revolution has changed all that. For example, the FBI's NCI computers receive more than 200 million inquiries annually. More than 50 percent of these requests come from private employers; once the information is in their possession, there is little the government can legally do to prevent its abuse or misuse. In addition, it is no secret that some local police officials occasionally use the NCI computers to run checks for private sources. Since such use does not constitute a violation of federal law, there is little or nothing the FBI can do to prevent it.

By itself, the high-tech revolution poses little or no threat to our privacy and freedoms. Computers do not dictate how those in government and business will use their awesome powers. Yet, in a world where over 60 percent of humanity lives under some type of repressive regime, where more than 100,000 political dissidents annually disappear without a trace, and where the political leadership in more than fifty countries makes widespread use of the latest tools of high technology to curtail privacy and freedom, there is ample basis for concern—even in the United States. This possibility is especially frightening since many of the legal safeguards that have served American citizens so well in the past are not well suited to meet the challenges presented by the high-tech revolution. If we in the United States should eventually lose our privacy and freedoms, it will be more from neglect than some Machiavellian plan hatched by a malevolent political elite.

Conclusion

T HE high-tech revolution has had—and continues to have—a profound impact on our social, political, and financial institutions. EFT systems now handle much of the world's international financial transactions, and the personal computer has become a fixture in the modern home. And plans are also afoot to construct a generation of supercomputers that can mimic the human thought process, 400-pound robots guided by artificial intelligence that can police our streets and prisons, and living computer chips that can be implanted in the human brain to replace damaged cells. Ours is truly a brave new world.

But the high-tech revolution has also spawned new forms of abuses and crime. Hackers now traverse our global computer networks at will and with impunity; terrorists have turned their ire toward computers; technoethics are virtually nonexistent; and modern criminals exploit the loopholes in our existing legal system to evade prosecution. U.S. Senator William S. Cohen perhaps summarized it best when he observed that computers may well become the Achilles' heel of our society.

No institution in our postindustrial society is immune from criminal attack. High-tech espionage directed at the private sector is now a multibillion-dollar annual business; and the federal government, the largest computer user in the world, has fast become an ideal target for technocriminals. Robbing Uncle Sam electronically has become a rite of passage.

Historians remind us that the future is a direct outgrowth of the past. Unless we learn from the past, we are tragically committed to repeating it—and the future is fast taking shape. Based on present-day trends, we can already predict how computers may change our future.

Computer systems are already fast replacing business and government officials as the targets of the world's political malcontents. If international political turmoil continues unabated, the West's computer networks, EFT systems, telecommunication systems, and other high-tech targets will increasingly attract the ire of terrorists. Technoterrorism is merely a new symptom of a world in conflict.

Tomorrow's wars may be won or lost in our computer centers, and modern military machines live and die by their computers. The destruction of an enemy's computer systems could throw its military capabilities into the Dark Ages. Yet while the West spends hundreds of billions of dollars on its nuclear weaponry, many of its computer systems are lacking in security.

Computer experts have already detailed how vulnerable our global electronic banking systems are to theft and sabotage. Although no one is sure how much is lost to EFT crime annually, the consensus is that the losses run in the billions of dollars. Yet few in the financial community are paying any heed; nor does it appear that this will change in the foreseeable future.

Protection of privacy will be one of the most crucial issues in upcoming years. When it comes to privacy, the Swedes are second to none. The Swedish version of the United States' Privacy Act was first passed into law in 1812. So it came as a shock in early 1986, when it was disclosed that a group of government researchers had collected and stored in computers data on the social and political affiliations of more than 15,000 of their fellow citizens. A government official was quoted as saying, "They know more about these people than they themselves."

In Orwell's *1984*, the citizens of Oceania lived under the watchful eye of Big Brother and his secret police. In the West, we all stand under the watchful eye of our giant computer systems. All that stands between us and Big Brother is the delicate political fiber we call democracy; if it were to collapse under the pressure of a profound social trauma, the edifice for a dictatorial takeover is already in place.

Some egalitarian theorists believe that the high-tech revolution will close the gap between the haves and the have-nots, that it will bring about a more equitable distribution of power and wealth in the postindustrial society. Out of our vast data banks, they reason, will emanate power and wealth for the lower strata of our society.

Yet it cannot be overlooked that the high-tech revolution has given a small group of technocrats a monopoly over the flow of information in our society. In the computer age, power and wealth have become synonymous with control over our data banks. And because computers are presently the monopoly of the more-affluent segments of our society, there is justifiable concern that they may only widen the gap between the haves and the have-nots. Marx's capitalist class may find itself displaced by an information elite.

As a species in the chain of evolution, we are still in our infancy. However, unlike other species before us, we have constructed tools of mass destruction. The high-tech revolution now gives us the tools with which to steal with impunity across oceans, control and manipulate the thoughts and movements of millions of our fellow human beings at the press of a button, and hold an entire society hostage. But if properly employed, the high-tech revolution could also dramatically improve our lives on this planet. The choice is ours. Humanity's future need not be one of high-tech terror.

Bibliography

Allen, Brandt. "Embezzler's Guide to the Computer," 53 *Harvard Business Review* 79–89 (July 1975).

American Bar Association, *Report on Computer Crime* (Chicago, Ill.: American Bar Association, 1984).

Becker, Robert S., *The Data Processing Security Game* (New York: Pergamon Press, 1977).

Bequai, August, *How to Prevent Computer Crime: A Guide for Managers* (New York: John Wiley & Sons, 1983).

_____ . *White Collar Crime, A 20th-Century Crisis* (Lexington, Mass.: D.C. Heath & Company, 1978).

Carroll, John M., *Computer Security* (Los Angeles, Calif.: Security World Publishing Company, 1977).

"Computer Abuse: The Emerging Crime and the Need for Legislation," 12 *Fordham Urban Law Journal* 73–101 (1983–84).

Haley, J.T., "Trade Secrets and Computer Software," 37 *Washington State Bar News* 51–59 (Sept. 1983).

"Legislative Issues in Computer Crime," 21 *Harvard Journal on Legislation* 239–254 (winter 1984).

McFarlane, Gavin, "Criminal Trials and the Technological Revolution," 133 *New Law Journal* 327–329 (April 8, 1983).

Myers, J., "Frauds and Computers," 133 *New Law Journal* 71–72 (Jan. 21, 1983).

Parker, Donn B., *Fighting Computer Crime* (New York: Charles Scribner & Sons, 1983).

Schabeck, Tim A., *Computer Crime Investigations Manual* (Madison, Wis.: Assets Protection, 1979).

Whiteside, Thomas, *Computer Capers: Tales of Electronic Thievery, Embezzlement, and Fraud* (New York: Thomas Y. Crowell Company, 1978).

Index

Abacus, 2
Access controls, 8
Access devices, 146, 151
Addressable converter, 19
Afghanistan, 137
Agricultural jobs, 21
Air traffic control, 16–17, 126
Airline reservation system, 12, 136
American Bank and Trust Company of
New York, 131
American Bankers Association, 70, 150,
151, 163
American Bar Association (ABA), 51, 110,
111, 117, 150; Computer Crime Task
Force, 117
American Civil Liberties Union (ACLU),
118
American Cyanamid, 137
American Express, 70, 72, 143
American Federation of Information Pro-
cessing Societies, 18
American Hospital Supply Corporation, 54
American Institute of Certified Public
Accountants (AICPA), 56
American Medical Association, 53
American Society for Industrial Security,
46, 51, 79, 94, 117
American Telephone and Telegraph Com-
pany, 21
Anderson, Han Shan S. Scott, 34
Andropov, Yuri V., 86
Angry Brigade (Great Britain), 130
Apple Computer, 58
Arab Bank of Jordan, 131
Argentine Revolutionary Army, 130
Armed Resistance, 131
Armed Revolutionary Nuclei (Italy), 134
Arms sales, 91, 100
Arthur Tree (New York), 41
Artificial intelligence (AI) programs, 10
Asian computer market, 2
Asian Triad syndicates, 71
Assassins, the, 132

Association of Chief Police Officers of
England, Wales, and Northern Ireland,
110, 122
Atomic bomb secrets, 88
Atomic demolition munitions (ADMs), 141
Australia, 13–14, 17, 67, 124–125
Austria, 80, 81, 87, 91, 92, 94
Automated payment systems. See Electronic
funds transfer (EFT)
Automated teller machines (ATMs), 70, 143,
144, 147, 149, 150, 152, 161–162
Automation. See Robotics
Automobile industry, 12, 21

Baader-Meinhof group. See Red Army Faction
(West Germany)
Babbage, Charles, 3
Bank of America, 148
Bank Protection Act, 152
Bank Secrecy Act, 68
Bank Wire (BW), 147
Banks, 12, 17, 45, 46, 48, 49, 50, 52;
automated teller machines, 70, 143, 144,
149, 150, 152, 161–162; electronic bank
cards, 69–70, 143, 148–149; electronic
banking, 67; electronic funds transfer, 12,
143–164; home banking, 11, 143,
148–149; money laundering, 66–68; ter-
rorist robberies, 131, 136
Banque pour l'Amerique du Sud (Belgium),
131
Barclays Bank (U.K.), 121
Barger, Jennie L., 49–50
Basque terrorists, 134, 136
Bayton, Texas, 136
BDM Corporation, 140
Belgium, 85–86, 131, 137
Bell Telephone Laboratories, 5
Bhopal, India, 137
Bilbao, Spain, 136
Bingham, Jonathan, 72–73
Biochemical weapons, 137–138, 141–142
Bishop, Arthur, 167

Black Hand, 132
Black Liberation Army, 131
Blackmail, 151, 158–159
Blair, Janet, 101
Block, William S., 153
Bloodstock Research Information Services, 34
Bloomquist, Sherlene, 15–16
"Blue boxes," 32
Bolivian terrorists, 130, 132
Bologna, Italy, train station bombing, 134
Bologna, Jack, 63
Bombings, 13, 20, 21, 23, 52, 126–138 *passim*, 151
Books and magazines on computers, 5
Boston Edison Company, 166
Boston University, 52
Boston Water and Sewer Commission, 20
Botulism, 137, 141–142
Boy Scouts, 32
Brave New World (Huxley), 15
Brazil, 2, 121, 156
Brighton, England, bombing, 13
Brink's robbery (Syracuse, N.Y.), 149
British Petroleum (BP), 147
Brookhaven National Laboratory, 41
Bruchhausen, Werner, 91
Budget and Accounting Procedures Act, 99
Bulgaria, 82
Bunch, Dennis L., 15
Burroughs Corporation: ILLIAC, 9; UDEC, 3
Business Research Corporation, 22
Business Roundtable, 92
Business Week, 51

Cable TV, 19
Calabrian gangsters (Italy), 132
Calculators, 2–3
California: Criminal Justice Information Center, 74; Department of Human Resources, 23; home computers, 148; prisons, 74; welfare fraud, 166
California State Polytechnic University, 59
Campos, Vera, 155–156
Canada, 20, 35, 82, 87, 120–121, 123–124; International Development Agency, 52; Police College, 122, 124; Royal Canadian Mounted Police (RCMP), 124
Canard Enchaine, Le (France), 162
Canary Islands, 132
Capone, Al, 67
Carbonari, 132
Caribbean region, 67
Carlos the Jackal (Illich Ramirez-Sanchez), 130, 134
Carlson, Paul, 82
Carnegie-Mellon University, 116

Casey, William J., 78
Caufield Institute of Technology (Australia), 124–125
Cemente La Forge Computer (Canada), 35
Central Intelligence Agency (CIA), 78, 82, 88, 89, 90, 130, 168
Central processing unit (CPU), 6, 7
Certified Food, 48
Chase Manhattan Bank, 143, 145, 148, 158
Chemical Bank of New York, 143, 148, 163
Chemical weapons, 137–138, 141–142
Chilean terrorists, 130
China, 2, 77, 78, 79, 91
Chipex, 91
Chrysler Corporation, 69
Chub & Son's Electronic Insurance Department, 139
Chui, Chen, 39–40
Church, Frank, 18
CII-Honeywell-Bull (France), 129
Cirrus Systems, 147
Citibank (New York), 67–68, 161–162
Citicorp, 143
Citizens & Southern National Bank (Atlanta), 147
City University (London) Business School, 46
Civil liberties, 18–19, 170–172
Civil strife, 21–22
Clearing House Interbank Service (CHIPS), 146–147
Clydesdale Bank (Scotland), 147
Coachman, Albert W., 102
Coca-Cola, 54
Codex Corporation, 66
Cohen, William S., 177
Colombian mobsters and terrorists, 67, 132
Colombo Mafia family, 64
Columbia University, 32, 116
Committee for the Liquidation or Deterrence of Computers (CLODO), 129
Commodity Control List (U.S. Dept. of Commerce), 90
Communication networks, 138
Compuserve, 37
Computer books and magazines, 5
Computer chips, 5–6; living chips, 27; super-chips, 13; theft and counterfeiting of, 70–71
Computer crime: and computer error, 151, 157; and criminal justice system, 113; estimated costs of, 51, 119; and fear of lawsuits, 113–114; "invisible," 112–113; public perception of, 111–112; in U.S. government departments and agencies, 97–108; versus violent crime, 114

Computer crime training, 120, 122, 124, 126, 127, 128
Computer dependency, 12–14
Computer error, 55–56, 151, 157, 170
Computer failure, 13
Computer Fraud and Abuse Act of 1984, 174
Computer market, 1–2
Computer operators, 7
Computer security, 8–9, 42, 54, 107–108, 163–164
Computer tasks, range and variety of, 10–12
Computer technology, 174; basics of, 6–10
Computer training programs for prisoners, 73–76
Computers: counterfeit, 71; and electronic funds transfer, 146; mainframes, 5, 9; microcomputers, 5, 10; minicomputers, 5, 10; personal computers, 1–2, 4, 5, 10–11, 34–35; supercomputers, 4, 9–10
Computerworld, 54, 57, 62, 66, 110
Confesore, Alfonse, 69
Congressional Clearinghouse, 144
Connecticut police department, 114
Consolidated Edison, 21
Control Data Corporation (CDC), 74, 79, 81; Economic Information Systems, 22–23; supercomputers, 4, 9
Control Data Institute, 155
Controls, 8, 107
Coordinating Committee for Multilateral Export Controls (Cocom), 92
Corinet computer network, 43
Corporate abuse, 172–176
Counterfeiting, 58, 68–69, 71, 151, 163
Cowlin, Geoffrey, 161
Cox, Rodney, 161
Cray, Seymour, Research Corporation, 4, 9–10
Credit bureaus, 115, 172; Atlanta, 143; Kansas City, 57
Credit cards, 69–70, 163
Credit data banks, 54, 57; pirating of, 71–72
Criminal justice system, 113
Criminal laws, 42
Cryptography, 9, 42, 162, 163
Cuba, 87, 95, 131, 132, 134
Cubbage, Michele, 49
Cyclix Communication, 37

Dade County, Florida, 55, 72
Dallas Municipal Court, 57
Dalton School (New York), 35
Darwish, Ismail, 133
Dashew Business Machine Corporation, 69
Data banks, 11, 19, 174

Data base, 6–7
Data base administrators, 7
Data bases, government, 72
Data bases, pirating of, 71–72
Data centers, 139
Data communications, 6, 7, 55
Data encrypting, 9, 42, 162, 163
Data Entry Management Association, 25
Data entry operators, 7
Data manipulation, 151, 159–161
Data processing, 7
Data Processing Management Association (DPMA), 24, 54; Computer Crime Committee, 117
Data retrieval services, 22
Da Vinci, Leonardo, 2
Deep Throat (movie), 64
Defense Intelligence Agency, 102
Defense Marketing Services Corporation, 91
De Filippo, Mathew, 65–66
De Geyter, Marc Andre, 91
Demon BBS (New York), 41
Denelcor, 10
Denmark, 86, 121, 126
De Paul University, 38
Deutsche Beryllium, 90–91
Deutsche Integrated Time (West Germany), 81
Dialog Information Services, 22
Digital Equipment Corporation, 22, 31, 81
Dime Savings Bank (New York), 52
"Dirty dialing," 36
District of Columbia, 53
Dow Jones computers, 41
Draper, John, 32
Drexel University, 39
Drug Enforcement Administration (DEA), 72
Drug trafficking, 65, 132, 144
Dual-use technologies, 91
Due process, 171, 172

East Asian Anti-Japan Armed Front, 130
East Germany (GDR), 79, 131
Economic Information Systems, 22–23
Edgerly, Eryie Ann, 49–50
EDP, 75
Education, 11, 29
Educational Fund for Individual Rights, 24
Electronic bank cards, 69–70, 143, 144
Electronic banking, 67
Electronic benefits transfer (EBT), 73
Electronic bulletin boards, 11–12, 29, 31, 33, 36, 37, 39–42
Electronic catalogs, 72
Electronic cottage industries, 4, 11

Electronic funds transfer (EFT), 11, 12, 143–164, 177, 178
Electronic Funds Transfer Act of 1980, 154, 173–174
Electronic Funds Transfer Association, 117
Electronic interceptions, 151, 161–162
Electronic lawyers, 11
Electronic mail system, 11, 36, 37, 38, 42
Electronic newspapers, 11
Electronic payment systems. *See* Electronic funds transfer (EFT)
Electronic Peace Corps (proposed), 43
Electronics, 85
Emerson Electric, 22
Employees: sabotage by, 21, 52, 56–57; surveillance of, 25–26, 172–173
EMV Associates, 27
Equifax, 173
Equity Funding, 52–53
Errors, 8
ETA systems, 10
Ethics, 23–25, 39
Exchange EDP Network, 147
Export Administration Act, 90, 92
Export controls, 90, 92–93, 94, 95
Extortion, 151, 161–162

Factories, 90, 139
Fairchild Semiconductor, 4
FALN (Fuerzas Armadas de Liberacion) (Puerto Rico), 23, 131
Fanuc (Japan), 92
Fed Wire, 68, 146
Federal Bureau of Investigation (FBI), 17, 46, 50, 57, 62, 98; Academy, 122; computer fraud classes, 119, 120, 122; and electronic funds transfer, 153, 155, 160; and hacking, 32, 34, 35, 36, 38, 40, 119; and law enforcement, 111, 112, 118; National Crime Information Center (NCI), 167, 175; and Soviet espionage, 77, 78, 87, 90, 93, 94; and terrorism, 137, 140
Federal Computer Systems Protection Act, 117
Federal Deposit Insurance Corporation (FDIC), 156
Federal Reserve, 144–145, 153, 157; Fed Wire, 68, 146
Federal Reserve Bank of Philadelphia, 136
Federal Trade Commission, 174
Fein, Leslie, 153
Fencing operations, 65–66
Ferdinand, Archduke of Austria, 133
Financial thefts, 58–59
Fingerprint scanners, 163
Finneran, William B., 19

Fire, 8, 17, 20, 134, 136
First Data Corporation, 20
First Federal Savings & Loan Bank (Lincoln, Nebr.), 147
First Interstate Bank, 163
First National State Bank (Newark, N.J.), 154–155
First Variable Rate Fund for Government Income, 155
Flooding, 8, 20
Florida, 74, 115
Food and Drug Administration (FDA), 114
Food stamp program, 46, 72–73
Forbes magazine, 61
Ford Foundation, 140
Ford Motor Corporation, 14
Foreign investments, 91
Fortune magazine, 46
Four Seas Gang (Taiwan), 71
Framingham, Mass., State Prison, 75; Con'puter Systems Programming, 74
France, 110, 121, 132, 145, 162; and industrial espionage, 86, 88, 89, 91, 92; and terrorism, 23, 129, 132, 133, 136
Frascati nuclear research laboratory (Rome), 129
Fraud, 8, 56, 69, 70, 104, 151, 154–156
Fresno State College, 52
Front, the (Italy), 134
Fuels, 136–137
Fujitsu, 10
Future Computing, 10

Gambino Mafia family, 64, 70, 75
Gambling, 61, 63–64
General Accounting Office, 73, 97, 98, 102, 104, 105, 107
General Dynamics Corporation, 26, 58
General Electric, 22
General Motors, 69
General Services Administration (GSA), 98, 99, 105, 168; Quality of Workplace Commission, 100
General Tire Corporation, 58
Genetic screening technique, 174
Gennano-Anguilo gang, 71
Genovese Mafia family, 67
Germany, 84. *See also* East Germany; West Germany
Giacalone, Anthony, 67–68
Ginny teller machines, 70
Glendale Federal Savings & Loan Association, 147
Glickman, Dan, 115
Global computer networks, 43

Gompers Secondary School (East San Diego), 29
Goodgame, Gary, 160
Government data bases, pirating of, 72
Gravier, David, 131
Great Britain, 21, 50, 52, 78, 81, 87, 110, 121–122; computer market, 2; Scotland Yard, 17, 122, 161; and terrorism, 13, 130, 134, 138
Greenbaum, Gus, 69
Grumbles, Robert, 121
Grumman Aerospace Corporation, 42, 166
GTE Telenet Communications Corporation, 36, 37, 38, 41, 42, 53
Guardian (London), 122
Gulf Oil plant bombing (Bayton, Tex.), 136

Hacking, 29–43, 119, 121, 123, 124, 138
Hallers, James L., II, 34
Hancock, Robert F., 52
Hanford, Wash., nuclear reactor, 137
Hansen, Mike, 160
Hansen, Rosemary, 159
Hardware, 6; theft and counterfeiting of, 58
Harper, James Durwald, Jr., 82
Harris gang, 75
Harris poll, 169
Harvard University, 3
Hawkins, Paula, 163
Headley, Susan, 34–35
Heath, Edward, 22
Hewlett-Packard, 111
Hitachi, 10, 50
Hollerith, Herman, 3
Hollywood, 39
Home banking (HB), 11, 143, 148–149
Honeywell Corporation, 52, 74
Hong Kong, 71, 91, 94, 95, 121, 127
Hospitals, 12–13, 20, 39–40, 173
Houston police, 109
Howard County, Md., police department, 35
Human rights, 18–19, 170–172
Hussein, Abdulkadir Mohammed, 154–155
Hutton, E.F., 153
Huxley, Aldous, 15

ICI (formerly Imperial Chemical Industries) (Netherlands), 161
Idaho National Energy Laboratory, 140
Illinois Bureau of Investigation, 62
Immigration and Naturalization Service, 99
India, 91, 94, 137
Indian Point, N.Y., power plant, 136
Indiana National Bank, 145
Industrial espionage, 22–23, 32, 50, 52, 90–91; Soviet, 77–95

Industrial Revolution, 21
Info World, 32
Infocorp, 31
Information Industry Association, 117
Informational catastrophes, 8, 19–20
Input, 6, 55
Input Inc., 144
Institute of Strategic Trade, 89
Insurance industry, 172
Integrated circuit, 4, 5
Intel Corporation, 4, 65, 70
Intelligence agencies: Soviet, 80; U.S., 168
Interbank Card Association, 149
Intercomputer networks, 36–37
International Business Machines Corporation (IBM), 3, 20, 26, 65, 79, 126; Mark I and 360 computers, 3, 5–6; MIS Training Institute, 46–47; versus National Semiconductor Corporation and Hitachi, 50
International Data Corporation (IDC), 1
International Society for the Abolition of Data Processing, 18
Interpol, 161
Investext, 22
Iran, 129, 134
Iraq, 134
Irish Republican Army (IRA), 129, 130, 132, 133, 134
Irving Trust Company (New York), 160
Islamic Guerillas of America, 131
Israel, 134; Lod Airport attack, 130; Mossad, 79
Israeli Mafia, 70–71
Italy, 86, 129, 132, 134, 139

Jackson, Sheila, 170
Jacobins (France), 132
Japan: computer crime, 121, 123, 149–150; computer market, 2; industrial espionage, 77, 79, 80, 86, 91, 92, 95; law enforcement, 110, 123; Nippon Telegraph and Telephone Public Corporation (NTT), 123, 150; *Police Department White Paper*, 123, 154; robotics, 26; *soroban*, 2; Study Group on Computer System Security Regulations, 123; supercomputers, 4; and terrorism, 130; test-tube computers, 27
JCPenney Company, 70
Jenkins, Rhys, 161
Job displacement, 13, 21, 22, 26
Johnson & Johnson Company, 138
Jones, Shirley, 170
Jones, Stephen, 45
Jones, William, 170
Justice Commandos of the Armenian Genocide (JCAG), 132

Kastenmeier, Robert W., 19
Kessler, Albert Franz, 81
Kidnapping, 131
Kiplinger Washington Letter, 53–54
Knox County, Tenn., police, 168
Kreisky, Bruno, 1
Kusserow, Richard P., 139
Kuwait, 134

Labor unions, 69
Langevin, Theode Charles, 153
Lansky, Meyer, 61, 69
Latin America: computer market, 2; terrorists, 130, 131, 132, 134
Law enforcement, 42, 109–128
Lawrence, D.H., 1
League of Terror, 129, 130–132
Leavenworth, Kans., federal prison, 74, 75
Legal data banks, 11
Leibniz, Gottfried Wilhelm, 3
Lemay, James, 73–74
Lenin, Nikolai, 83–84
Lewis, Ben, 157–158
Liability law, 113–114
Libya, 77, 80, 91, 129, 131, 134
Liechtenstein, 92, 94
Loansharking, 68
Lockheed, 89
Lomonosov, Mikhail, 83
London Clearing Bank Employer's Federation, 138
London Clearing Banks, 147
London Daily Star, 121
Long Island Lighting, 53
Loren Industries, 53
Los Alamos National Laboratory, 9, 40, 41, 115
Los Angeles County, 40, 55, 72, 166, 169, 170
Lothrop, Woodward A., 70
Lovelace, Lady, 3
Lufthansa Airlines hijacking, 130

M5 terrorist group (France), 133
McKnight, Gerald, 45
Mafia. *See* Organized crime
Mainframe computers, 5, 9
Malaysia, 71, 95
Maluta, Anatole, 91
Manufacturing jobs, 21
Mao Tse Tung, 49
Marine Midland Bank (New York), 152
Market Data Retrieval, 29
Marshall, Sonnie, 157–158
Marshall Flight Center (Huntsville, Ala.), 139
Marxist-Leninist ideology, 83

Maschinenfabrik Ausburg-Nuernberg AG (West Germany), 135
Mass media, 138
Massachusetts, 17, 21, 74
MasterCard, 70, 163
MasterCharge, 149
Master Teller, 70
Mathias, Charles, Jr., 42, 58
May 19th Communist Organization, 131
MCI, 41
Medard H. Nelson Elementary School (New Orleans), 29
Medicine, 11
Mendeleyev, Dmitri, 83
Menendez, Jose Louis Llovio, 95
Merit Systems Protection Board, 103
Metallurgy, 85
Metropolitan Life Insurance Company, 21, 52
Mexico, 2
Mexico City, 136
Microchip, 5–6
Microcomputers, 5, 10. *See also* Personal computers
Microprocessors, 4, 6
Militarily Critical Technologies List (U.S. Defense Dept.), 90
Military, the, 3, 79–95 *passim*, 131, 135
Military Personnel Records Center (St. Louis, Mo.), 17
Milwaukee 414s, 40, 41, 53, 115
Minicomputers, 5, 10
Minnesota, 74, 168
Minnesota Educational Consortium, 33
MIS Training Institute, 46–47
Missile systems, 85, 91, 131
Missing children, 166
MIT: Cookie Monster, 32; Laboratory for Computer Science, 38
Modem, 7, 12, 31, 37
Monde, Le (France), 162
Money cards, 69–70, 143, 144
Money Exchange, 152
Money laundering, 66–68
Monolithic Memories, 48, 61
Morse, Samuel, 19
Most teller machines, 70
Mueller, Richard, 81–82
Muhammad Ali Professional Sports (MAPS), 158
Muller-Butcher, Brian, 82

National Academy of Sciences, 92
National Advisory Commission on Criminal Justice Standards and Goals, 140
National Aeronautics and Space Administration (NASA), 54, 77, 98, 105

National Association for State Information
Systems, 117
National Association of Accountants, 24
National Association of Working Women, 25
National Bonded Company, 48
National Bureau of Standards, 99
National Center for Computer Crime Data, 51
National Commission on Electronic Transfers,
144
National Communications Security Committee,
42
National Crime Information Center (NCI),
167, 175
National Institute for Occupational Safety and
Health, 25
National Institutes of Health, 27
National Law Journal, 23
National Security Agency (NSA), 17, 19, 168
National Semiconductor Corporation, 50
National Telecommunications and Information
Security Committee (NTISC), 99
NATIONE, 147
NATO, 92, 135, 137
Navy Federal Credit Union, 154
Nelson, Bill, 110
Neopolitan Camorra (Italy), 132
Nerve gases, 137, 142
Nestar Systems, 58
Netherlands, 48, 82, 86, 161
Networking, 11, 105
New Orleans police, 170
New York City, 40, 46, 135, 161, 166
New York State, 74; Commission on Cable
Television, 19
New York Times, 29, 86
New York University, 21
New Yorker, The, 50
New Zealand, 127
Nilson Report, 69
1984 (Orwell), 165-166, 178
Nippon Telegraph and Telephone Public
Corporation (NTT) (Japan), 123, 150
Norway, 17, 121, 125, 126, 156
Nuclear missile warning systems, 17, 20
Nuclear power plants, 136, 137
Nuclear Regulatory Commission (NRC),
140
Nuclear terrorism, 139-141
Nuclear weapons, 135, 138, 141
Nunn, Sam, 93

Oak Ridge, Tenn., nuclear facility, 138, 140
Office of Technology Assessment (OTA), 99,
102, 135
Ohio Scientific Users of New York (OSUNY),
40

Omar, Ali M., 154-155
Omega 7, 132
Omnibus Crime Control and Safe Streets Act,
163
One Eye Jack gang, 71
OPEC headquarters attack in Vienna, 134
Operation Exodus, 82, 93
Optimum Services, 48
Organization for Economic Cooperation and
Development, 17
Organized crime, 61-76, 132, 133, 144
Orwell, George, 19, 165-166, 178
"Orwell, George A.," 105
Output, 6, 55; theft of, 105-106

Pacific Telephone and Telegraph Company,
40, 45
Pacifist and Ecologist Committee, 23, 136
Pakistan, 77, 79, 131
Palestine Liberation Organization (PLO), 130,
131, 133, 134
Pan American World Airways, 69
Panama, 67
Paperwork Reduction Act, 99
Paraguay, 130
Pascal, Blaise, 3
Passport reader system, 167
Passwords, 9, 33, 37
Patents and licenses, 90
Patriarca Mafia family, 66
Patrick, Neal, 40
Pavlov, Ivan, 83
PC Week, 58
Penkovsky, Oleg, 88
Penn Central Railroad, 66
People's Security Bank (Oxon Hill, Md.), 49
People's Will, 132
Peraino, Joseph, 64
Personal computers, 10-11, and hacking, 34-
35; market, 1-2, 4, 5
Personal identification number (PIN), 73, 146,
147, 151
Personnel screening, 8-9
Peru, 132
Peter the Great of Russia, 80
Philadelphia Family Court, 143
Philadelphia Money Access, 143
Philips Data Systems (France), 129
Physical attacks, 151, 152
Pipelines, 136-137
Planning and coordination, 106-107
Planning Research Corporation, 73
Plus Systems, 70
Point-of-sale (POS), 70, 145, 147-148
Poison, 137-138, 141-42
Poland, 77, 79, 82, 121

Police, 109–128, 161, 166, 168–170
Polish American Machinery Corporation, 79
Pornography, 64–65
Portable computers, 13
Power outages, 8, 135
Power plants, 135–136
President's Council on Integrity and Efficiency, 102
Prester, Andre L., 155–156
Price Waterhouse and Company, 54
Princeton University, 33
Prison computer training programs, 73–76
Privacy, invasion of, 13, 18, 19, 165–176 *passim*, 178
Privacy Act of 1974, 174
Processing alterations, 105
Programming, 7, 55
Property, tangible/intangible, 116
Prostitution, 64
Protected location, 8
Psychopathic killers, 166–167
Public opinion, 111–112
Publicity, fear of, 113
Purdue University, 58

Qaddafi, Muammar, 134

"Raid button," 63
Ramirez-Sanchez Illich (Carlos the Jackal), 130, 134
Rand Corporation, 92
Raytheon Corporation, 54
Reagan, Ronald, 85, 94, 131
Red Army (Japan), 130, 131, 133, 134
Red Army Faction (Baader-Meinhof group) (West Germany), 130, 131, 134, 138
Red Bank, N.J., schools, 39
Red Brigades, 131, 134, 138
"Remorseful Rapist," 169
Reserve Fund of New York, 146
"Reverse engineering," 22
Revolutionary Coordinating Junta, 130–131
Revolutionary Fighting Group, 131
Ribicoff, Abe, 117
Rifkin, Stanley Mark, 159–160
Riggs National Bank, 67, 155–156
Rison, Tyron, 133
Robinson, Scott, 74
Robotics, 12, 14, 21, 26
Rostow, Melvin, 106
Rote Zellen (West Germany), 134–135
Russalmaz (Soviet Union), 159, 160

Sabotage, employee, 21, 52, 56–57
St. Louis police department, 119
San Francisco police, 109, 168–169

San Jose State University, 34
Sandia National Laboratories, 63
Santa Barbara earthquake, 20
Santa Clara County, Calif., 119
Savannah River, S.C., nuclear weapons plant, 137
Scandinavia, 125–126
Schneider, Jerry Neal, 45
Schools, 29, 39
Search and seizure, 171
Sears Roebuck and Company, 15–16
Securities and Exchange Commission, 155
Securities counterfeiting, 68–69
Security Pacific National Bank (Los Angeles), 40, 159–160
Selective Dissemination of Information, 22
Semiconductor Industry Association, 92
Serbian Black Hand Society, 133
Shanklin, Richard P., 143
Shiite terrorists, 134
Sicilian Mafia, 132
Siegel, Benjamin (Bugsy), 69
Silicon chip, 5–6
Singapore, 71, 94, 95, 127
60 Minutes (TV program), 49
Skinner, Todd, 101–102
Slavenburg Bank (Rotterdam, Neth.), 48
Sloan-Kettering Cancer Center (New York), 39–40, 41, 115
Slyngstad, Stanley, 49
Small Business Administration (SBA), 117
Small Business Administration Act, 117
Smart cards, 164
Smith, Arlene, 106
Smith, Harrold Rossfields, 157–158
"Smith, James, Jr.," 97
Smith, Wayne, 153
Social Revolutionaries, 132
Social Security Administration (SSA), 12, 97, 98, 100, 101–102, 105, 106
Software, 6; pirating of, 41–42, 58; U.S. sales, 4, 5
Somalia, 130, 154, 155
Soroban, 2
South Africa, 81, 94
South Carolina, 20
South Korea, 71, 95, 98, 121
South Korean jetliner downing, 17, 85
South Yemen, 131
Southern Illinois University, 53
Southland Corporation, 147
Soviet Lithuania, 46
Soviet Union, 77–95; Academy of Sciences, 83; Aeroflot, 89; computer crime in, 46, 121; Defense Council, 89; Gosplan (State

Planning Agency), 89; GRU (military intelligence), 86, 87–89, 90, 92; intelligence agencies, 80; International Department of the Central Committee of the Communist Party, 131; KGB (State Security Committee), 78–95 *passim;* Military Industrial Commission (VPK), 77, 84–85, 88, 89; minorities, 88; plant purchases, 90; scientists, 83; T-2 toxin, 137; Techmashimport, 91; techniques of obtaining U.S. technology, 90–91; support of terrorism, 131, 134

Spain, 86, 91, 136

Sperry Corporation, 135; UNIVAC I, 4

Sprint, 41

Squibb, E.R., & Sons, 65

SRI International, 138

Stalin, Josef, 83

State Papers (Lenin), 83–84

States' rights groups, 118

Stein, Lou, 159, 160

Stillwater, Minn., Correctional Facility, 74

Stone, Geraldo, 167

Stonehenge, 2

Storage. *See* Data base

Strategic Air Command Headquarters (Omaha), 52

Stress, 25–26

Strikes, 21

Sunshine State Bank (Miami), 66–67

Superchip, 13

Supercomputers, 4, 9–10

Superprograms, 10

Surveillance, 174–176

Sweden, 26, 52, 81, 84, 87, 92, 94; Bromma airport, 126; Ministry of Defense, 17; Ministry of Justice, 125–126; Police Academy, 126; Privacy Act, 178

Switzerland, 110; and computer crime, 127, 149, 162; and industrial espionage, 80, 81, 82, 87, 91, 92, 94

Syracuse, N.Y.: Brink's robbery, 149

System abuses, 104–105

System operator ("syop"), 41

Systems analysts, 7

Taiwan, 71, 94

Tap, 33

Tcimpidis, Tom, 40

Technology, 6–10, 174

Telecommuting, 4, 11

Telenet System, 35, 38, 41

Telephone bill paying (TBP), 148

Telphone system, 12, 19, 21, 172; and hacking, 32, 33, 35, 36, 138

Tenerife, Canary Islands, airport crash, 132

Tennessee work release program, 73–74

Tennyson, Alfred, 143

Terminals, 7, 25, 146

Terrorism, 13, 17, 23, 129–142, 165; in history, 132–133; nuclear, 139–141; its targets, 134–139

Test-tube computers, 27

Texaco Company, 52

Texas: prisons, 74

Texas A&M University, 34

Texas Instruments, 4, 79

Thatcher, Margaret, 13

Theft, 58, 66, 151, 152–154

Third World, 43

3M, 54, 74

Time-sharing, 7, 20, 105, 115

Timecor (Boston), 4

Toshiba Corporation (Japan), 4

Total Assets Protection, 111

Touch-sensitive display screen, 13

Toxic agents, 137–138, 141–142

Toynbee, Arnold, 16

TRW Data Systems, 71, 88, 111, 172, 173

Turing, Alan, 3

Turner-Curtis gang, 75

2001: A Space Odyssey (movie), 10

Tylenol, 138

Unauthorized transactions, 152–154, 157–158

Union Bank (Los Angeles), 160

Union Bank of Switzerland, 156

United California Bank (Los Angeles), 55

United Freedom Federation, 21

United Freedom Front, 131

United Kingdom. *See* Great Britain

United States: attacks on military bases abroad, 132, 133; computer crime in government departments and agencies, 97–108; computer industry, 1; crime in, 45–46; export controls, 90, 92–93, 94, 95; intelligence agencies, 168; northeastern blackout (1965), 135; personal computer market, 4, 5; police agencies, 166–169; prison population, 74; research and development expenditures, 4; robotics in, 26; terrorism in, 23, 129–140 *passim*

U.S. Air Force, 100, 133

U.S. Army, 97, 98, 104, 132, 141, 142

U.S. Bureau of Justice Statistics, 114, 144, 156

U.S. Capitol building, 137

U.S. Census Bureau, 3, 4, 19

U.S. Chamber of Commerce, 51, 66, 92

U.S. Comptroller General's Manual for Guidance of Federal Agencies, 99

U.S. Congress, 51, 99, 140, 173. *See also* U.S. House of Representatives; U.S. Senate
U.S. Constitution, 170–172
U.S. Customs Service, 53, 71, 81, 84, 93, 167, 170
U.S. Department of Agriculture, 54, 73, 97–98, 104, 105
U.S. Department of Commerce, 10, 50, 81, 84, 93, 94; *Commodity Control List*, 90; Operation Exodus, 82, 93
U.S. Department of Defense, 17, 23; Advanced Research Projects Agency Network, 105; and computer crime, 98–106 *passim*; and hackers, 31, 36, 42, 135; and industrial espionage, 90, 92, 93, 94; Inspector General's Office, 101, 103; *Militarily Critical Technologies List*, 90
U.S. Department of Energy, 59, 107–108, 129, 136, 137, 140
U.S. Department of Health and Human Services, 100, 104, 139
U.S. Department of Justice, 51, 62, 69, 74, 118, 149; and computer crime, 103, 107; and industrial espionage, 82, 93, 94
U.S. Department of Transportation, 97
U.S. Executive Branch and industrial espionage, 93–94
U.S. Government Accounting Office (GAO), 16, 136, 139
U.S. House of Representatives: Banking Committee, 150; Commerce Committee, 140; Subcommittee on Science and Technology, 115
U.S. Internal Revenue Service (IRS), 63, 73, 97, 98, 168
U.S. Navy, 80, 98, 105, 140; Naval Ocean Systems Center, 105; Naval Research Laboratory, 105
U.S. Office of Management and Budget (OMB), 42, 99, 100
U.S. Privacy Commission, 173
U.S. Secret Service, 101, 102, 120
U.S. Senate, 34, 93, 98; Committee on Government Operations, 17, 74–75; Judiciary Committee, 70, 139–141, 144; Permanent Subcommittee on Investigations, 62, 78; Subcommittee on Security and Terrorism, 129
U.S. State Department, 129, 168
U.S. Supreme Court, 137
U.S. Treasury Department, 68, 99; Enforcement Communication System (TECS), 72, 167
University of California, 35, 37, 57
University of Chicago's Billings Hospital, 173
University of Florida's Center for Intellectual Machines and Robots, 26

University of Illinois, 9, 159
University of London, 121
University of Maryland: Center for Philosophy and Public Policy, 175; Hospital, 59
University of Minnesota Graduate School of Business Administration, 16
University of Oslo: Norwegian Research Center for Computers and Law, 156
University of Southern California, 53
University of Toronto, 59
Uruguay terrorists, 130
USA Today, 110, 114

Vector Graphics, 58
Venetians, 78
Virginia National Bank, 155–156
VISA, 70, 145, 163
Visual display terminal (VDT), 25

Wall Street Journal, 56, 67, 133
Wang Laboratories, 22, 58, 66
Washington State Division of Vocational Rehabilitation, 49
Weather Underground, 131
Webster, William, 78
Weinberger, Caspar, 92
Weizenbaum, Joseph, 19
Welfare fraud, 166
Welfare recipients, 15, 17, 21
Wells, H.G., 15
Wells Fargo Bank, 157, 163
West Germany, 26; Federal Criminal Office (BKA), 165; and industrial espionage, 77, 81, 84, 86, 91, 92; law enforcement and police training, 110, 127; personal computer market, 1–2; and terrorism, 130, 132, 133, 134–135, 141, 142
Western Europe, 1–2, 95
Western Washington University, 32
Westinghouse, 22, 48
White-collar workers, 21
Whiteside, Tom, 50
Wilde, Oscar, 45
Wilson, Herbert F., 149
Wire transfer (WT), 146–147
Wiretap statutes, 116, 175
Wisconsin, 37
Wisconsin State Journal, 37
Worker surveillance, 25–26, 172–173
World War I, 84, 132–133
World War II, 3, 84
Wozchod Handels Bank (Zurich), 160
Wright-Patterson Air Force Base, 130
Wristwatch computer, 13

Zuse, Konrad, 3

About the Author

A UGUST BEQUAI, in his many roles as author, lecturer, instructor, and attorney, is recognized as one of the United States' foremost experts on law and industrial security. The author of more than 100 articles on various aspects of law and technology, Mr. Bequai has written eight books: *Computer Crime, Computers and Business, White-Collar Crime: A 20th-Century Crisis, Organized Crime: The Fifth Estate, The Cashless Society: EFTs at the Crossroads, How to Prevent Computer Crime: A Guide for Managers, Making Washington Work for You,* and *Technocrimes*. He is currently completing a book entitled *Computer Contracting*.

Mr. Bequai has lectured before numerous management, security, banking, and other professional groups and has taught for The George Washington University, American University, and New York University. Presently in the private practice of law in Washington, D.C., specializing in law and security, he is the former chairman of the Federal Bar Association's Subcommittee on White-Collar Crime and the former vice chairman of Washington, D.C.'s Bar Committee on Regulating Agencies. He currently sits on the advisory boards of the *Journal of Media Law and Practice, Advanced Management Journal, French Computer Law Journal, Business Ethics Reporter, U.K. Computer Law and Security Report,* and *Human Resources Law Advisor*.

Mr. Bequai has also served as project director for the study on computer crime/security funded by the U.S. Department of Justice and as a consultant to the U.S. Congress, White House, and various government agencies. He is listed in *Who's Who in the World, Who's Who in the East, Who's Who in the Law,* and the U.K.'s *Men of Achievement*. Mr. Bequai holds a B.A., M.A., J.D., and LL.M.